First World War
and Army of Occupation
War Diary
France, Belgium and Germany

21 DIVISION
62 Infantry Brigade
Northumberland Fusiliers
12th Battalion
1 January 1915 - 31 July 1917

WO95/2155/1

The Naval & Military Press Ltd
www.nmarchive.com
Published in association with The National Archives

Published by

The Naval & Military Press Ltd

Unit 10 Ridgewood Industrial Park,

Uckfield, East Sussex,

TN22 5QE England

Tel: +44 (0) 1825 749494

www.naval-military-press.com

www.nmarchive.com

This diary has been reprinted in facsimile from the original. Any imperfections are inevitably reproduced and the quality may fall short of modern type and cartographic standards.

© Crown Copyright
Images reproduced by permission of The National Archives, London, England, 2015.

Contents

Document type	Place/Title	Date From	Date To
Heading	WO95/2155-1		
Miscellaneous	Adjutant General's Office at The Base		
Miscellaneous	A Form. Messages And Signals.		
Heading	21st Division 62nd Infy Bde 12th Bn North'd Fus. Sep 1915-Jly 1917 Arrangements With 13 Bn. Aug 1917 As 12/13 Bn		
Heading	62nd Inf. Bde. 21st Div. Battn. Disembarked Boulogne From England 10.9.15 War Diary 12th Battn. The Northumberland Fusiliers. September (9.9.15-29.9.15) 1915		
War Diary	Folkestone	09/09/1915	09/09/1915
War Diary	Boulogne	10/09/1915	10/09/1915
War Diary	Watten	10/09/1915	10/09/1915
War Diary	Eperlecques	20/09/1915	20/09/1915
War Diary	Wittes	21/09/1915	21/09/1915
War Diary	Lieres	22/09/1915	22/09/1915
War Diary	Allouagne	24/09/1915	24/09/1915
War Diary	Noeux-Les-Mines	25/09/1915	25/09/1915
War Diary	Loos	25/09/1915	26/09/1915
War Diary	Hill to	26/09/1915	26/09/1915
War Diary	Noyelle-Les Vermelles	17/09/1915	27/09/1915
War Diary	Witternesse	27/09/1915	27/09/1915
War Diary	21st Division 12th Northumberland Fusiliers Vol 2 Oct 15		
War Diary	Marbecque	01/10/1915	02/10/1915
War Diary	Strazeele	05/10/1915	13/10/1915
War Diary	Bailleul	14/10/1915	14/10/1915
War Diary	Armentieres	15/10/1915	22/10/1915
War Diary	Epinette	24/10/1915	28/10/1915
Heading	21st Division Nov 15		
War Diary	Armentieres	28/10/1915	28/11/1915
Heading	21st Division 12th Northumberland Fus Vol 4 December 1915 121/7911		
War Diary	Armentieres	01/12/1915	31/12/1915
Heading	12th Northumberland Fusiliers Vol 3		
Heading	12th Northumberland Fus Vol III		
War Diary	Armentieres	01/01/1915	31/01/1915
Operation(al) Order(s)	12th (S) Bn. Northumberland Fusiliers. O.O. No. 20	09/01/1916	09/01/1916
Miscellaneous			
Operation(al) Order(s)	62 Inf. Bde. O.O. No. 45	29/01/1916	29/01/1916
War Diary	Armentieres	01/02/1916	29/02/1916
Map	Rough Sketch To Explain Minor Operation Carried Out By 12th Battn Northumberland Fusiliers 11.1.16		
Map	Not to Be Taken Beyond Battn Hd Div		
Operation(al) Order(s)	Operation Order No. 37	01/02/1916	01/02/1916
Operation(al) Order(s)	62 Inf. Bde. O.O. No. 46.	04/02/1916	04/02/1916
Operation(al) Order(s)	Operation Orders. No. 38	07/02/1916	07/02/1916
Miscellaneous	A Form. Messages And Signals.		
Operation(al) Order(s)	Operation Order No. 39	10/02/1916	10/02/1916
Miscellaneous	12th North'd Fus.	12/02/1916	12/02/1916

Operation(al) Order(s)	Operation Order No. 40	12/02/1916	12/02/1916
Operation(al) Order(s)	62 Inf. Bde. O.O. No. 47	12/02/1916	12/02/1916
Miscellaneous	12 North'd Fus.	11/02/1916	11/02/1916
Miscellaneous	12 North'd Fus.	15/02/1916	15/02/1916
Miscellaneous	12 North'd Fus.	16/02/1916	16/02/1916
Miscellaneous	12 North'd Fus.	17/02/1916	17/02/1916
Operation(al) Order(s)	62 Inf. Bde. O.O. No. 48	18/02/1916	18/02/1916
Miscellaneous	12 North'd Fus.	18/02/1916	18/02/1916
Operation(al) Order(s)	Operation Order No. 42	19/02/1916	19/02/1916
Operation(al) Order(s)	Operation Order No. 41	16/02/1916	16/02/1916
Operation(al) Order(s)	62 Inf. Bde. O.O. No. 50	23/02/1916	23/02/1916
Map			
Operation(al) Order(s)	Operation Order No. 43	25/02/1916	25/02/1916
Operation(al) Order(s)	Operation Order No. 44	28/02/1916	28/02/1916
Heading	12. Hath Fab Vol 7		
War Diary	Armentieres	01/03/1916	22/03/1916
War Diary	La Creche	23/03/1916	31/03/1916
War Diary	Coisy (Six Miles N NE Of Amien)	01/04/1916	08/04/1916
War Diary	Laneuville	09/04/1916	14/04/1916
War Diary	Ville	15/04/1916	15/04/1916
War Diary	Meaulte	16/04/1916	30/04/1916
Operation(al) Order(s)	62 Inf. Bde. O.O. No. 62	30/04/1916	30/04/1916
War Diary	Meaulte	01/05/1916	02/05/1916
War Diary	La Neuville	03/05/1916	13/05/1916
War Diary	Buire	14/05/1916	21/05/1916
War Diary	Fricourt	22/05/1916	27/05/1916
War Diary	Meaulte	28/05/1916	02/06/1916
War Diary	La Meauilte	03/06/1916	11/06/1916
War Diary	Buire	12/06/1916	20/06/1916
War Diary	Fricourt	21/06/1916	27/06/1916
War Diary	Reduvets	28/06/1916	28/06/1916
War Diary	Ribemont	29/06/1916	29/06/1916
Heading	62nd Inf. Bde. 21st Div. War Diary 12th Battn. The Northumberland Fusiliers. July 1916		
War Diary	Ribemont	30/06/1916	30/06/1916
War Diary	Fricourt	01/07/1916	04/07/1916
War Diary	St Sauveur Near Ailly-Sur-Somme	05/07/1916	06/07/1916
War Diary	Molliens Vidame	07/07/1916	10/07/1916
War Diary	Meaulte	11/07/1916	11/07/1916
War Diary	Mametz Wood	11/07/1916	23/07/1916
War Diary	St Pol	23/07/1916	23/07/1916
War Diary	Averdoingt	24/07/1916	24/07/1916
War Diary	Izel-Lez-Hameaux	25/07/1916	26/07/1916
War Diary	Wanquetin	27/07/1916	27/07/1916
War Diary	Arras	28/07/1916	31/07/1916
Heading	62nd Brigade. 21st Division. 1/12th Battalion Northumberland Fusillers August 1916		
War Diary	Arras	01/08/1916	18/08/1916
War Diary	Agnes-Lez-Duisans	19/08/1916	31/08/1916
Heading	62nd Brigade. 21st Division. 1/12th Battalion Northumberland Fusiliers September 1916		
War Diary	Arras	01/09/1916	04/09/1916
War Diary	Grand Rullecourt	05/09/1916	13/09/1916
War Diary	Dernancourt	13/09/1916	14/09/1916
War Diary	Becordel	15/09/1916	16/09/1916
War Diary	Flers	17/09/1916	18/09/1916

Type	Description	From	To
War Diary	Near Flers.	18/09/1916	26/09/1916
War Diary	Gueudecourt.	26/09/1916	30/09/1916
War Diary	Bernafay Wood	30/12/1916	30/12/1916
War Diary	Buire	01/10/1916	03/10/1916
War Diary	L'etoile	04/10/1916	07/10/1916
War Diary	Lapugnoy	08/10/1916	09/10/1916
War Diary	Fouquieres	10/10/1916	10/10/1916
War Diary	Vermelles Quarry Sector.	11/10/1916	11/10/1916
War Diary	Trenches	12/10/1916	12/10/1916
War Diary	Quarries Hulloch	13/10/1916	20/10/1916
War Diary	Trenches Hulluch	21/10/1916	31/10/1916
War Diary	Reserve (Bde)	01/11/1916	06/11/1916
War Diary	Quarries Sector	07/11/1916	28/11/1916
War Diary	Quarries	29/11/1916	30/11/1916
War Diary	Hulloch	01/12/1916	24/12/1916
War Diary	Hulloch	24/12/1916	28/12/1916
War Diary	Allouagne	28/12/1916	31/01/1917
War Diary	C Camp (A 16b.)	01/02/1917	01/02/1917
War Diary	Popperinghe	02/02/1917	15/02/1917
War Diary	Bethune	16/02/1917	16/02/1917
War Diary	Sailly	16/02/1917	16/02/1917
War Diary	Quarries	17/02/1917	22/02/1917
War Diary	Vermelles Quarries Sector	22/02/1917	27/02/1917
War Diary	Vermelles	27/02/1917	28/02/1917
War Diary	Quarries	01/03/1917	01/03/1917
War Diary	Annezin	02/03/1917	03/03/1917
War Diary	La Pierriere	04/03/1917	08/03/1917
War Diary	Rely	09/03/1917	09/03/1917
War Diary	Hestrus	10/03/1917	11/03/1917
War Diary	Hericourt	11/03/1917	11/03/1917
War Diary	Halloy	12/03/1917	27/03/1917
War Diary	Boisleux St Marc	28/03/1917	29/03/1917
War Diary	Boyelles	30/03/1917	31/03/1917
War Diary	Boiry Becquerelle	01/04/1917	03/04/1917
War Diary	Berles-Au-Bois.	04/04/1917	15/04/1917
War Diary	Bellacourt.	16/04/1917	30/04/1917
Map	Sketch Showing Dispositions at 6 PM		
Diagram etc	Sketch Showing Dispositions at 6 pm 13th 4-17.		
War Diary	St. Leger	01/05/1917	11/05/1917
War Diary	Blairville	12/05/1917	31/05/1917
War Diary	Croisilles.	01/06/1917	04/06/1917
War Diary	Trenches Croisilles	05/06/1917	07/06/1917
War Diary	Moyenville	08/06/1917	15/06/1917
War Diary	Croisilles	16/06/1917	19/06/1917
War Diary	Basseux	19/06/1917	30/06/1917
Operation(al) Order(s)	62 Inf. Bde. O.O. 119.	11/02/1917	11/02/1917
Operation(al) Order(s)	62 Infantry Bde. O.O. 120.	11/02/1917	11/02/1917
Miscellaneous	To-13th Northd Fus B.A. 530-12th February 1917.	12/02/1917	12/02/1917
Miscellaneous	Second Omnibus Train. 1 Coach, 30 covered wagons. 17 flat trucks.		
Miscellaneous	First Omnibus Train. 1 coach, 30 covered wagons, 17 flats.		
Miscellaneous	Instructions For Move To 1 Corps Area.	10/02/1917	10/02/1917
Miscellaneous	13th. (S) Battalion Northumberland Fusiliers. Preliminary Order.	12/02/1917	12/02/1917
Operation(al) Order(s)	13th Northumberland Fusrs. Of Operation Order No 3	14/02/1917	14/02/1917

Type	Description	Date From	Date To
Miscellaneous	12th Northd. Fus.	13/02/1917	13/02/1917
Miscellaneous	62nd Inf. Bde. (for information)	15/02/1917	15/02/1917
Miscellaneous	Proposed Movements Of 62nd Infantry Brigade		
Miscellaneous	21st Division. All Units-For information.	14/02/1917	14/02/1917
Miscellaneous	Disposition Of 62nd Infantry Brigade.	14/02/1917	14/02/1917
Miscellaneous	21st Division.	15/02/1917	15/02/1917
Miscellaneous	62 Infantry Bde. O.O. 121.	18/02/1917	18/02/1917
Miscellaneous	12 Northd Fus.	14/02/1917	14/02/1917
Operation(al) Order(s)	13th. Nrthd. Fusrs. Operation Order No E	16/02/1917	16/02/1917
Operation(al) Order(s)	62 Infantry Brigade O.O. No. 122.	18/02/1917	18/02/1917
Miscellaneous	March Table.	17/02/1917	17/02/1917
Operation(al) Order(s)	62 Infantry Brigade O.O. No. 123.	18/02/1917	18/02/1917
Operation(al) Order(s)	13th. Northd. Fusrs. Operation Order No. T	16/02/1917	16/02/1917
Operation(al) Order(s)	62 Infantry Brigade O.O. No. 124.	20/02/1917	20/02/1917
Operation(al) Order(s)	13th Northumberland. Fusrs. Operation Order No.6.	21/02/1917	21/02/1917
Operation(al) Order(s)	62 Infantry Brigade O.O. 125.	26/02/1917	26/02/1917
Operation(al) Order(s)	62 Infantry Brigade O.O. No. 126.	26/02/1917	26/02/1917
Operation(al) Order(s)	13th Northumberland Fusiliers Of Operation Order No 7.	26/02/1917	26/02/1917
Operation(al) Order(s)	13th Battalion Northumberland Fusiliers Of Operation Order No 8	27/02/1917	27/02/1917
Operation(al) Order(s)	62 Infantry Brigade O.O. No. 127.	27/02/1917	27/02/1917
Miscellaneous	12 Northd Fus.	27/02/1917	27/02/1917
Miscellaneous	12 Northd Fus.	28/02/1917	28/02/1917
Operation(al) Order(s)	13th Battalion Northumberland Fusiliers Of Operation Orders No 9	28/02/1917	28/02/1917
War Diary	Boyelles	01/07/1917	04/07/1917
War Diary	Hindenburg Line.	04/07/1917	28/07/1917
War Diary	Boyelles	29/07/1917	31/07/1917

WO 95/21551

XXI   12   Northum
                                        Vol. 8

Officer i/c
   Adjutant General's Office
     at the Base.

    The War Diary for this Battalion is being submitted rather late on account of operations in trenches.

                            L Bowell   2/Lt. for
                                         Lt. & Adjt.
                     12th S. Bn. Northd. Fusiliers.

"A" Form. Army Form C. 2121.
MESSAGES AND SIGNALS.
No. of Message ....

Prefix .... Code .... m.	Words	Charge	This message is on a/o of:	Recd. at .... m
Office of Origin and Service Instructions.				Date ....
....	Sent		.... Service.	From ....
....	At .... m.			
....	To			
....	By	(Signature of "Franking Officer.")	By ....

TO

| * | Sender's Number. | Day of Month. | In reply to Number. | A A A |

From			
Place			
Time			

The above may be forwarded as now corrected.   **(Z)**

.... Censor.   Signature of Addressee or person authorised to telegraph in his name.

* This line should be erased if not required.

21ST DIVISION
62ND INFY BDE

12TH BN NORTH'D FUS.
SEP 1915 - JLY 1917

Amalgamated with
13 BN. AUG 1917
as
12/13 BN

62nd Inf.Bde.
21st Div.

Battn. disembarked
Boulogne from
England 10.9.15.

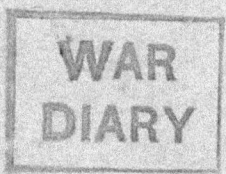

12th BATTN. THE NORTHUMBERLAND FUSILIERS.

S E P T E M B E R

(9.9.15 - 29.9.15)

1 9 1 5

WAR DIARY or INTELLIGENCE SUMMARY

Army Form C. 2118

Place	Date	Hour	Summary of Events and Information	Remarks and references to Appendices
FOLKESTONE	9.9.15	11.40pm	The Bn. embarked at FOLKESTONE	
BOULOGNE	10.9.15	1.15am	Disembarked at BOULOGNE & marched to rest camp	
"	10.9.15	5.00pm	marched to PONT DES BRIQUES Rly Stn and entrained to WATTEN	
WATTEN	11.9.15		detrained at WATTEN and marched to EPERLECQUES arriving about 3.15 am, where the Bn went into billets and continued training	
EPERLECQUES	20.9.15	7.0pm	The Bn. marched out and proceeded by road to WITTES arriving about 12.30am on the 21.9.15. Here the Bn. bivouacked	
WITTES	21.9.15	7.0pm	Marched to LIERES where the Bn. went into Billets. Time of arrival 11.0 pm. Inhabitants rather difficult.	
LIERES	22.9.15	5.25pm	Marched to ALLOUAGNE where the Bn. went into Billets. Time of arrival 9.30 pm.	
ALLOUAGNE	24.9.15	5.1pm	Left ALLOUAGNE and proceeded by rd to NOEUX-LES-MINES where the Bn. bivouaced. Raining and cold.	Map. 1/40000 36c FRANCE
NOEUX-LES-MINES	25.9.15	10.30am	marched to NOYELLES-LES-VERMELLES where the Bn. rested and two heavy guns were in action. Wounded even met all along the rd.	
"	"	3pm	The Bn. moved off following S.E. VERMELLES & 10 road R. left of which was extended behind the crest of the hill about 4.28 c and moved to the attack. The 124 Bdo.? was extended on left of LONE TREE about 5.0pm but unable to move over the crest of the hill and eventually came against the german trenches. filled up to count forwards and back of an outpost line. Here the Bn. first came under shell fire about 7.10 pm	
		9.25 am	The Bn. moved into L.25 and came under shell fire on the 7? Bn was already	

WAR DIARY
or
INTELLIGENCE SUMMARY
(Erase heading not required.)

Army Form C. 2118

Place	Date	Hour	Summary of Events and Information	Remarks and references to Appendices
LOOS	25/9/15		The Bn. moved through LOOS and halted under cover of houses by church square. Another sister hop. Reinforcing companies. The extract returned & did the Bn. of under Capt. L.H. PHILLIPS went forward to report on best route to Tower Bridge and visible hops. Here the Bn. had three dead casualties from shell fire. Here shells must have been very fast as they came along the rest of the garden wall. The Bn. moved back into the street the men still keeping steady. Lt. Col. MARWICK went back to Bde. H.Q. Returned and moved the Bn. to 968a. The Bn. here lay in lines of Platoons at 50 yds distance. Two platoons of 1/4 S. were sent forward to dining two wide entrenching tools under 2nd Lt. R.M. HILL & 2nd Lt. F. WILSON to help the 10th & Bde. interval later the remainder of 1/4 S. were ordered to entrench 100 yards Conds. Capt. F. G.F. EDLMANN.	Map. 40000 36c. France.
		10.30pm		
		11.45pm		
LOOS	26.9.15	2.30am	2 patrols under 2nd Lt. T. PARKER went forward to trenches to find the best way forward in case of being called upon to reinforce.	
			Shrapnel began & was fairly heavy. A party of rifle gren were sent from trenches & Bn. stood by. Instructions to Bn. to charge with bayonet in case of enemy approach.	
		5.30am	High explosive pitched in town behind Bn. H.Q. and shells moving explosive were frequent. Some casualties. Bn. was quiet & steady.	
		7am 7.30am	Wilson lying in field and road. Orders received given for attack on Hill 70	

WAR DIARY
or
INTELLIGENCE SUMMARY

(Erase heading not required.)

Army Form C. 2118

Place	Date	Hour	Summary of Events and Information	Remarks and references to Appendices
LOOS	26.9.15	5 am	Telephone returned to be with orders. C.O. Gates informed of operations intensive bombardment commenced. Enemy still give no reply. Telephonic comm. anyway. Casualties Capt W. ? R.H.E and 2nd Lt R.G. Trenchman wounded.	
		8.30am	Bn moved out in position to assault.	Map.
		9 am	Assault commenced "C" "D" "A" "B" Cos. according by platoons at 100yds distance. Wounded reported attack progressing well, enemy running after enemy first line trench. The attack appears to have come into machine gun & rifle fire. Attack held up and heavy casualties. Troops in rear tried to advance one but further progress impossible. C.O. slightly hit in toe and cannot walk in officers hosp. The crest of the hill was held by enemy. Line? but M.G. may have cut troops. Officer? but back to first line trench. Enemy attempting to to follow our crest but were swept and easily repulsed. P.G. report having taken enemys first line trench, now nearly and bayonetted several germans but were afterwards were nearly fired on by M.G.'s while in pursuit of enemy. Obliged to retire again to crest and afterwards to first line trench.	1/40000 36c FRANCE
		4.8pm	The 46th Bde left the trenches and 8th "York" tea and 8.C. York R. also moved but were badly enfiladed from the HULLOCH R and ? 31 WAY of the LE?OIRE? R. claimed it necessary to abandon the trench. Lt Col WS. leaving expected this which was with Lt Col MARWICH to reconnoitre to on the matter to retire being given the line	

WAR DIARY or INTELLIGENCE SUMMARY

Army Form C. 2118

Place	Date	Hour	Summary of Events and Information	Remarks and references to Appendices
				Map: 1/40,000 36C FRANCE
NOYELLES-LES-VERMELLES	27.9.15		Officers mentioned above arrived the earlier hours to warn the remainder of 8 & 9 not to return. It being found impossible to evacuate the trench the Cmdg. Officer removed the wounded and O. Col. Warwick was short through the shoulder, he was placed in a dugout until the South returned. In the meantime, he collected all available men and commenced putting LOOS in a state of defence. 1st & 2nd M. SHAMS also collected all available men and commenced putting LOOS in a state of defence, to Glosters handed over to Col. ?,?,? ?,?,? ???th also came in with R.B. Col. ?,?,?,?,? reports he was relieved by the 2nd Division Engrs. and Capt. GALLATLY. Similarly other members of 12th North Fus. were collected under Major BRAMWELL.	
		4.30 am	The Bn. entailed at NOYELLES-LES-VERMELLES. Moved by N.S. to NOEUX-LES-MINES when they entrained on FERQUETTE. Rway. and land end. Moved by R.S. & WITTERNESSE arriving at 8.30 am.	
WITTERNESSE				

D. Bramwell Poe
Major
Cmdg. 12th (Ser) Bn. North's Fus.

| WITTERNESS | 29/9/15 | 8.30 am | The Battalion remained in billets at WITTERNESS | Map 36 Sheet 1 |

121/743

21st Brown

12th Northumberland Fusiliers
vol 2

Oct 15

Army Form C. 2118.

WAR DIARY
INTELLIGENCE-SUMMARY.

October 1915

12/Northumberland Fusiliers.

(Erase heading not required.)

Place	Date	Hour	Summary of Events and Information	Remarks and references to Appendices
MARBECQUE	1/10/15	7.10am	Left WITTERNESS, moved by road to MARBECQUE, arrived at MARBECQUE at 1.15pm and billeted there	
	2/10/15	8.10am	Left MARBECQUE and proceeded by road to STRAZEELE	
STRAZEELE	5/10/15	—	2nd Lieuts Clothier and Bailey joined the Battalion from 3rd Bn N.F.	
	9/10/15	—	A draft consisting of 10 2nd Lieuts and 1050 other ranks joined from the 15th Battalion N.F.	
	10/10/15	—	Lieuts Hoch.L.C. and Brunck joined from the 15th Battalion	
	13/10/15	12pm	The Battalion left STRAZEELE and marched to BAILLEUL arrived at 4.55pm and billeted for the night	
BAILLEUL	14/10/15	10.30am	The Battalion left BAILLEUL and moved by road to ARMENTIERES arriving at 12.15pm, billeted at the ASILE PUBLIC DE AHENNES and were attached to the 149th Inf Bde for training in trench warfare	

WAR DIARY or INTELLIGENCE SUMMARY

Army Form C. 2118

(Erase heading not required.)

Instructions regarding War Diaries and Intelligence Summaries are contained in F. S. Regs., Part II. and the Staff Manual respectively. Title Pages will be prepared in manuscript.

Place	Date	Hour	Summary of Events and Information	Remarks and references to Appendices
ARMENTIERES	15/75	9am	Officers and N.C.O's of two sections per Coy went into the trenches for 24 hours instruction	
	16/75	9am	At 9am the remaining officers in C of S proceeded to the trenches	
		5pm	The Officers of N C.O.'s of the first two sections per company returned to the trenches with their men.	
	14/75	5pm	The remaining men of the Battalion proceeded to the trenches	
	19/75	5pm	A & C Companies proceeded to the trenches until 6pm 20th	
	20/75	5pm	B & D Companies proceeded to the trenches Machine gunners were served in the trenches for 48 hours under the Bde Machine Gun Officer 149th Infy Brigade	

WAR DIARY
or
INTELLIGENCE SUMMARY
(Erase heading not required.)

Army Form C. 2118

Place	Date	Hour	Summary of Events and Information	Remarks and references to Appendices
ARMENTIERES	21/10/15	5pm	"B" & "D" Coys returned from the trenches	Major Shuter France
	22/10/15		The Battalion proceeded with training in billets and a draft of 40 rank and file joined from the 3rd Battalion	
ERQUINGHEM	24/10 to 26/10 1915		During the bombardment the Battalion commenced duty by Bn. HQ. and Nos. 45, 46 & 44 Sections also Nos. 46 & 44 Sikh Trenches occupying Nos. 45, 46 & 44 trenches also Nos. 46 & 44 Sikh trenches during which time things were later to considered "normal" in this sector, the Divisional Commander (Maj. Gen. Snow - Isaacs) visited the Battalion. Our casualties were slightly wounded.	
	26/10/15	4.30pm	Lieut. Bailey and 32 N.C.O. men proceeded to BAILLEUL to represent the Battalion at a review of the 2nd Army by H.M. the King	

J. Greening Poen.
Major Comdg.
12th (S) Bn Northumberland Fus

28-10-1915

12th N. Otsuschi Tai:
Vol: 3

121/7624

21st Kuwaun

Nov 15.

Army Form C. 2118

WAR DIARY
or
INTELLIGENCE SUMMARY
(Erase heading not required.)

Instructions regarding War Diaries and Intelligence Summaries are contained in F.S. Regs., Part II. and the Staff Manual respectively. Title Pages will be prepared in manuscript.

Place	Date	Hour	Summary of Events and Information	Remarks and references to Appendices
ARMENTIERES	28/10	—	The Battalion continued to hold the trenches No 45, 46 + 47 L'EPINETTE	Reference MAP 1: HOOGE
	29/10		Part of "A" Cy. and the whole of "C" and "D" Companies moved out of trenches to billets. The remainder of "A" Company and the whole of "B" remaining in.	
	30/10			
	31/10		Capt. H.R. Gallerly was taken off the strength of the Battalion and appointed Staff Captain 62nd Inf. Brigade, the appointment to take effect from Sept 22nd 1915. Lieuts. Caton, L'Estrange Sickle and Goulsworthy returned from a course of instruction at the Divisional Grenade School.	
	1/5		Companies proceeded with training from billets. Lieuts. Johnson, R.B., Lovell, P.B., Brunton, J., and Reynolds, R. reported themselves for duty from the 28th Bn. of London Regt (Artists Rifles) having been posted from the Battalion.	
	2/5		The Battalion (less a detachment of "A" + the whole of "C" Company) took over Nos 44 + 48, 44 Support, S.P. + 48 Support trenches, the detachment of "A" + upwards above and "C" Company were retained and proceeded to billets.	
			The Battalion remained in trenches until the evening of Nov 6th when they were withdrawn to billets. Casualties Nil.	
	6/5		The Battalion was billeted at the RUE-DE-PAIX which headquarters at the RUE-DE-STRASBOURG. Divine service was held in billets.	

WAR DIARY
or
INTELLIGENCE SUMMARY
(Erase heading not required.)

Army Form C. 2118

Place	Date	Hour	Summary of Events and Information	Remarks and references to Appendices
ARMENTIERES	Nov 8th/1915	-	Training proceeded under Company Commanders, each Company being inspected by the Commanding Officer in turn.	
	10th		The Battalion relieved the 13th (S)Bn Northumberland Fusiliers in Trenches 48, 49 and 80 having on its right the 10th YORKS REGT and on its left the 11th D.L.I. Casualties No. 10th — one wounded 14th — one wounded 15th — five wounded Much work was rendered necessary by rain and four valuable work was carried out by the Royal Engineers by revetting trenches, fixing V shaped frames and the construction of gas dug-outs for the use of the men. Lieut REYNOLDS and 3 N.C.O's proceeded to the Divisional Grenade School.	
	15th			
	16th		The Battalion was relieved by the 13th (S) Bn Lancashire Fus. and proceeded to billets in the RUE DE PAIX, headquarters in RUE DE STRASSBOURG	

WAR DIARY or INTELLIGENCE SUMMARY

Army Form C. 2118

Place	Date	Hour	Summary of Events and Information	Remarks and references to Appendices
ARMENTIERES	Nov 17th 1915		The Battalion continued training etc	
	18th 1915		The commanding officer made an inspection of Companies. Also in marching order and two "Inspection of Accessories".	
	19th		The town was heavily bombarded but little damage was done. resulted except damage to Private property, as one of the Battalion was injured.	
			Two Companies of the Battalion were detailed as Brigade reserve and two as Divisional reserve during the period out of trenches	
	22nd		The Battalion proceeded to take over trenches 48, 49 and 80 from the 13th Bn. Northumberland Fusiliers who were ordered to take over the trenches occupied by the 12th Battalion	
	23rd		2nd Lieut Reid was wounded in the ankle during the night when out with a patrol, he was removed to ENGLAND	
	28th		The Battalion left trenches relief completed by 4.10 p.m. the	

WAR DIARY or INTELLIGENCE SUMMARY

Army Form C. 2118

Place	Date	Hour	Summary of Events and Information	Remarks and references to Appendices
ARMENTIERES	28th		13th Bn Northumberland Fusiliers took over trenches 48, 49 & 80 being on their right the 10th Battalion LINCOLNSHIRE REGT who replaced the 11th EAST YORKSHIRE REGT who have left the Brigade to join another Division.	

J. Armungole
Lt. Colonel.
commanding 12th I Service Bn Northumberland Fusiliers

62/51

12th November: Paris

Vol: 4

12/ December 1915
12/1794

WAR DIARY or INTELLIGENCE SUMMARY

Army Form C. 2118

Place	Date	Hour	Summary of Events and Information	Remarks and references to Appendices
ARMENTIERES	Dec 1915 1st	10a	The Battalion proceeded with training out of trenches, two machine gunners were wounded whilst in trenches with the 13th (S) Bn. Northumberland Fusiliers. The Divisional Commander inspected the Battalion in marching order,	Reference Map 1:20000
	3rd	9.30am	and at 11 a.m inspected the 1st line Transport. Lieut C.G. Mackay joined for duty.	
	4th	4.30	Several shells fell in the town, one which fell near headquarters injuring the Sentry and killing a child	
	5th	5pm	The Battalion took over from the 13th Bn Northumberland Fusiliers at 5pm. Nos. 48, 49 & 80 trenches on our right being 10th YORKS REGT. Lieut A.R. Luck and 35 O.R.s joined for duty from the 15th Battalion	
	6th		Trenches were found to be in a very bad state, practically all parapits in the fire trenches, at already strengthened with 'U' frames had collapsed, while in the communicating trenches water was standing to a depth varying from 6 inches to 3 feet. Weather very mild & slushy, occasional rain storms.	
	7th		Enemy did not pay any attention to our trenches. By constant pumping water was prevented from rising in the communicating trenches and dry standing was provided in most of the fire trenches. Weather mild, no rain until after dusk when rain fell steadily for two & a half hours. Wind South.	
	8th		The 21st Divisional Artillery shelled the enemy's support trenches & certain points behind his line between midday & 1pm. the battalion snipers shot to their loop holes & men with sniperscope rifles to their allotted positions to await themselves of any targets offered, the enemy did not retaliate, weather mild & clear, wind south-west.	
	9th		Armentieres was shelled from midday until 2 p.m by the enemy, our artillery retaliated vigorously; day dark, windy, heavy rain at intervals, roads are very much in communicating trenches. On our right the 10th YORKS REGT was relieved in the evening by the 1st Bn L. INCOLNSHIRE REGT.	

Army Form C. 2118

WAR DIARY
or
INTELLIGENCE SUMMARY
(Erase heading not required.)

Instructions regarding War Diaries and Intelligence Summaries are contained in F. S. Regs., Part II. and the Staff Manual respectively. Title Pages will be prepared in manuscript.

Place	Date	Hour	Summary of Events and Information	Remarks and references to Appendices
ARMENTIERES	1915. DEC 10th	—	The enemy again shelled ARMENTIERES, but again paid no attention to the trenches. Weather mild, wind South, water lower in communicating trenches, which are still usable although the water is in many places above the knee.	Reference sheet 1
	11th	—	Heavy rain having fallen during the night & at intervals during the day portions of the main communicating trench had become waist deep in water by 4 p.m. inspite of all available pumps. Portions of support trench 79 (S.S) had to be abandoned temporarily owing to depth of water, men being transferred into 80 support trench. Weather mild, clear and rainy. There were bright intervals, wind South West.	
	12th	—	The Battalion left trenches, relief completed by 7.15 p.m. The 13(S) Battalion Northumberland Fusiliers took over 78, 79 and 80 trenches with their supports & storey points. There were no casualties in the 12(S) Bn during this seven days tour of duty. The battalion proceeded to their billets in the RUE DE LA PAIX vacated by the 13th battalion, where the men's feet were looked upon arrival, a foot inspection held, the state of men's feet after seven days in mud & water was remarkably satisfactory.	
	13-14th	—	Large working parties for the trenches were despatched each day. The men not thus employed continued their training, particular attention being paid to practice in the use of anti-gas helmets.	
	15th	—	On Dec 15th one man was killed in trench 80 whilst on a working party. During the day the 21st Divisional Artillery cut a good deal of wire all along the front of the 62nd & 63rd Infantry Brigades.	
	16th	—	On the night of the 15th – 16th "A" and "D" Companies were in Brigade Reserve in the Subsidiary Line, and "B" and "C" Companies in Divisional Reserve at the Rue DE LA PAIX, in readiness to be used in the event of the enemy making a counter attack, following on a cutting out expedition, carried out by the 8th (S) Bn Somerset Light Infantry, upon the enemy trenches opposite trench 72.	

WAR DIARY or INTELLIGENCE SUMMARY

Army Form C. 2118

(Erase heading not required.)

Instructions regarding War Diaries and Intelligence Summaries are contained in F.S. Regs, Part II. and the Staff Manual respectively. Title Pages will be prepared in manuscript.

Place	Date	Hour	Summary of Events and Information	Remarks and references to Appendices
ARMEN-TIERRES	Dec 16th		The 'cutting out' expedition was completely successful, no counterattack was attempted and neither the Divisional or the Brigade Reserve were called upon.	References Map 1/10,000
			On this date Lt-Col Pole went to England on short leave, Capt F J F Edlmann taking command of the battalion in his absence, 2nd Lt Land Southampton & Col Joicey were attached for 48 hours for instructional purposes.	
	18th		The Battalion relieved the 13th (S) Battalion in trenches 78.79 and 80. The battalion on the night was the 10th (S) battalion of the YORKSHIRE REGIMENT, that on the left the 1st Battalion EAST YORKSHIRE REGIMENT. The relief was completed by 7.15 p.m.	
	19th		From 5 A.M. in the morning very heavy artillery fire continued to be heard on the left. It is 21st Divisional Artillery became very active from 8 A.M. the Germans retaliating on trenches 74 to 77. About 40.7.7cm shells were fired into 79 support trenches, our casualties one man killed. Enemy's minenwerfer and catapults did very extensive damage on our right to the trenches held by the 10th (S) battalion of the YORKSHIRE REGIMENT. A Reinforcement of 57 N.C.O's and men arrived from the 3rd battalion Northumberland Fusiliers.	
	20th		During the night 19th - 20th additional sentries were posted and gas gongs placed in position, strong patrols at frequent intervals examined our front, this being considered necessary owing to the activity of the enemy to the North. There was no artillery activity, but after stand to in the evening the enemy's machine guns shot down AUSTRALIA ROAD and SPAIN AVENUE with precise aim as if previously arranged schemes without however inflicting any casualties.	
	21st		Quiet day, trenches becoming dryer owing to free weather and successful drainage schemes devised by the 97th Field Coy R.E. Casualty, 1 man wounded by bullet in "S.P.Z". A patrol from Trench 76 threw some bombs into enemy's trench opposite at 10 p.m.	

Army Form C. 2118

WAR DIARY
or
INTELLIGENCE SUMMARY
(Erase heading not required.)

Instructions regarding War Diaries and Intelligence Summaries are contained in F. S. Regs., Part II. and the Staff Manual respectively. Title Pages will be prepared in manuscript.

Place	Date	Hour	Summary of Events and Information	Remarks and references to Appendices
ARMENTIERES	Dec 22		Cloudy day, wind South-West. The Divisional Artillery firing at intervals from 11.10AM to 3.15 p.m. cut the enemy's wire opposite PONT BALLOT, and damaged the enemy's parapit in the salient opposite trench 80. The enemy retaliated with a few 7.7 cm shells behind 79 & 80 trenches doing no damage. At night the enemy's machine guns were again very active, but caused no casualties. The food & water supply in S.P.2 was overhauled, it was being increased from 24 to 40 gallons; this being considered sufficient for 40 men for 72 hours. A Patrol from trench 80 reached the enemy's parapit & brought back a full reel of his barbed wire.	Reference Map 1/40000
	23.		Heavy rain; the enemy shewed no activity except that two 7.7 cm shells were fired into S.P.2, one of which wounded a man. After dusk the enemy's machine guns traversed the ground between AUSTRALIA ROAD and AUSTRALIA AVENUE COMMUNICATING TRENCH; one man on sentry outside Battalion Headquarters wounded by SPAIN dropping bullet; working parties and ration parties continually interfered with but no other casualties.	
	24.		South West wind, occasional rain, until nose rose members of the divisional grenade school came up to trench 80 & fired 50 rifle grenades into the enemy's salient; enemy retaliated with 20. 7.7 cm shells into PONT BALLOT, without result. Capt Shann & seven privates proceeded on short leave to England, this being the first short leave granted to this battalion. Casualty, one man was killed outside the artillery forward observation station by a stray bullet. The battalion was relieved after dark by the 13th (S) Battalion Northumberland Fusiliers, 2nd Lt d'Arafton commanding; 78, 79 and 80 trenches were handed over, together with support trenches and S.P.2. The 1st Battalion of the East Yorkshire Regiment. The relief was completed without any casualty by 7.25 p.m. The 1st Battalion of the East Yorkshire Regiment being on the left and the 1st Battalion Lincolnshire Regiment on the right. The battalion went into the billets in the RUE DE LA PAIX vacated by the 12th S Battalion Northumberland Fusiliers. Battalion Headquarters 60 RUE SADI CARNOT.	

Army Form C. 2118

WAR DIARY
or
INTELLIGENCE SUMMARY
(Erase heading not required.)

Place	Date	Hour	Summary of Events and Information	Remarks and references to Appendices
ARMENTIERES	Dec 25		Lt.-Col Warwick, who had been wounded at the battle of LOOS arrived from England and assumed command of the battalion vice temp Lt.-Col Ipatam-Pole to whom two months sick leave has been granted. The enemy dropped a few shells near the Railway station at midday, but otherwise the day was quiet.	Reference Map Trench
	26		Marching to where training in billets	
	27		The Divisional Cavalry & Cyclist troops arrived by G.R. Gurugen and our a bombardment of the enemy trenches and him slags ensued our 12 H.F. ten. 4½ to shells fell in the fair of the town commencing to Billeno	
	28		in which the Battalion was Marching to report training in billets	
	29		Nothing to report	
	30		The Battalion took over trenches 49 & 80 from the 13th Br London Territorials the 10th YORKS REGT occupying the right sector of the line of trenches held by the 62nd Inf Bde on	
	31		Nothing extraordinary has happened on was was killed and was wounded on the night of 30-31st Lieut A. H. Arthur was slightly wounded in the leg by the explosion of a rifle grenade fired into our trenches from the GERMAN lines. Keates, Fair Rain this afternoon wind South	

W.Warwick
Lieut Colonel
12nd (S) Bn Yorkshireland Shaddle

12 d Southumberld Prov. G.W.

Vol. 3 -

Tan '16

12ᵉ Northumberland ?as

21   Vol VII

62 &c

WAR DIARY
or
INTELLIGENCE SUMMARY
(Erase heading not required.)

Army Form C. 2118

Instructions regarding War Diaries and Intelligence Summaries are contained in F. S. Regs., Part II. and the Staff Manual respectively. Title Pages will be prepared in manuscript.

Place	Date	Hour	Summary of Events and Information	Remarks and references to Appendices
ARMENTIERS	1915 Jan 1st	1.30am	A message was received on the afternoon of the 31st warning the Battalion that "Quinson" in night would be active and perhaps use gas", (imitiarily 1.30am). At 1.30am a heavy bombardment commenced accompanied by the discharge of red rockets by the enemy; a considerable number of Shrapnel shells well directed against our trenches and Battalion Headquarters; no damage being done. The trench garrisons fired rapid fire at intervals during the night. The enemy replied with rapid fire as what was known to be midnight (his new year's eve) Berlin time.	
	2nd		Wind South West, dull atmosphere, the night was very quiet, several casualties occurred during the evening and night of 1st; 2nd Lieut A. MCARTHUR was wounded in the leg outside Clary of returning from a minor (GERMAN) rifle grenade, since coming into trenches rifle and machine gun fire has caused much annoyance to parties of our men working behind the lines.	
	3rd		A quiet day, considerable firing by day and a lot of machinegun fire at night, one man killed and two wounded.	
	4th		Nothing unusual has happened, the G.O.C. 2nd Division inspected Battn Headquarters and trenches and expressed his approval of the way in which trench hygiene was carried out, and complimented the Commandant upon the state of his Command	

Army Form C. 2118

WAR DIARY
or
INTELLIGENCE SUMMARY
(Erase heading not required.)

Place	Date	Hour	Summary of Events and Information	Remarks and references to Appendices
ARMENTIERES	January 1916 5th		During the night 4–5th enemy were quiet, it is thought that a less active unit relieved those who occupied the line when the Battalion took over. During the day trench 80 and PONT BALLOT were shelled, there were no casualties. A building known to unite existing trenches as CAMBRIDGE HOUSE about 500 yards due west of PONT BALLOT was heavily shelled with H.E. shells of large calibre. One man was killed by a bullet near 79 support trenches. The Battalion was relieved by the 13th Bn. NORTHD FUSRS and returned to billets in the RUE DE LA PAIX.	Sheet 36 map 1 HQ00-0
	6–7		The Commanding Officer inspected the two drafts, which reached the Battalion during the last tour of duty and one from the 3rd Battalion Northumberland Fusiliers. in trenches, one of 99 Non commissioned officers and men which arrived on Jan 3rd also from the 3rd Battalion, & one of 40 Non commissioned officers and men which arrived on Jan 5th. The General Officer commanding the 62nd Infantry Brigade having given orders that a raid be made by a party from the 12th Service Battalion on Northumberland Fusiliers upon the German salient opposite PONT BALLOT (c.29.A.4.1.) before the next tour of duty in trenches, preparations were hurried on as soon as the Battalion reached billets. An enlarged map having been prepared from air-plane photographs of the trenches in question, a similar system of trenches was put in a field suitable for practice work a little West of ARMENTIERES. CAPTN R.B. SINGLEHURST commanding D'Coy having been selected to direct the enterprise, it was decided to draw the detachment from volunteers from 'D' Coy. The reason for this was that 'D' Coy have frequently occupied trench 80 opposite the front of the enemy's line to be entered, and also further away that by drawing upon one Coy	

WAR DIARY or INTELLIGENCE SUMMARY

Army Form C. 2118

Place	Date	Hour	Summary of Events and Information	Remarks and references to Appendices
ARMENTIERES	Jan 7. 1916		only. Party, & c. coy could be pursued. D. Coy was therefore placed at all fatigues and the work of filling the trenches and digging them out to a depth of 6 inches was completed by the afternoon of Dec 7th the marking out being done under the supervision of Major Philpotts R.E. commanding the 97th Field Coy R.E.	Map ref Sheet 36 1/40,000
	Jan 8.		On the afternoon of Jan 7th the raiding detachment practiced entering and bombing along the whole system of trenches. The practice was repeated at night. Practices on the model trenches were carried out by day & night, and the final arrangements as to the composition of the parties settled upon.	
	Jan 9.		Further practices were carried out during the day, and one by night at which Brigadier General WILKINSON, G.O.C. 62nd Infantry Brigade was present. After the evening practice was completed Capt SINGLEHURST, Lieut PHILIP and No 11348 Sergt W.H. SCOTT made an extensive reconnaissance of the German wire and ditch in front of the proposed point of entry. The party got through the wire, crossed his ditch and reached the parapet of his trench; this reconnaissance proved subsequently of great value and contributed largely to the success of the final enterprise.	
	Jan 10.		Practices were again carried out by day and night; Lieut SPARKS R.E. and a party of 5 sappers participating. A final practice was carried out at 10.25 p.m. This practice was most satisfactory, every man knowing thoroughly well where to go and what to do. Bridges & mats for crossing the enemy's obstacles were carried, and a model of the wire & ditch built in front of the model trenches, these were thoroughly tested. Major General JACOB. G.O.C. 21st Division addressed the Raiding detachment in the morning.	
	Jan 11.		At midday the 21st Divisional Artillery cut the wire in front of the point to be attacked and heavily shelled	

Army Form C. 2118

WAR DIARY
or
INTELLIGENCE SUMMARY
(Erase heading not required.)

Instructions regarding War Diaries and Intelligence Summaries are contained in F. S. Regs., Part II. and the Staff Manual respectively. Title Pages will be prepared in manuscript.

Place	Date	Hour	Summary of Events and Information	Remarks and references to Appendices
ARMENTIERES	1916 Jan 11.		The enemy's trenches not only opposite PONT BALLOT, but also in several places along the Divisional front. Lt PHILIP observed the bombardment from Bo trench (C.28.B.7.3) and reported 15th prevent observation officer when he was satisfied as to the gap cut in the enemy's wire. The raiding party consisting of Capt R.B. SINGLE HURST, Lt A.C. SPARKS. R.E., Lt G.M. PHILIP, 2nd Lt C.P. STERLING, 2nd Lt G.H. CORKE, 2nd Lt G.D. MURRAY, Coy Sergt Major A. HILTON (no 5064) and 62 N.C.O's & men of the 12th Service Bn Northumberland Fusiliers and 5 sappers from the 97th Field Coy R.E. left ARMENTIERES at 8.30 p.m. All badges were removed and service caps exchanged for 'P'hive anti gas helmets at the dressing station of the 13th (S) Bn Northumberland Fusiliers at HOUPLINES. Faces were blacked & bayonets dulled, equipment was not worn, ammunition being carried in tunic pockets. The detachment was divided into five parties, four parties under officers and one under No 10402 Corporal (Lance Sergeant) J. SIMM of the battalion grenadiers. Each party consisted of two grenade throwers, two bayonet men, two carriers, two spare men and three extra bayonet men; each party carried 96 mills grenades. Extra to these parties were 6 men to act as escort to prisoners and 6 men to act as stretcher bearers and a party of five sappers led by Lt SPARKS. R.E. Lt PHILIP and Sergt SCOTT had previously reconnoitred the enemy's wire and reported a broad gap in it in front of the proposed point of entry: up to the S.of. Lt PHILIP had laid a line of string. The men of the 13.S.Bn who were holding the trenches during hour withdrawn from Bays 1 and 2 of trench 80, the raiding detachment assembled in those Bays at 10.40 p.m. At 11.10 p.m Lt PHILIP and Sergt SCOTT with the first party went over our parapet at Bay 1, Trench 80 (C.29.C.1.8½) and advanced steadily to the enemy's ditch laying a double line of white tape as they went. This party carried bridges for crossing the ditch which were placed across it without the party being observed, no complete had the Artillery destroyed the wire that the mats were not required. The remainder from parties followed in quick	Ref. MAP Sheet 36 1 40,000

1875 Wt.W593/826 1,000,000 4/15 I.B.C. & A. A.D.S.S./Forms/C. 2118.

WAR DIARY
or
INTELLIGENCE SUMMARY
(Erase heading not required.)

Army Form C. 2118

Instructions regarding War Diaries and Intelligence Summaries are contained in F. S. Regs., Part II. and the Staff Manual respectively. Title Pages will be prepared in manuscript.

Place	Date	Hour	Summary of Events and Information	Remarks and references to Appendices
ARMENTIERES.	1916. Jan 1st		succession, the portions keeping up the roar. The 21st Divisional artillery assisted by the 2nd Divisional Artillery and the heavy artillery of the 2nd Army opened fire at 11:15 p.m. forming an effective barrage of fire in a semi circle 50 yards beyond the limits of the sector attacked by the Infantry. At 11:17 p.m. 2/Philip and his party jumped into the German trench. Followed by the four other parties and the Royal Engineers. The Germans were taken completely by surprise and offered very little resistance, two prisoners were taken and about twenty of the enemy were killed while attempting to escape; the fire parties cleared their allotted section of the trenches, while the party of Royal Engineers planted no machine gun emplacements on mine shafts; two charges were successfully exploded by them in two concrete structures. Twenty minutes after the entry of our first party into the enemy's trenches Capt SINGLEHURST gave the signal to withdraw and all the parties returned to our lines. Our casualties were six killed and twelve wounded, one sapper was also wounded most of the casualties suffered were due to the enemy's artillery fire directed onto "no mans land" and our own wire; one Sergt was however killed before the attack while cutting our opening through our wire, and one man was in the German trench. The two prisoners were sent at once to the Advanced Brigade Headquarters of the 62nd Infantry Brigade. thence to the 21st Divisional Headquarters. Both prisoners belonged to the 133nd Saxon Regiment. and supplied much valuable information when subsequently interrogated. After the return of our raiding detachment, CAPT SINGLEHURST, 2Lt LANCELOT BURRELL, 2Lt LESLIE REYNOLDS and No 5064 Coy Sergt Major A. HILTON went out again under heavy fire and assisted in the	Ref. Map NO 36 1/40,000.

Army Form C. 2118

WAR DIARY
or
INTELLIGENCE SUMMARY
(Erase heading not required.)

Instructions regarding War Diaries and Intelligence Summaries are contained in F.S. Regs, Part II. and the Staff Manual respectively. Title Pages will be prepared in manuscript.

Place	Date	Hour	Summary of Events and Information	Remarks and references to Appendices
ARMENTIERES	1916. Jan 11th		bringing in of our wounded from between the trenches. There was sufficient light from the moon, which was 5 days old, to enable 2/Lt BORRELL, who was in charge of the signals to observe the entry of our parties into the enemy's trenches from our own parapet; he was thus able to keep Advanced Brigade Headquarters constantly informed as to the progress of the operations. The detachment remained under cover in 79 trench until the enemy's artillery fire had ceased and then returned to Billets in ARMENTIERES. The G.O.C. 21st Division addressed the Officers & men who had taken part in the raid and congratulated them on their success; messages of congratulation were also received from the Corps Commander of the 11th Corps and from the 1st Canadian Division.	Ref map sheet 36 1/40,000
"	12th		The Battalion relieved the 13th (S) Bn Northumberland Fusiliers in trenches 78,79 and 80 trenches. The relief being completed by 8.45 p.m. The Bn on the right – the 10th (S) Bn Yorkshire Regiment, the Bn on our left the 9th (S) Bn King's Own Yorkshire Light Infantry. Total strength of the battalion of this date was 897 all ranks; total number of rifles in firing & support trenches 545.	
"	13th		A very quiet day, weather clear, wind South West; both our own and the enemy's air planes were very active. The state of the trenches is greatly improved, and in the fire trenches there is dry standing in nearly every bay.	
"	14th		The enemy hoisted a white flag in the salient opposite 80 trench (C.29.A.4.1). It remained up for a quarter of an hour and was fired at by the men in trench 80. The enemy were more active than recently, and sent over a considerable number of rifle grenades into trench 80; two men were wounded and one killed, all by grenades before midday. At 1 p.m. the 21st Divisional Grenade School came up to 80 trench & fired 50 rifle grenades at the enemy trenches, the enemy retaliated and one man was killed by a grenade in 79 trench.	

1875 Wt. W593/826 1,000,000 4/15 J.B.C. & A. A.D.S.S./Forms/C. 2118.

WAR DIARY
or
INTELLIGENCE SUMMARY

(Erase heading not required.)

Army Form C. 2118

Instructions regarding War Diaries and Intelligence Summaries are contained in F. S. Regs., Part II. and the Staff Manual respectively. Title Pages will be prepared in manuscript.

Place	Date	Hour	Summary of Events and Information	Remarks and references to Appendices
ARMENTIERES.	1916. Jan 14.		More rapid fire than usual was directed upon the enemy's communication trenches and roads in rear of this trenches; this fire was very quick during 'stand to' and seems to have caused the enemy much annoyance as he retaliated with 7.7 cm shells or 80 trench mortar, no casualties resulted.	Ref map sheet 36 1/40,000
	" 15.		A very quiet day, the enemy contenting himself with shelling the Distillery and FERME DE LA BUTERNE. weather very fine, wind South West.	
	" 16.		Very fine dry weather continues, the trenches have improved immensely, the fire trenches being quite free from water, rapid progress has been made on the Strong Points and wire entanglements in front are can of the Strong Points. After dusk enemy's machine guns unusually active, enfilading 78 trench & shooting down AUSTRALIA ROAD. Casualties one man killed by a bullet in 79 trench, one wounded on the AUSTRALIA ROAD tramway. 2 Lt Johnstone joined the Battalion, having come from 15th Reserve Battalion.	
	" 17.		Very clear morning, our own and the enemy's air-planes very active from 9 AM till midday; the enemy shelled S.P.2 at 10.15 AM and 3.45 p.m with 10.5 cm H.E. shells; one of the last group fell into the trench but no casualties resulted. Enemy machine guns were again active, and the 94th Bde R.F.A shelled BLACK REDOUBT between 6 P.M - 7 P.M which had the result of silencing the most troublesome of the machine guns.	
	" 18.		Fine day, wind South West; the enemy shelled S.P.2 at 10 A.M and again at 4 p.m; there were no casualties. The Btⁿ was relieved by the 13th (S) Bn Northumberland Fusiliers in trenches 78, 79, 80 and outposts being handed over & relief complete by 3.45 p.m. The 12" S. 13th returning to Billets in the RUE DE LA PAIX.	

WAR DIARY or INTELLIGENCE SUMMARY

Army Form C. 2118

Place	Date	Hour	Summary of Events and Information	Remarks and references to Appendices
ARMENTIERES	1916 Jan 19-29		The Battalion was in rest billets, and supplied working parties for the trenches daily. The Coys most so employed continuing training; one Coy was on duty in the subsidiary line from AUSTRALIA ROAD to SPAIN AVENUE communication trench nightly.	Ref. Map sheet 36 1/40,000
	23.		A draft of 19 other ranks arrived from the base, 12 men coming from the 3rd Bn and 7 of the 12th (S) Bn. wounded returning from Base hospital.	
	24.		The Battalion relieved the 13th (S) Bn. West Yorks in trenches 78, 79 & 80 & the supports. The enemy were unusually active during the relief, which in consequence took rather longer than usual; it was completed by 9.15 pm. There was one man wounded during the relief, one man during the day wounded on a working party, and one later on sentry.	
	25.		The Battalion on the night was the 10th Service Battalion Yorkshire Regiment, and on the left the 9th(S) Bn K.O.Y.L.I. An unusually clear day, not a cloud to be seen. The enemy began to shell HOUPLINES soon trenches at 8 A.M and continued without intermission until 4.30 p.m.; their fire was evenly distributed over all trenches and works in rear but no damage whatever was done.	
	26.		Major T. McL. JARVIS, 10th(S) Bn QUEEN'S ROYAL WEST SURREY Regt was attached in trenches in instruction until 28th. At 9.55 p.m the 64th Brigade, on our left carried out a 'cutting out' enterprise against trenches opposite BURNT FARM; hostile artillery retaliation on the heavy on of Bn dunderion. The enemy shelled the whole Divisional front purposely; during the day we suffered one casualty only, 2/Lt G. D. MURRAY, being killed by a 7.7 cm shell in S.P.2. 2/Lt MURRAY joined the battalion on Oct 9th 1915 from the 11th Bn. At 9.50 p.m the enemy opened rapid fire.	
	27.		This day being the German Emperor's birthday, officers & men were quite prepared for unusual 'frightfulness'	

1875 Wt. W593/826 1,000,000 4/15 J.B.C. & A. A.D.S.S./Forms/C. 2118.

WAR DIARY
or
INTELLIGENCE SUMMARY

(Erase heading not required.)

Army Form C. 2118

Place	Date	Hour	Summary of Events and Information	Remarks and references to Appendices
ARMENTIERES	Jan 27		Promiscuous shelling began at 8.30 A.M. and continued until 4.30 p.m., front line trenches, supports & communication trenches all coming in for a share; a most remarkable number of 7.7 cm shells fired by the enemy were blind, fully 70 per cent failing to explode. There was considerable rifle fire at 'stand to'. A patrol went out at 7 p.m. to examine a supposed enemy sap opposite the junction of 8 & 8½ trenches at a point C.29.a.4.5½; the officer in charge 2 Lt MATHER reported much noise in the German trenches; the supposed sap being shell holes made by our heavy guns whilst the enemy have dug out to trenches. At 9.50 p.m. the enemy opened rapid and machine gun fire along the Divisional front, a few minutes later opened a heavy bombardment of all our fire trenches; our artillery retaliated, the bombardment lasted about half an hour; our casualties were seven wounded. At 4.15 A.M. the enemy again bombarded our trenches, no more casualty being suffered sustained; Wind West, day dull & atmosphere moist.	Ref Map Sheet 36 — 1/40,000
	Jan 28		The bombardment of our trenches and strong points continued from 8.30 A.M. - 4.30 p.m.; battalion headquarters & SPHIN AVENUE communication trench being specially attended to. Our wires to the artillery were broken several times, but communication was kept open all day between Bn. HQ and 'D' Battery of the 97th Field Howitzer Bde. Total casualties for the 24 hours, 1 killed by rifle bullet, four wounded by shrapnel, the result of over 1000 shells of all sorts.	
	Jan 29		Misty morning, very little artillery activity in consequence. In the afternoon the wind veered round to the East and armoured between East and South East for 48 hours. Machine guns active after dusk but little or no artillery fire by either side	

WAR DIARY
or
INTELLIGENCE SUMMARY
(Erase heading not required.)

Army Form C. 2118

Place	Date	Hour	Summary of Events and Information	Remarks and references to Appendices
ARMENTIERES	1916 Jan 29		The following honours were announced in connection with the raid on the enemy's trenches on Crepa Mds. January 11th — CAPT. R.B. SINGLEHURST, and Lieut. G.M. PHILIP to receive the military medal. This distinction was also conferred on Lt A.C. SPARKS R.E. To receive the Distinguished Conduct Medal, No 11348 Sergt W.H. SCOTT, No 5064 Coy Sgt Major A. HILTON., No 14265 Pte H. HODGKINSON No 15377 Pte (Lance Cpl) T.J. JONES.	Ref Map Sheet 36 1/40,000
	Jan 30.		Wealth colder, wind still in the East; special precautions were therefore taken against hostile gas attack. There was again a thick mist & in consequence very little artillery activity. There were three men wounded this day, two being caused by a rifle grenade. The Battalion was relieved in trenches 78.79.80 and supports by the 13th (S) Bn Northumberland Fusiliers, the relief being complete by 8.50 p.m; the 12th (S) Bn returning to Billets in the RUE DE LA PAIX.	
	Jan 31.		The Battalion rested in Billets, the day being occupied with the usual inspections in the afternoon; Coys were marched to the Divisional Baths at PONT DE NIEPPE.	

M. Vincent Luddard
Capt. 12" (S) Bn Manchester

12th (S) Bn. Northumberland Fusiliers.

Ref. Map 1/10.000.   O.O. No. 20.   9.1.1916.

1. An attack will be made on the enemy's position East of ARMENTIERES on the night of January 11th 1916.

OBJECTS.
   (a) Capturing as many Germans as possible and gaining information from them.
   (b) Killing as many Germans as possible.
   (c) Destroying M. Gun emplacements and mine shafts.
   (d) Decreasing the morale of the enemy.
   (e) Discovering what arrangements (if any) exist for using poisonous gas or liquid fire.

ATTACKING FORCE. 2. The attacking force will be commanded by Captain R. B. SINGLEHURST and will consist of 6 Officers 54 N.C.O.'s and men (volunteers) made up as follows.

   No. 1 Squad commanded by Lt. G. M. Philip.
   No. 2   "   "   "   2/Lt. G. D. Murray.
   No. 3   "   "   "   2/Lt. G. H. Corke.
   No. 4   "   "   "   2/Lt. G. P. Sterling.
   No. 5   "   "   "   L/Sgt. Simm.

   and

Lieut. Sparks and 5 R. & F. R.E., 97th Fd. Coy. to whom special orders have been issued.

OTHER DETAILS. 3. 1 N.C.O and 8 men to act as escort for prisoners. 6 stretcher bearers (with 3 stretchers) this party will leave Bay 1, Trench 80, as soon as the bombardment commences, and lie down on the Western side of the enemy's wire.

OBJECTIVE. 4. The objective will be the enemy's front line, communication trenches and dug outs from C.29.c.5.8 to C.29.a.4.0 and as far back as the PONT BALLOT - LA FRESNELLE Road.

WATCHES. 5. Signal watches will be carried and set at 6 p.m. Sunday 9th, 9 a.m. Monday and at 7 p.m. at B.H.Q. Watches will be finally checked and set at 6 p.m. on Tuesday at Brigade Headquarters.

RECONNAISSANCE. 6. Lieut. Philip and scouts drawn from No. 1 squad will reconnoitre the enemy's wire and ditch between 7 p.m. and 10 p.m., they will cut any barbed wire necessary (but not smooth) and report to the O.C.

EQUIPMENT & DRESS. 7. Cap and shoulder badges will be left at Billets, bayonets will be darkened, all ranks will blacken their faces and hands, gas helmets rolled up will be worn in lieu of the S. Dress Cap and satchels left at the dressing station 13th Bn. N. F. Magazines will contain 10 rds in addition 4 full chargers of S.A.A will be carried in the pockets of trousers.

A.B. 64, letters, oil bottles and personal property will be left at Billets.

Bayonets will be fixed and no equipment will be worn.

COMMUNICATION 8. 2nd Lieut. BORRELL will arrange for communication to be established between the O.C. and Bay 1, Trench 80 at 11.15 p.m., thence to Bn. Headquarters, 13 N.F.

POSITION. 9. The O.C. attacking party will be just inside the enemy's trench (with two orderlies and two immediately outside) from 11.15 p.m. until withdrawal commences.

ARTILLERY. 10. The 21st Divnl. Artillery will cut wire in front of the enemy's trench during the day and place a barrage of fire on the flanks of the sector to be attacked, and at every point for 50 yds outside the area of operations on the East side.

ASSAULT. 11. The attacking party will be drawn up inside Bays 1 & 2 Trench 80 by 10.45 p.m. Scouts and matmen in front, the remainder of squads in rear.

Stretcher bearers will be in rear and quite clear of the attacking party.

(Scouts) At 11 p.m. Lieut PHILIP and the scouts will leave the parapet and make their way towards the enemy's wire and select crossing points indicating them to the squads as they arrive.

Lieut. PHILIP will by means of a liquid compass direct the advance and arrange for two lines of white tape to be laid from Bays 1 & 2, Trench 80, to the enemy's wire and from it to the point of trench to be entered.

(Main attack). At 11.5 p.m. the remainder of the force will advance under the O.C. to the wire where they will be met by the scouts from No. 1 squad.

At 11.15 p.m. the trench will be entered. Squads will at once proceed to the trenches allotted to them, prisoners taken will be passed back, any who resist will be bayonetted, squads will bomb their way through the trenches, examine all dug outs, remove shoulder straps from dead Germans.

Prisoners. Prisoners will be brought back as taken and conducted to Advanced Brigade Headquarters via LONDON RD and AUSTRALIA ROAD.

WITHDRAWAL. 12. The force will withdraw at 11.35 p.m. the signal to do so will be several long blasts on the whistle sounded by all Officers & N.C.Os.

Officers i/c Squads will watch the time carefully and should the O.C. not be able to make himself heard they will retire their squads and sound their whistles at 11.35 p.m.

No equipment or rifles will be left behind.

The party will be warned to look out for the tapes.

SHELTER. 13. 2nd Lieuts BORRELL and HARROWER will note men's names, take possession of captured articles and conduct men to shelter on arrival at Trench 80.

Machine Guns. (a) The Bde. M. Gun Officer, 64 Inf. Bde. is arranging to open bursts of fire on the enemy's parapet from

C.29.c.5.8. to C.29.a.4.0 from Trench 81, between 11 p.m. and 11.10 p.m.

From 11.10 p.m. to 11.15 p.m. bursts of fire will be directed from this gun at a height of 5 yards above the German parapet.

(b) From 11.35 p.m. to 11.40 p.m. M. Gun from Trench 81 will traverse the enemy's parapet with rapid fire from C.29.a.4.2 to C.29.a.7.5, and M. Guns from Trenches 80, 79, 78, 77, 75 and 74 will similarly traverse enemy's parapet from C.29.c.6.7 to I.5.c.7.1.

GRENADIERS. 14. Bombs will be fired from the WEST Spring Gun into the enemy's trench from C.29.c.5.8 to C.29.a.4.0 between 11 p.m. and 11.10 p.m.

Aid Posts. 15. In dug outs under 2nd Lieut. MATHER.

16. Reports to Advd. Bde. H. Qrs. after 10 p.m.

G. White. Lieut & Adjt.
12th (S) B. Northd Fus.

A

A95
D111
A92
D95
C95
A97
D94
B97
/2guns 94°
C94
B97

Tracing
1/10,000

Red 18 pounders.
Blue 4.5 Howitzers
Green 9.2 howitzers

a94
a94

Tracing
1/10,000

Red 18 pounders.
Blue 4·5 Howitzers
Green 4·2 Howitzers

62 Inf. Bde. O.O. No. 45.   Copy No. 1

Ref. 1/10,000 Map
& Trench Sketch.
                                                        Jan. 29th 1916.

1. The front now occupied by 21 Div. will be held by two Brigades in the front line, and one in Reserve, from the night of 1/2 February.
   The boundary between the two Brigades in front line will be from level crossing North of FME DES JARDINS (I.2.b.5.6.) to the FME de la BUTERNE (inclusive to the right Brigade) thence to Rd. Junction at C 28.d.7.2. and along road to where Trench 77 cuts, ~~road~~ (JAPAN Rd) and thence due East to the German lines.

2. On the night 1/2 February, 62 Inf. Bde. will become Divisional Reserve, till the night of Feb. 7/8th, when it will relieve 63 Inf. Bde. in the right sector.

3. The following reliefs will take place on night of Feb. 1/2 :-

   (a) 1/Lincoln R, will be relieved by 4 Middlesex R, 63 Inf. Bde, in Trenches 74, 74s, 74ss, 75, CHICKEN FARM, 75s, 76, 76s, 77, (as far as where JAPAN road cuts trench) 77s, S.P.X. and S.P.Y.; and by 9 K.O.Y.L.I., 64 Inf Bde, in remainder of Trench 77.

   (b) 13 North'd Fus, will be relieved by 9 K.O.Y.L.I. in Trenches 78, 79 and 80, and their support trenches, and S.P.Z.

   Details of relief will be arranged between Battns. concerned, and will be reported to this Office.

4. Machine Guns will be relieved under arrangements to be made by the Bde. Machine Gun Officer, with Bde. M. Gun Officers of 63 and 64 Inf. Bdes.

5. O.C.'s 13 North'd Fus, and 1/Lincoln R, will be responsible for their sectors till the reliefs are complete when they will report to this Office.

6. On completion of reliefs Battns. will be billeted as follows:-

   13 North'd Fus, at the HOSPICE CIVILE in RUE des PATURES and COLLEGE de GARCONS in RUE du COLLEGE, at present occupied by 10 K.O.Y.L.I.

   1/Lincoln R, in Blue Factory in RUE JULES LEBLEU and the HOSPICE MAHIEU in RUE DENIS PAPIN, at present occupied by 8 Somerset L.I. (63 Inf.Bde).

7. Bde. Hd. Qrs, will remain in its present position.

8. Please acknowledge.

Issued at 6-45 p.m.
   by Orderly.
                                              Major,
                                              Bde. Major,
                                              62 Inf. Bde.

   Copy No.1 - 13 North'd Fus.
       : 2 - 1/Lincoln R.
       : 3 - 12 North'd Fus.
       : 4 - 10 York R.
       : 5 - Bde. M. Gun Officer.
       : 6 - Retained.

Copy No. 1 - 12 North'd Fus.
:   :   2 - 10 York R.
:   :   3 - 1/Lincoln R.
:   :   4 - 13 North'd Fus.
:   :   5 - 63 Inf. Bde.
:   :   6 - Bde. M. Gun Officer.
:   :   7 - Bde. Signalling Officer.
:   :   8 - Retained.

WAR DIARY or INTELLIGENCE SUMMARY

Army Form C. 2118

(Erase heading not required.)

Place	Date	Hour	Summary of Events and Information	Remarks and references to Appendices
ARMENTIERES	Feb 1–6th		The 12th Service Battalion Northumberland Fusiliers, retired in billets in ARMENTIERES, continued working parties being provided daily to work in the trenches of the 63rd Infantry Bde now holding the left sector of the Divisional front – Trenches 67 – 71 (I.16.c.6.7.10. I.5.A.2.7). From Feb 1st the front line of the 21st Division was held by two Brigades, the Third Brigade being in Divisional Reserve in ARMENTIERES. The junction of the two Brigades was fixed at the front where JAPAN ROAD runs into Trench 77. (I.5.A.2.7)	Ref Map sheet 36 1/40,000. (edition 6) from Feb 1st onwards reference was all to the revised edition of sheet 36.
	Feb 7th		A Reinforcement of 1 officer and 22 other ranks arrived. The officer was 2nd Lt A. MALCOLM who went to the 15th Reserve battalion, when this battalion went abroad. The battalion relieved the 8th Service Battalion Lincolnshire Regiment in trenches 67, 68, 69, 70 & 71 (I.16.c.6.7.10. 1.10.B.7.3) The disposition of companies was as follows – Relief was complete at 8.15 p.m. "A" Coy from 67 to 68 inclusive, "C" Coy 69 and half 70, "B" Coy half 70 and 71 including the salient known as the "MUSHROOM", "D" Coy LILLE POST Strong point and 67 strong support. On the left was the 10th Yorkshire Regiment, on the right the 1st Battalion WORCESTERSHIRE REGT, 9th battalion on the right was left Battalion of the Second Army, 23rd Division, 1st Army. The 12th (S) Batn Shropshire on the extreme right flank of the two Bns of the 62nd & 1st Bn LINCOLNSHIRE REGT occupied the subsidiary line of trenches in rear of the two Bns of the 62nd Infantry Bde occupying the right sector of the Divisional front.	
	Feb 8th		Fine day, wind South West, day passed very quietly; after dark all available men worked on the parapet of the front line trenches & on the wire in front of them, both of which were found to be in a deplorable condition. "B" Coy relieved the Platoon holding the MUSHROOM after 12 hours.	

Army Form C. 2118

Instructions regarding War Diaries and Intelligence Summaries are contained in F.S. Regs., Part II and the Staff Manual respectively. Title Pages will be prepared in manuscript.

WAR DIARY
or
INTELLIGENCE SUMMARY
(Erase heading not required.)

Place	Date	Hour	Summary of Events and Information	Remarks and references to Appendices
ARMENTIERES	Feb 9th 1916		Wind veered round to the East, but was too high for use of gas; raining and cold. It gun commanding.	Ref map sheet 36 $\frac{1}{40,000}$ (Edition 6.)
	Feb 10th		'B' Coy was slightly wounded in the "MUSHROOM", but remained at duty. At 3 pm the enemy fired four eight inch shells at trench 70, but caused no casualties. Wind remained in the East, but was too high to cause uneasiness, very cold & raining. 'B' Coy holding	
	Feb 11th		the MUSHROOM was relieved by 'E' Coy at 5 p.m. Wind back to South West and weather fine & dry; enemy's artillery very active, our frontline & support trenches shelled in the afternoon. At stand-to the PONT BALLOT salient which had been located to a number of phosphorous bombs, the enemy shelled by our artillery during the day, was stood to by the Division front, fired rapid and his field guns strafed at	
	Feb 12th		incoming enemy all along the Division front. During night the 1st Bn WORCESTER REGT relieved by 1/1st Bn SHERWOOD FORESTERS. Our frontline trenches. On our right all our frontline who shelled during the afternoon, also 67 support Enemy's artillery again very active, the latter rather severely. Weather fire & clear, wind South-West. Coy Sergt Majr GARDINER trenches.	
	Feb 13th		(No 8369) of 'B' Coy killed. Shelling two severe, enemy put some 7·7 cm shells into LILLE POST. The Battalion was relieved by the 13th (S) Bn Northumberland Fusiliers, in trenches 67,68,69,70 and 71; the relief being complete at 10·45 p.m; on our left the 10th Bn Yorkshire Regt had been relieved earlier in the evening by the 1st Bn LINCOLNSHIRE REGT; the 10th (S) Bn Yorkshire Regt went into the Subsidiary Line (right sector) and the 12th (S) Bn Northumberland Fusiliers into the Bde Reserve billets in the BOULEVARD	
	Feb 14,15		FAIDHERBE. Casualties during this tour in the trenches 7 killed and 17 wounded. The Bn in Bde Reserve, numerous working parties provided daily for the trenches in the right sector.	

WAR DIARY or INTELLIGENCE SUMMARY

Army Form C. 2118

Place	Date	Hour	Summary of Events and Information	Remarks and references to Appendices
ARMENTIERES	Feb 16th		12th (S) Bn. relieved the 10th (S) Bn. Yorkshire Regt. in the right sector of the Subsidiary Line (19.C.7.3. to C.28.A.12) Strong Points S.P.X. and S.P.Y. and PORT EGAL, REDOUBT. Bn. Headquarters at SQUARE FARM (19.B.2.4)	Ref. Map Sheet 36 1/40,000 (Edition 6)
	Feb 17 & 18		Battalion supplied large working parties for work in front line trenches by day and night. Weather rainy & cold, wind South West.	
	Feb 19		62nd Infantry Bde relieved in the Right Section of the 2nd Divisional front by the 64th Infantry Bde. 12th (S) Bn. KINGS OWN YORKSHIRE LIGHT INFANTRY in the right section of the Subsidiary line, relief complete at 11.35 p.m.	
	Feb 20-25		12th (S) Bn. Northumberland Fusiliers relieved by the 9th (S) Bn. KINGS OWN YORKSHIRE LIGHT INFANTRY in the right section of the Subsidiary line, relief complete at 11.35 p.m. The Battalion received the congratulations of the Divisional Commander "for the excellent way they had carried out their duties during their recent tour in the trenches." The Battalion in Divisional Reserve in ARMENTIERES; every day large working parties were provided for work on the trenches. Bn. Billets occupied were — A & B Coys COLLEGE DES GARCONS, C & D Coys. HOSPICE CIVILE, Head quarters 35 RUE NATIONALE.	
	Feb 25		The 62nd Infantry Bde relieved the 63rd Infantry Bde in the left sector, the 12th Northumberland Fusiliers relieved the 8th (S) Bn. LINCOLNSHIRE REGT in trenches 77, 78, 79, 80, 81, 82. The relief was completed at 8.30 pm. the (6 huh?) Brigade continued to occupy the right sector of the Division from. 12th (S) Bn. Northumberland Fusiliers holding from (1.5.A.2.7 to C.23.C.2.2) 10th (S) Bn. Yorkshire Regt. on the left, the 9th (S) Bn. K.O.Y.L.I on the right.	
	Feb 26		A very quiet day, artillery fired several rounds at P.M.E. HELA BUTERNE and DISTILLERY, there was little rifle fire from enemy trenches.	
	Feb 27, 28		Little rifle fire, artillery fired H.E. and several elongated MINENWERFER bombs at ground between 8 B S and Battalion Headquarters, several shells were blind, no damage was done. A quiet day, enemy shews HOUPLINE'S little rifle fire some machine gun fire at night.	

Army Form C. 2118

WAR DIARY
or
INTELLIGENCE SUMMARY
(Erase heading not required.)

Instructions regarding War Diaries and Intelligence Summaries are contained in F.S. Regs., Part II. and the Staff Manual respectively. Title Pages will be prepared in manuscript.

Place	Date	Hour	Summary of Events and Information	Remarks and references to Appendices
ARMENTIERES	1916 Feb 29.		A quiet day, the hostile Artillery put a little shrapnel into the subsidiary line (left sector) and SPAIN AVENUE. There were no casualties. Hostile machine guns very active from "Strand" in the evening (5 p.m.) until midnight. The dispositions of companies were as follows. A Coy his trenches 77~78~78 support. D Coy trenches 79~80~80 support. B Coy trenches 81 and 82. C Coy in Reserve in the subsidiary line with one platoon in S.P.2. Battalion Grenadiers in the Subsidiary Line. M Mansurl Lewl Col Comg. 12th Notts & Derby 1/3/16.	Ref map sheet 36 1/40,000 (Edition 6)

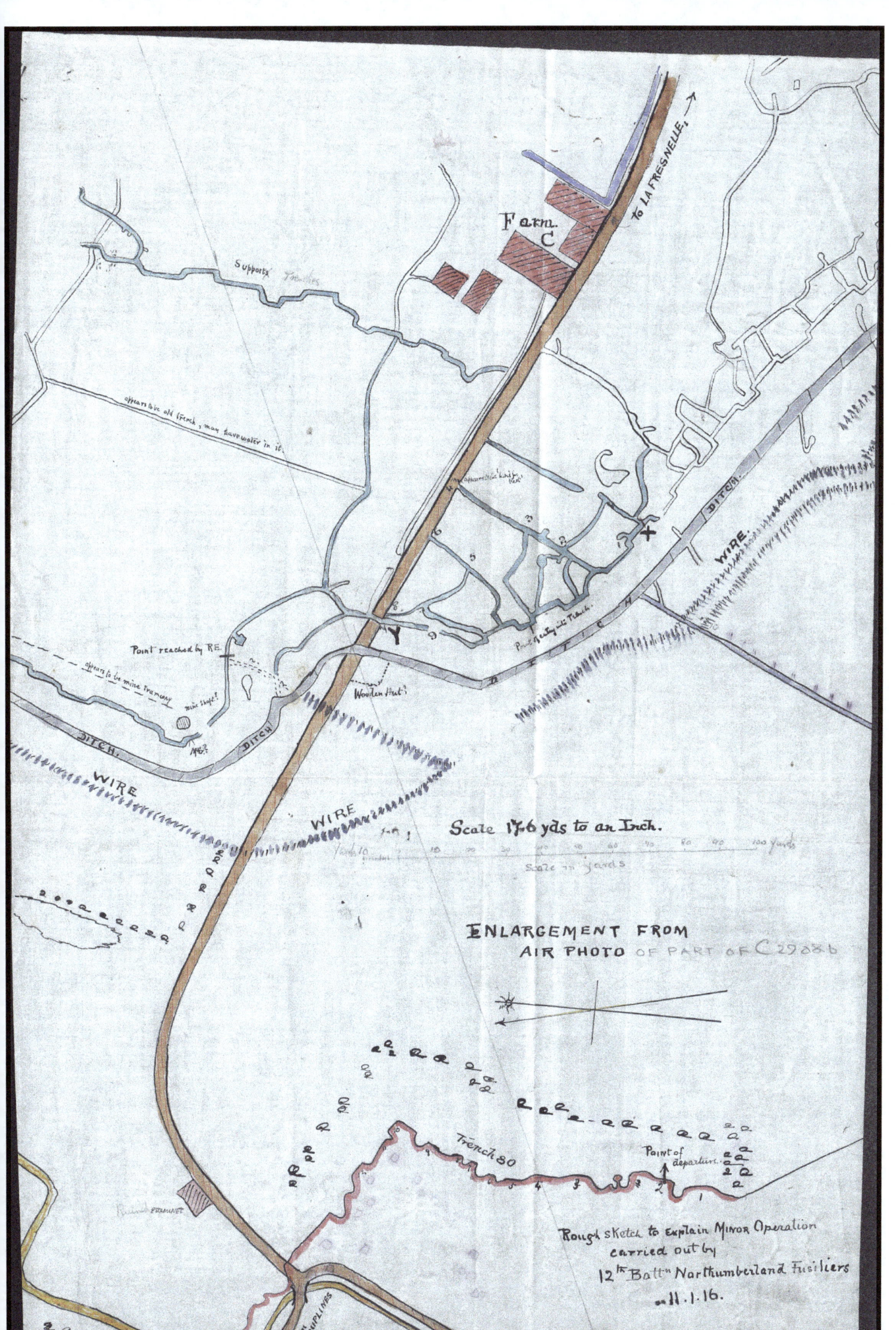

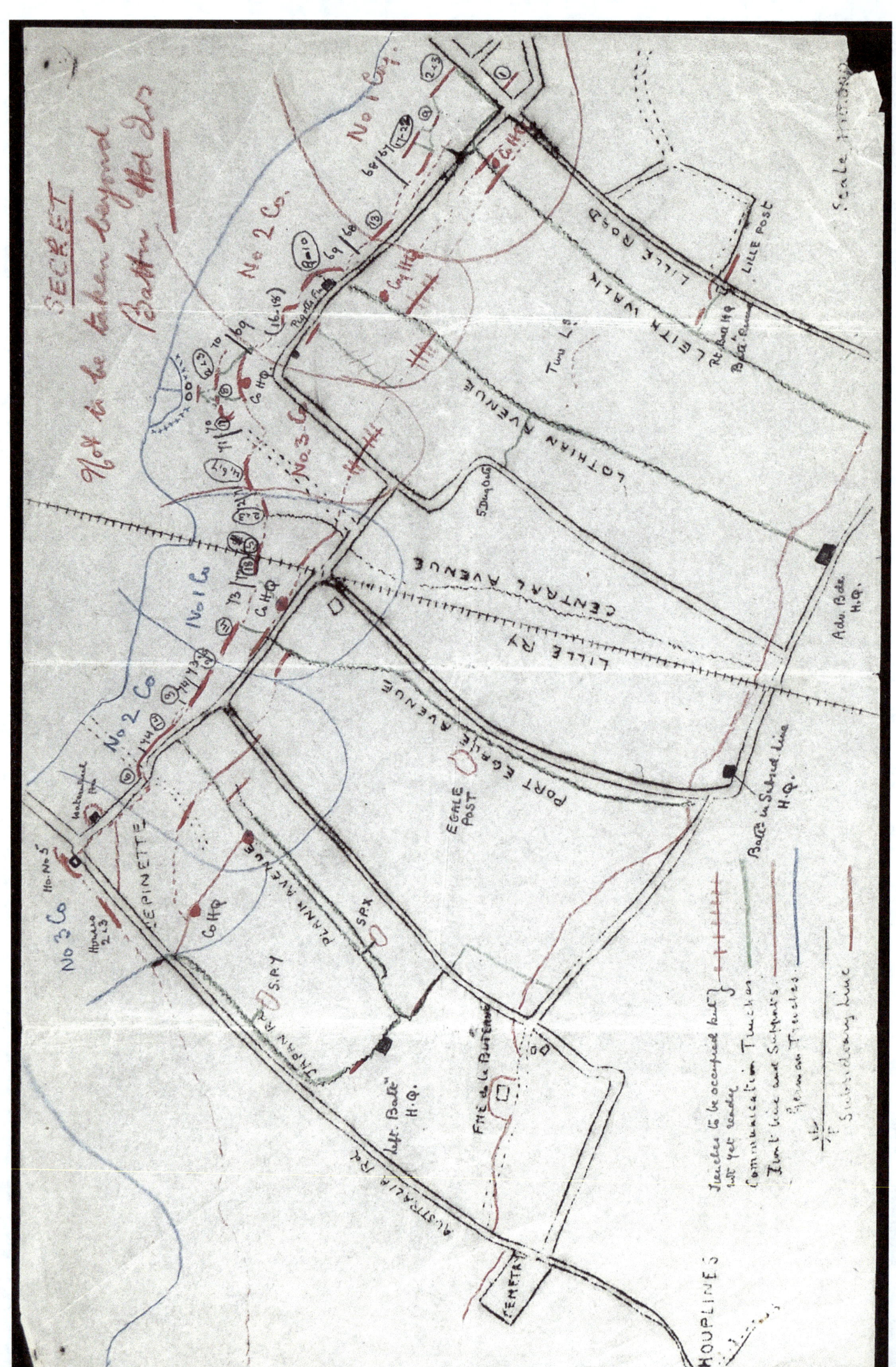

13th. Northd. Fus.   OPERATION ORDERS No. 37   Copy No. 1

SPAIN AVENUE (TRENCHES)

Ref. Trench Sketch Map & Sheet 36.   Feby. 1st. 1916.

(1) The 9th. K.O.Y.L.I. will relieve the Battn. this evening, taking over the trenches as follows :-

A Coy.	9th. K.O.Y.L.I.		78 & 78S.
B "	"	"	79 & 79S, 79SS
C "	"	"	80 & 80 S
D "	"	"	SPZ & Subsidiary Line.

(2) The relief will be carried out via following routes :-
78 Trench. Incoming troops via HOUPLINES-EPINETTE Road. Outgoing troops at discretion of O.C.Coy. If SPAIN AVENUE is used relief of 79 must be completed first.

Trench 79. Traffic both ways via SPAIN AVENUE.

Trench 80 Incoming troops via GLOSTER AVENUE & 80S. Outgoing troops via SPAIN AVENUE.

(3) O.C's Coys. will report personally at H.Qrs. when their relief is complete.

(4) All down traffic in SPAIN AVENUE will be suspended from 6 p.m. to 6.30 p.m.

(5) Guides from each trench and SPZ will meet incoming troops at HOUPLINES Trench Tram Terminus at 6 p.m. They are to be given slips bearing the number of the trench to which they are guiding.

(6) A & B Coys. will occupy billets in HOSPICE CIVILE, RUE DES PATURES. C & D Coys. COLLEGE DE GARCONS, RUE DU COLLEGE. Officers' billets are as follows :-

H. QRS.	35 RUE NATIONALE
A. Coy.	22 RUE SADI CARNOT
B. Coy.	14 RUE SADI CARNOT
C. Coy.	6 RUE DU COLLEGE
D. Coy.	37 RUE NATIONALE

Grenadiers will be billeted with A & B Coys. and Signallers with C & D Coys.

(7) All N.C.O's and men are to wash their feet and change their socks immediately on arrival in billets. Platoon Commanders are responsible for this.

(8) All ranks are to be shown the way into the cellars as soon as possible after arrival in billets.

(9) All Officers are to make themselves acquainted with whereabouts of H.Qrs. at once and will send an orderly there who knows their own H.Qrs. on arrival in billets.

(10) Copy of trench store receipts to be sent in to the Adjutant tonight for transmission to 62nd INF. BDE.

Issued by Orderly at 5 p.m.

No. 1 Copy Retained.
"   2 "   A Coy.
"   3 "   B Coy.
"   4 "   C Coy.
"   5 "   D. Coy.
"   6 "   Grenadier Officer.

Capt. & Adjutant,
13th. Northd. Fusiliers.

62 Inf. Bde. O.O. No. 46.   Copy No. 4 **Secret**

Ref. 1/10,000 Map
& Trench Sketch attached.   Feb. 4th 1916.

1.   62 Inf. Bde. will relieve 63 Inf. Bde. in the Right
        Sector of 21 Div. front, on night of Feb. 7th/8th.
            Two Battalions will hold the sector with two Battalions
        in Bde. Reserve, one of which will occupy the Subsidiary
        Line.

2.(a)   12 North'd Fus. will relieve 8 Lincoln R. in Trenches
        67 - 71 (both inclusive), finding 1 Officer and 40 men in
        LILLE POST.

  (b)   10 York R. will relieve 4 Middlesex R. in Trenches 72 -
        point in 77 where JAPAN Road cuts Trench, finding garrisons
        of EGALE POST, S.P.X., and S.P.Y.

            These reliefs will commence at 5 p.m., 12 North'd Fus.
        using LEITH WALK and LOTHIAN AVENUE, and 10 York R. PORT
        EGALE AVENUE, PLANK AVENUE, and AUSTRALIA Road.

            Details of relief will be arranged between the Battns.
        concerned.

3.   1/Lincoln R. (in Bde. Reserve) will relieve 8 Somerset
        L.I., in the Subsidiary Line from LILLE Road to FME de la
        BUTERNE (inclusive) at 9 p.m.

            Details of the relief to be arranged between the Battns.

4.   The relieved Battns. will be responsible for their
        sectors till the relief is complete, when O.C. relieving
        Battns. will report to 63 Inf. Bde.

            G.O.C. 62 Inf. Bde. will assume Command of the Sector
        as soon as the whole relief is complete.

5.   The necessary reconnaissance for the relief will be made
        by Commanding Officers, and Company Officers on Feb. 6th
        and 7th.

6.   The Bde. M. Gun Officer will arrange for the relief of
        M. Guns of 63 Inf. Bde. with Bde. M. Gun Officer, 63 Inf.
        Bde. on night of Feb. ~~7th/8th~~. 6th/7th

7.   The Bde. Signalling Officer will arrange with Bde.
        Signalling Officer, 63 Inf. Bde. for the relief of the
        Signallers by midday Feb. 7th.

8.   13 North'd Fus. will take over the billets at present
        occupied by 10 York and Lancs. R. (H.Q. 20 Boulevard Faid-
        herbe) on the night of Feb. 7th/8th.
            Arrangements to be made between Battns. concerned.

9.   The Right Battn. will evacuate wounded to 63 Fd. Ambce.
        and Left Battn. to 64 Fd. Ambce.

10.   Reserves of S.A.A., Grenades, and Trench Stores will be
        handed over by midday on Feb. 7th.

11.   Hd. Qrs., 62 Inf. Bde. will move to present HD. Qrs.,
        of 63 Inf. Bde. at No. 3 RUE BAYARD at 6 p.m. on Feb. 7th.

                                            W.Weltheed Major,
                                                Bde. Major,
Issued at 8 p.m.   62 Inf. Bde.
by Orderly.

13th. Northd. Fusiliers.   OPERATION ORDERS. No. 38.   Copy. No. 1

ARMENTIERES.   7/2/16.
Ref/ Trench Sketch Map.

1.   The 62nd. Brigade will relieve the 63rd. Brigade in trenches
     67 - 71 inclusive tonight.

2.   The Battalion is placed in 62nd. Bde. Reserve tonight.

3.   Present billets will be vacated at 6.30 p.m. and new billets
     will be taken as follows :-
     A Coy.   Rue Marle.   Dufor-Lesernez Warehouse.
     B Coy.   Rue de la Gare.   Mahieu Warehouse.
     C Coy.   "   " "   "   Dansette Warehouse.
     D Coy.   "   " "   "   Dafour-Daren Warehouse.

     Officers' billets will be as follows :-
     H.Qrs.   42 Rue Marle.
     Ord.Rm. 20 Boulevarde Faidherbe
     A & C Coy. 1 Rue Jacquard.
     B Coy.   20 Boulevarde Faidherbe
     D Coy.   6   do.   do.
     The key of 6 Boulevarde Faidherbe is to be obtained at No.8
     Boulevarde Faidherbe.
     Signallers and Grenadiers will be billetted in Mahieu Warehouse.

4.   All reserve S.A.A. and Grenades in waistcoats, will be handed
     over to the 8th. Lincoln Regt. who will take over our billets.

5.   A wagon will be at Bn.Hqrs. in Rue Nationale at 6 p.m. to move
     Officers' baggage.

6.   Reports up to 6 p.m. to 35 Rue Natioale, afterwards to 42 Rue
     Marle.

Issued at 5.30 p.m. by Orderly.

Copy No.1 Retained.
  "   " 2 A Coy.
  "   " 3 B "
  "   " 4 C "
  "   " 5 D "

                                        B. Masseh-Palmer
                                        Capt. & Adjutant,
                                        13th. Northd. Fusiliers.

"A" Form.   Army Form C. 2121.
           MESSAGES AND SIGNALS.   No. of Message_____

Prefix_____Code_____m. | Words | Charge |
Office of Origin and Service Instructions. | | | This message is on a/c of: | Recd. at_____m.
                         | Sent | | | Date_____
  Secret | At____m.| |_____Service. | From_____
                         | To | | |
                         | By | | (Signature of "Franking Officer.") | By_____

TO { ~~1 Lincoln R.~~
     13 Nattd Fusrs

| Sender's Number | Day of Month | In reply to Number | AAA |
| BM. 746 | 9th | | |

13th Nattd Fusrs will relieve 1/Lincoln R. in
subsidiary line from LILLE ROAD to
FME de la BUTERNE inclusive tomorrow night
Feb 10th AAA 13th Nattd Fusrs will reconnoitre
the line tomorrow and make the necessary
arrangements with 1/Lincoln R AAA O.C. 1st Lincoln R
will be responsible for the line till the
relief is completed when O.C. 13 Nattd Fusrs
will report to this Office.

From   62 Inf Bde
Place
Time   7.15 pm
   The above may be forwarded as now corrected.   (Z)   W Wetheradmaj.
                                           Censor.   Signature of Addressor or person authorised to telegraph in his name.
                                  * This line should be erased if not required.

13th. Northd. Fusiliers.   OPERATION ORDERS No. 39.   Copy. No. 1.

Ref. Map 1/40000 Sheet 36   ARMENTIERES 10/2/16.

(1) The Battn. will relieve the 1st. Lincoln Regt. in the Subsidiary Line from CHAPELLE D'ARMENTIERES (I 9.c Central) to FME DE LA BUTERNE (C 28 c 1.5) both inclusive tonight.

(2) Companies will be disposed in the following order from the right, A, C, B, D.

(3) Guides for D Coy. will be at Level Crossing at C 27 a 2.1 at 6 p.m.. Guides will meet the remainder at I/d.4.9 at 6.p.m.

(4) O.C's Coys. Grenadiers and Signalling Officer will reconnoitre the line during the morning.

(5) Relief will be reported to Hqrs. by telephone by O.C's Coys. The Grenadier Officer will report his dispositions personnally at Hqrs. at I 9 b 1.4 as soon as relief is complete. He will also arrange with Grenadier Officer 12th. Northd. Fusiliers to send 2 squads Battn. Grenadier Platoon to relieve Grenadiers in defence of the Mushroom and report arrangements made.

(6) In the event of an action C Coy. will furnish a reinforcement of 1 Sergt. and 20 men to EGALE POST.

(7) The utmost precautions are to be taken to conceal from the enemy the occupation of the Subsidiary Line. O.C's Coys. will detail 1 Aeroplane Picquet for each Platoon, furnished with glasses and whistle during daylight to give warning of approach of Hostile aircraft. On the warning being given (three blasts) all ranks will at once take cover. If cover is not available they are to stand still- in the shade if possible -until the aircraft has passed when two blasts will be sounded on the whistle and work may be resumed.

(8) All fires -Officers' and men's-must be lighted before dawn, in order that during daylight no smoke may be visible from the enemy's line. Any fire found smoking will immediately be extinguished by throwing on earth.

(9) D Coy. will furnish a working party of 5 N.C.O's and 100 men to report to 98 Fd. Coy. R.E. at 5 p.m. to-day at ROND POINT. Tools and gum boots to be taken. Transport has been arranged to take up these men's valises to the Dump on the left of line. Men will work until 12 m.n. and return to Subsidiary Line. 2nd. Lt. C.Deuchar will be in charge of this party.

(10) The following Guards will be furnished :-
By B Coy. 1 N.C.O and 3 men Dump by Central Avenue.
           1 N.C.O and 6 men over 62nd. BDE. S.A.A. reserve in Square Fm. The Sergt. of this Guard is responsible for the issue of S.A.A. to fire trenches in accordance with signed requisitions received by him from H.Qrs. These requisitions are to be preserved.
By A Coy. 1 N.C.O. and 3 men at Brick Yard.
           1 N.C.O. and 3 men (by day) at Rd. Cross Roads Junction at I 9 C 4.5 and 1 N.C.O. and 6 men by night at same crossing.
           1 N.C.O. and 3 men at LITTLE RED HOUSE by Rly. Crossing.

(11) The following will be furnished daily by C Coy. whilst in Subsidiary Line to report to R.E. at R.E.Dump at 5.30 p.m.
     1 Sergt. and 15 men.

(12) Reports to 5.30 p.m. to 42 RUE MARLE afterwards to Hqrs. in Subsidiary Line.

Issued by Orderly at 4.30 p.m.
No. 1 Copy. Retained
 " 2 "   A Coy.
 " 3 "   B "
 " 4 "   C "
 " 5 "   D "
 " 6 "   Gren. Officer
 " 7 "   Sign.   "

Capt. & Adjutant,
13th. Northd. Fusiliers

SECRET.

To:- 12 North'd Fus.
    13 North'd Fus.
    10 York R.
    1/Lincoln R.

1. Three sets of 'gridiron' trenches recently dug by the enemy were disclosed by an air photograph taken on Feb. 9th. Similar preparations have been reported from the LOOS Salient.

    The gridirons are as follows:-

    (i) C 29.d.7.0. Eight parallel trenches about 200 yards long and 30 yards apart facing S.W. at right angles to the communication trench running from I.5.b.6.8. to C.29.d.9.5.

    (ii) C.30.c.5.4. Eight similar trenches running due N & S with southern ends on GUN AVENUE.

    (iii) C.30.a.2.10. Four similar trenches facing S.W. with left (S.E.) ends on the communication trench which runs along the road from C.30.a.1½.8. to C.24.c.9.5.

2. These may be defensive or offensive, or merely intended to deceive.

    If offensive they probable foreshadow an attack on the EPINETTE Salient.

    There may be similar trenches at other parts of our front, so every one must be prepared for eventualties.

3. To provide for this, work is being pushed on at the retrenchment just behind the EPINETTE Salient, and also on the Support Trenches running from 77s through CHICKEN FARM to PLANK AVENUE.

4. Immediate steps must be taken to improve the wire in front of the support trenches as well as that in front of the front line.

5. Every Company must prepare definite schemes for counter-attack; and each Platoon and Grenadier Squad must know exactly what action they would take, and this must

be frequently practiced in the Trenches.

6. Till further orders the Battalion in the Subsidiary Line will find the garrisons of I Officer and 20 men in S.P.X. and S.P.Y., and I Officer and 40 men (which will be reduced by day to I Officer and 20 men) in FORT EGAL REDOUBT

In the event of actual attack the Battalion in the Subsidiary Line will at once make up each of these garrisons to I Officer and 40 men.

7. Till further orders the Battalion in the Subsidiary Line, as well as Supporting Points, Supports and firing line will stand to arms from 5 a.m. till full daylight.

Companies in the Subsidiary Line should be prepared to counter-attack on their own initiative, should communication be temporarily cut off.

Major,
Bde. Major,
62nd Infantry Bde.

Feb 12th 1916.

13th. Northd. Fusiliers ~~ROUTINE~~ ORDERS No. 40   Copy No. 1

Operations

Secret

SUBSIDIARY LINE.   12.2.16.
Ref. 1/10000 Map & Trench Sketch.
1. Three sets of "GRIDIRON" Trenches recently dug by the enemy were disclosed by an air photograph taken on the 9th. inst. Similar preparations have been reported from the LOOS Salient.
   The Gridirons are as follows :-
   (1) C 29.d.7.0. Eight parallel trenches about 200 yds. long and 30 yds. apart facing S.W. at right angles to the Communication trench running from I.5.b 6.8 to C 29 d 9.5.
   (2) C 30 C 5.4 Eight similar trenches running due N. and S. with Southern ends on Gun Avenue.
   (3) C 30.a 9.10 Four similar trenches facing S.W. with left (S.E) ends on Communication Trench which runs along the road from C 30 a 1½.8 to C 24 c 9.5

2. These may defensive or offensive . If offensive they probably foreshadow an attack in the near future. There may be similar trenches at other parts of our front so everyone must be prepared for eventualities.

3. Immediate steps must be taken to improve the wire in front of the support trenches as well as that in front of front line.

4. Every Coy. must be prepared definite schemes for counter-attack, and submit same to H.Qrs. as soon as possible after they have been reconnoitred the trenches they are taking over tomorrow evening viz:-
   A Coy.   Trenches   67 and half 68 (right)) With Support
   C "   "   Half 68 (left) & 69.   )
   B "   "   70 & 71   )   Lines.
   D "   "   LILLE POST,
   Each Platoon and Grenadier Squad must know exactly what action they would take and this must be frequently practised in the trenches.

5. Until further orders Battn. in Subsidiary Line will find Garrisons of 1 Officer & 20 men in S.P.X. and S.P.Y and 1 Officer & 40 men (which will be reduced by day to 1 Officer & 20 men) in PORT EGAL REDOUBT. In the event of an action Garrisons will be immediately brought up to 1 Officer & 40 men.

6. The Garrisons of S.P.X & S.P.Y. will be furnished by B Coy. and that of PORT EGAL REDOUBT by C Coy. The extra N.C.O and men for the reinforcements are to be detailed at once and held in readiness to move at short notice . These men are not to be taken for working parties or fatigues.

7. Until further orders Battn. in Subsidiary Line will Stand to Arms from 5 a.m. until full daylight. Garrisons of Supporting points will do likewise. Coys. in Subsidiary Line should be prepared to counter-attack on their own initiative should communication be cut temporarily.
   A Coy. should use LOTHIAN AVENUE for this purpose.

   Issued by Orderly at 8.30 p.m.
   No. 1 Copy.   Retained
       2   =   O.C. A Coy.
       3   =   O.C. B "
       4   =   O.C. C "
       5   =   O.C. D "
       6   =   Grenadier Officer

   M J Massiah-Palmer

                                             Capt. & Adjutant,
                                             13th. Northd. Fusiliers.

62 Inf. Bde. O.O. No. 47.   Copy No. 3

Ref. 1/10,000 Map
& Trench Sketch.
                                              Feb 12th 1916.

1. 63 Inf. Bde. is relieving 64 Inf. Bde. in the left sector of the Divl. front during the early morning of Feb. 14th.

2. The following reliefs will take place on the evening of Feb. 13th:-

   (a). 1/Lincoln R. will relieve 10 York R. in Trenches 72 - 77 (up to Junction of JAPAN Road and Trench 77) leaving billets at 5 p.m.

   (b). 10 York R. (when relieved by 1/Lincoln R) will relieve 13 North'd Fus. in S.P.X., S.P.Y., EGAL POST and Subsidiary Line.

   (c). 13 North'd Fus. will relieve 12 North'd Fus. in Trenches 67 - 71 and LILLE POST, leaving Subsidiary Line when relieved by 10 York R.

   12 North'd Fus. when relieved, will return to billets at present occupied by 1/Lincoln R.

   Details of relief will be arranged on Feb 12th & 13th by the Battalions concerned.

3. 1/Lincoln R. & 10 York R. will use PORT EGALE AVENUE, PLANK AVENUE and AUSTRALIA Road.

   12 & 13 North'd Fus. will use LEITH WALK, and LOTHIAN AVENUE.

4. The relieved Battalions will be responsible for their sectors till the relief is complete, when O.C. relieving Battns. will report to this Office.

Issued at 7 a.m.
by Orderly.
                                              Whitehead Major,
                                              Bde. Major,
                                              62 Inf. Bde.

              Copy No. 1 - 1/Lincoln R.
               "   " 2 - 10 York R.
               "   " 3 - 13 North'd Fus.
               "   " 4 - 12 North'd Fus.
               "   " 5 - Retained

SECRET.

To:- 12 North'd Fus.
13 North'd Fus.
10 York R.
1/Lincoln R.

G

A combined shoot against enemy's trenches in PONT BALLOT Salient will be carried out on Feb 12th commencing at eleven a.m.

At 5-15 p.m. West Spring Guns and catapults will fire smoke bombs into PONT BALLOT Salient and from 5-20 p.m. to 5-30 p.m. all available 18 pounder Batteries will fire salvoes at trenches in PONT BALLOT Salient.

Between 5-15 p.m. and 5-30 p.m. three two minute bursts of rifle fire will enfilade both sides of salient and M. Guns will fire on L'AVENTURE and Communication Trenches in C 29.d. and b.

MWethered Major,
Bde. Major,
62nd Infantry Bde.

Feb 11th 1916.

Ref. Trench Map
   I/10,000.
                                                S E C R E T.

To:- 12 North'd Fus.
     13 North'd Fus.
     10 York R.
     1/Lincoln R.

------

1.   On the 15th February and following days, the Div. Art with three attached Batteries of 25th Division, Canadian Heavy Battery, 41 Siege Howitzer Battery, and Trench Mortars, will carry out a systematic bombardment of enemy's front and support trenches from I.5.c.8.2. to C.29.a.8.9. and his Communication Trenches and Works in vicinity of PONT BALLOT SALIENT.

2.   <u>On Tuesday 15th February</u>, the shooting will commence at I p.m. and continue intermittently until 5 p.m.

    Targets for) Front and Support trenches in squares
    Howitzers &)
    18-pounders.) C 29 c, as far North as C 29.a.9.5. The Howitzers will fire deliberately, and 18-pounders will fire salvoes at I-2 p.m. and I-4 p.m. and at irregular intervals between I-10 p.m. and 5 p.m.

    Targets for
    Trench Mortars - FARM "BOX" (C 29.c.8.4.)

3.   <u>On Wednesday, 16th February</u>, shooting will commence at 12 noon and continue until 5-10 p.m.

    Targets for) FARM "COX" (C 29 c.7.8.) Front and
    Howitzers &)
    18-pounders.) Support trenches from C 29.c.8½.5. to C 29 a.7½.4. The Howitzers will fire deliberately and 18-pounders will fire salvoes at 12-2 p.m. and 12-4 p.m. and at irregular intervals from 12-10 to 5-10 p.m.

                                                  P.T.O.

-2-

4. The Canadian Heavy Battery and other batteries will be ready for counter battery work.

5. The 4I Siege Howitzers will co-operate each day by shelling certain of the following enemy strong points etc. behind his front line:-

   I 18 b,
   I 6 b,
   J 1 d,
   C 30
   I 5 b N.E.
   D 25 a

6. A Programme for the remaining days of the week will be published later.

7. Battalion Commanders will arrange for M. Gun and Rifle fire to be brought each night against all parts of the enemy's trenches, works and wire, which have been damaged by the Artillery.

 Trench Commanders will be in close touch with Artillery F.O.O's to note these places in order that no opportunity may be lost of interfering with the enemy's working parties.

            J Rwethuck Major,
            Bde. Major,
Feb 15th 1916.   62nd Infantry Bde.

SECRET.

To:- 12 North'd Fus.
13 North'd Fus.
10 York R.
1/Lincoln R.

In continuation of my B.M. 938 of 15/2/16, the bombardment for Thursday 17th February will commence at 12-30 p.m.

Targets for Howitzers and 18-pounders.
: Road Junction and buildings near ARRET, I 12 central. SPARROWS NEST, (I 5 d.0.1), Enemy front and support trenches (I 5 c and d).
Howitzers will fire deliberately and 18-prs will fire salvoes at 12-31 p.m. and single rounds of H.E. and bursts of shrapnel at irregular intervals afterwards.

Target for Trench Mortars.
: SPARROW'S NEST (I 5 d.0.1) and front trench (I 5 c 7 1).

J.R. Weltherd Major,
Bde. Major,
62nd Infantry Bde.

Feb 16th 1916.

S E C R E T.

To:- 12 North'd Fus.
    13 North'd Fus.
    10 York R.
    1/Lincoln R.

        In continuation of my B.M. 938 of 15/2/16, the bombardment for Friday, 18th February, will commence at 11-30 a.m.

Targets for Howitzers)   Front and Support Trenches
and 18-pounders.)   in I 5 b and C 29 d.
                              BRUNE RUE (I 5 b 4.8).
                              Howitzers will fire deliberately
                              and 18-pounders will fire salvoes
                              at 11-30 a.m. and bursts of fire
                              from 11-32 a.m. to 1-15 p.m.

Targets for Trench)   New emplacements near
Mortars.)   BRUNE RUE.

                                          Major,
                                          Bde. Major,
Feb 17th 1916.   62nd Infantry Bde.

62 Inf. Bde. O.O. No. 48.

Copy No. 1

18th February 1916.

1. 64 Inf. Bde. will relieve 62 Inf. Bde. on night of Feb. 19th/20th.

2. (a) 13 North'd Fus. will be relieved by 10 K.O.Y.L.I. in Trenches 67 - 71 and LILLE POST.

   (b) I/Lincoln R. will be relieved by 15 Durh. L.I. in Trenches 72 - 77.
   Relieving Battns. will pass "SANDBAG CORNER" (I 1 d 6.4.) and HOUPLINES Tram Terminus at 6 p.m.

   Right Battn. will use LEITH WALK and LOTHIAN AVENUE.
   Left Battn. will use PORT EGAL AVENUE, PLANK AVENUE and the HOUPLINES - EPINETTE Road.
   Details will be arranged between Battns. concerned.

3. 12 North'd Fus. in Subsidiary Line, PORT EGAL Redoubt, S.P.X. and S.P.Y. will be relieved by 9 K.O.Y.L.I.

   9 K.O.Y.L.I. will pass "SANDBAG CORNER" (I 1 d 6.4.) at 10 p.m.

4. I/E York R. will take over the billets now occupied by 10 York R. on night of 19th/20th.
   Arrangements to be made between Battalions.

5. On relief, 62 Inf. Bde. will become Divl. Reserve. Arrangements re billets are being issued separately.

6. Machine Guns will be relieved during night 18th/19th Feb.
   Details to be arranged by Bde. Machine Gun Officers.

7. Relief of Signals by 64 Inf. Bde. will be complete by midday Feb 19th.

8. Bde. Reserves of S.A.A., Grenades, Trench Stores etc., will be handed over by midday Feb. 19th.

9. The relieved Battalions will be responsible for their Sections till the relief is complete, when they will report by wire to this Office, the word "LONDON".

10. On completion of the whole relief Bde. Hd. Qrs., will move to 93 RUE SADI CARNOT.

Major,
Bde. Major,
62 Inf. Bde.

Issued at 7-15 p.m.
by Orderly.

Copy No. 1 - 13 North'd Fus.
  "   " 2 - I/Lincoln R.
  "   " 3 - 12 North'd Fus.
  "   " 4 - 10 York R.
  "   " 5 - 64 Inf. Bde.
  "   " 6 - 63 Inf. Bde.
  "   " 7 - 103 Inf. Bde.
  "   " 8 - Retained.

SECRET.

To:- 12 North'd Fus.
     13 North'd Fus.
     10 York R.
     I/Lincoln R.

1.   In continuation of my B.M. 938 of 15/2/16, the bombardment for Saturday 19th Feb. will commence at 1-20 p.m.

2.   Targets between 1-20 p.m. and 1-35 p.m.

      Howitzers. -   FARM "COX" (C 29 c 7.8.). Support Trenches in C 29 c a and b.

      18-pounders -   Front Trenches in C 29 c and a, and enfilade Support Trenches in C 29 c and Communication Trenches in C 29 a.

      Siege Howitzers - L'AVENTURE (C 30 Central).

      Trench Mortars - Point of Salient (C 29 a 5 0.)

3.   Targets from 1-35 p.m.

      Howitzers. -   Trenches near LE TEMPLE I 6 b 8.7. to C 30 d 7.1.
                      L'AVENTURE (C 30 Central) and new trench C 30 d 1.5. to C 30 c 4.9.
                      Road Junction C 30 a 1.8 and trench C 24 c 2.0 to C 23 d 9.0.

      Siege Howitzers - LA PREVOTE.

      Infantry. -
      (63 Inf. Bde)   Rifle and machine gun fire on to both sides of PONT BALLOT SALIENT.

      Cyclists.   Smoke bombs from catapults into PONT BALLOT SALIENT.

4.   At 1-45 p.m. the 18-pounders will re-commence fire on their original targets, and at 1-50 p.m. continue bursts of fire if suitable targets present themselves.

5.   A Howitzer Battery will shell ARRET (I 12 central) and LA FRESNELLE (I 12 b 9.9.) commencing at 1-20 p.m.

6.   The Canadian Heavy Battery and other Field Batteries have been told off for counter-battery work.

-2-

9.   The correct time will be given to all concerned by Divl. Signal Co. at 9 a.m. and 12 noon 19th Feb.

[signature] Major,
Bde. Major,
62nd Infantry Bde.

Feb 18th 1916.

13th. Northd. Fus.   OPERATION ORDERS No. 42   Copy. No. 1.
Ref. map sheet 36 & Trench sketch.   LILLE POST 19/2/16.

1. The 64th. Inf. Bde. is relieving the 62nd Inf. Bde. this evening
   The 10/K.O.Y.L.I. will relieve this Battn. leaving Level Crossing
   I 1 d 4.9. at 6 p.m.   Incoming troops will use Communication trench
   to Chapelle d'Armentieres and LOTHIAN AVENUE . Outgoing troops will
   use LEITH WALK and Communication trench from CHAPELLE D'ARMENTIERES

2. Coys. will be relieved in following order :-
   (1) D Coy. by D Coy. 10/K.O.Y.L.I.
   (2) A "   by B "   "
   (3) C "   by C "   "
   (4) B "   by A "   "

3. Guides will meet incoming troops at Level Crossing at I 1 d 4.9
   at 6 p.m. with exception of two platoons in the Mushroom and 70
   trench. These will be relieved in small parties during the afternoon
   and guides will meet them at Level Crossing at 3 p.m. and conduct
   them in via LEITH WALK. Guides for each trench and support trench
   are to be sent and are to be given slips bearing the number of the
   trench to which they are guiding.

4. The handing over of trench stores is to be carried out during the
   early afternoon to-day. Receipts will be taken in triplicate-
   one will be retained by O.C.Coy.- one handed over to Relieving Coy.
   and the third copy will be sent in to the Adjutant by 6 p.m. for
   transmission to 62nd. Inf. Bde.   All receipts must be taken on
   the forms issued for this purpose any necessary additions being made
   A & C Coys. will each hand over 50 pairs Gum Boots and will draw
   same from D Coy. to complete if they have not sufficient. All other
   Gum boots will be taken out. All 1" Very Pistols with xxxxxxxxxxx
   xxxxxxxxxxxxxxxxxxxxxxxxxxxx will be taken out of trenches and the
   4 new 1½" pistols with stocks which were issued on the 16th. inst
   as these are Regimental Property. Trench store dixies will be
   handed over. The position of trench stores is to be indicated on
   receipts taken and all S.A.A. is to be included. All tools except
   R.E.Tools will be taken out.

5. On relief the Bn. as part of the 62nd. Inf. Bde. will be in Div.Res.
   and will occupy billets in COISNE WAREHOUSE Rue de la Paix. Battn.
   H.Qrs. will be at 60 RUE SADI CARNOT. Coy. Officers H.Qrs. will be
   as follows :- A Coy. 33 RUE STRASBOURG
                 B "   127 RUE SADI CARNOT
                 C "   133 "   "   "
                 D "   3 PLACE DE LA REPUBLIQUE

6. Short reports on work done during occupation of trenches together
   with Intelligence reports and Grenade Officers Report will be sent to
   the Adjutant at 6 p.m.
   Statement of work in hand is to be sent to the Adjutant by 4 p.m.
   to-day.

7. As soon as the advanced parties of the 10/K.O.Y.L.I. come into trench
   advanced parties may be sent to take over billets.

8. O.C's Coys and the Grenadier Officer will report personnally at
   H.Qrs. LILLE POST on completion of relief. Transport for tools, Mess
   boxes etc., will be at Dump at 8 p.m.

   Issued by Orderly at 3.15 a.m.
   NO. 1 Copy   Retained.
       2   "   A Coy.
       3   "   B "
       4   "   C "
       5   "   D "
       6   "   Grenadier Officer.   Capt. & Adjutant,
                                            13th. Northd. Fusiliers.

13th. Northd. Fusiliers OPERATION ORDERS No 41   Copy No.
Ref/ Trench Sketch Map   LILLE POST 16/2/16.

1. D Coy. will relieve B Coy. in Trenches 70,71 and the MUSHROOM today commencing at 1 p.m. B Coy.(less 2 platoons) will garrison LILLE POST 2 platoons occupying 67SS and will be in Battn. reserve.
The two platoons of D Coy. in 67 SS will relieve first. The relief to be carried out by small sections at a time.

2. Officers will reconnoitre trenches to be taken over at once

3. Trench stores to be handed over and receipts obtained at once. B Coy will hand over all VERY pistols in possession to D Coy. Copy of receipts to be sent to the Adjutant.

4. D Coy. will draw extra rations of OXO, RUM or SOUP as issued, for grenadiers holding the Saps.

5. O.C.D Coy. will submit his defence scheme in writing as soon as possible after relief and will see that all ranks know what to do in event of attack.

6. Completion of relief will be telephoned to the Adjutant by O.C.D Coy by the word "THERMOS" preceded by the Officers name.

7. O.C's all Companies should make themselves acquainted at once with position of personnel of Trench Mortar Batteries and have orderlies instructed as to the quickest way to them. Trench Mortar Batteries stand in same relationship to O.C's Trenches as R.F.A. Batteries.

Issued by Orderly at 12 noon.

No. 1 Copy Retained.
    2 "   to A Coy (for information)
    3 "   " B "
    4 "   " C " (for information)
    5 "   " D "
    6 "   " Grenadier Officer.

                                        Capt. & Adjutant,
                                        13yh. Northd. Fusiliers.

62 Inf. Bde. O.O. No. 50.   Copy No. 5

Ref. 1/10,000 Map
& Trench Sketch.
                                              Feb. 23rd 1916.

1. 62 Inf. Bde. will relieve 63 Inf. Bde. in Left Sector of Divisional Front on the night of Feb. 25th/26th.

2. (a) 12 North'd Fus, will relieve 8 Lincoln R, (Right Battn) from Trench 77 (where JAPAN Road cuts trench) to PETTY CURY.
   12 North'd Fus, will pass TISSAGE, HOUPLINES at 6-30pm. [7.0]

   (b) 10 York R, will relieve 4 Middlesex R, (Left Battn) from Bay 19 Trench 83 to Trench 89 (both inclusive).
   10 York R, will pass TISSAGE, HOUPLINES at 7-0 p.m. [6.30]

   (c) 13 North'd Fus, will relieve 8 Somerset L.I. in Brigade Support ('2 Co's in Subsidiary Line, 2 Co's in billets HOUPLINES. Hd. Qrs., CHATEAU LA ROSE).
   13 North'd Fus, will pass TISSAGE, HOUPLINES at 10-30 p.m.

   (d) 1/Lincoln R, will relieve 10 York & Lancs. R, in Brigade Reserve, (Hd. Qrs, TISSAGE, HOUPLINES) at 9-30 p.m.

3. The Right Battn. will use SPAIN AVENUE, and GLOUCESTER AVENUE.

   The Left Battn. will use WESSEX AVENUE, CAMBRIDGE AVENUE, EDMEADS AVENUE, and IRISH AVENUE.

   Details of reliefs will be arranged between Battalions concerned.

4. Relieving Battalions, when relief is complete will report completion to 63 Inf. Bde by sending the word "HOUPLINES". G.O.C. 62 Inf. Bde, will take over Command of the sector on completion of the whole relief, when O.C. Battalions will be notified.

5. Billeting parties will take over and hand over billets during the day of Feb. 25th under Battn. arrangements.

6. Trench Stores, statement of work in progress, S.A.A. and Grenade Reserves etc, will be handed over by midday Feb. 25th.

7. Machine Guns will be relieved under arrangements to be made by Bde. M. Gun Officers, by midday Feb. 25th.

8. Signals will be relieved by midday Feb. 25th.

9. Bde. Hd. Qrs, will open at No. 3 RUE DE JESUITS when the relief is complete, and close at present Bde. Hd. Qrs. at the same hour.

Issued at 9 p.m.
                                              Major,
                                              Bde. Major,
                                              62 Inf. Bde.

        Copy No. 1 - 63 Inf. Bde.
             : 2 - 64 Inf. Bde.
             : 3 - 28 Inf. Bde.
             : 4 - 12 North'd Fus.
             : 5 - 13 North'd Fus.
             : 6 - 10 York R.
             : 7 - 1/Lincoln R.
             : 8 - Retained.

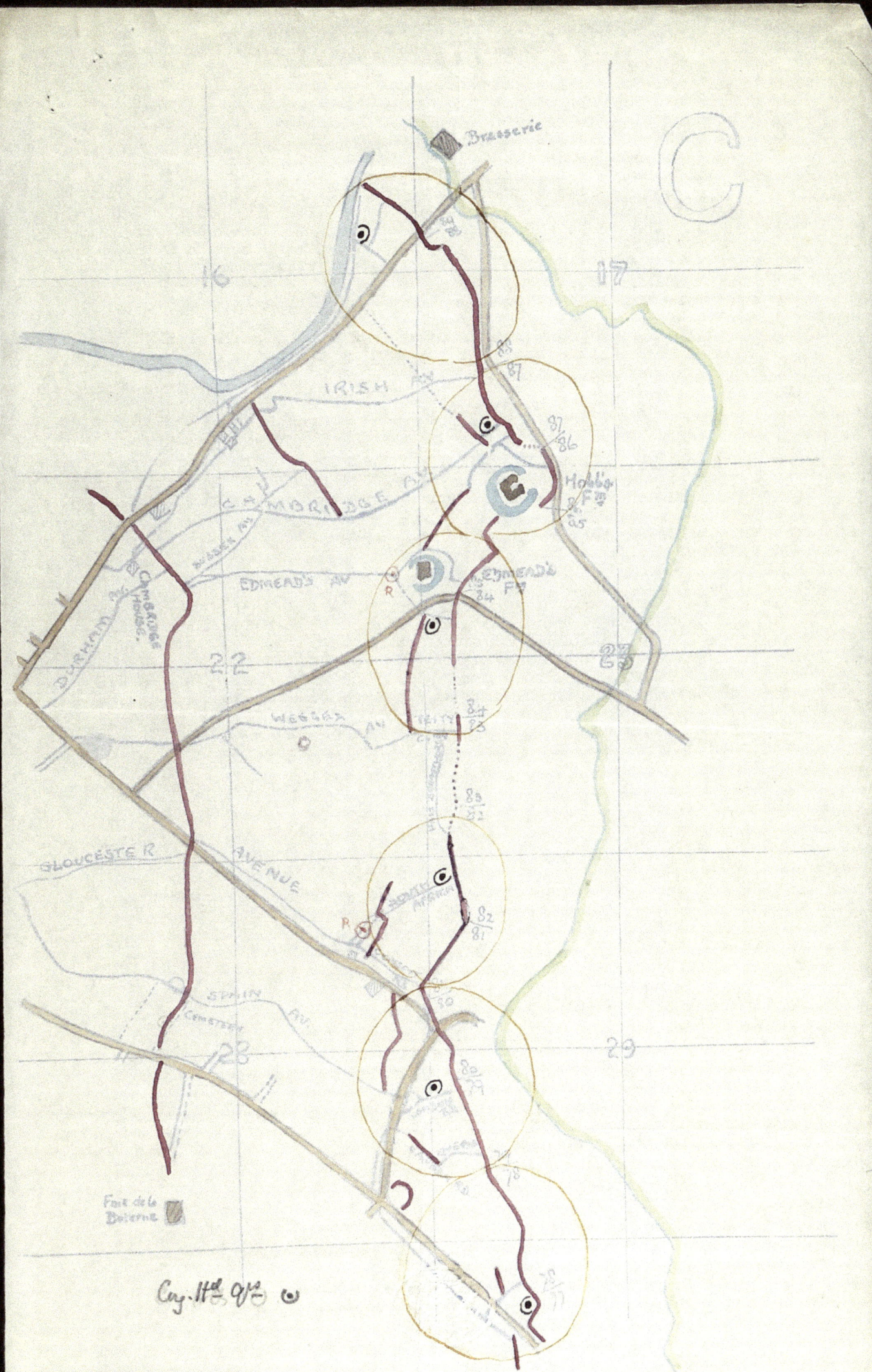

13th. Northd. Fus. OPERATION ORDERS No. 43. Copy No. 1
Ref. Map 1/40000 Sheet 36 & Trench Sketch ARMENTIERES 25/2/16.

1. The 62nd Inf. Bde. will relieve the 63rd. Inf. Bde. in the left sector of the Divisional front tonight. The Battn will be in Bde. support with 2 Coys. in the Subsidiary line and 2 in HOUPLINES relieving the 8/Somerset Light Infantry

2. A Coy. will occupy Subsidiary line on the right from FME de la BUTERNE (C 28 c 5.2) to GLOSTER AVENUE leaving sufficient dug-outs at Junction of GLOSTER AVENUE for the Battalion Grenadiers, who will occupy that portion of line immediately to the south of GLOSTER AVENUE. C Coy will occupy the line from GLOSTER AVENUE to the River LYS. B & D Coys. will occupy billets in the BRASSERIE HOUPLINES at C 21 b 5.1.
Battn. H.Qrs. will be at CHATEAU LA ROSE HOUPLINES.

3. Guides will meet Coys. at Rd. Junction at C 27 b 5.8 (near TISSAGE) Coys. will pass this Junction at following times.
A Coys. 10.30 p.m.
C   "   10.45 p.m.
B   "   11. 0 p.m.
D   "   11.15 p.m.

4. As soon as their relief is complete O.C's Coys. will send two Orderlies who know the position where Coy. Commanders will be sleeping, to Batt. H.Qrs. to report personally to the Adjutant.

5. Sentries will be posted over all Gas alarms and at all posts guarded be 8/Somerset L.I.

6. The utmost care is to be taken to conceal all troops from hostile aircraft and pickets over each platoon in A & C Coys. will be posted at daybreak and will remain on duty until dark. B Coy will furnish a picket at the BRASSERIE tomorrow during same hours, D Coy. on the 27th. and B Coy on the 28th. inst. There must be no smoke allowed during daylight. All fires must be lighted well before dawn. Any fire found smoking must be put out at once with earth

7. Two blankets per man will be taken. Transport for these will be at the Qr.Mr.Stores at 9.15 p.m. Blankets are to be neatly rolled in bundles by Coys. and taken to Stores by 9.10 p.m. D Coy. will furnish a loading party and the Orderly Officer will supervise loading. Mess cart at H.Qrs. at 9.30 p.m. for Officers Baggage.

8. A duplicate copy of trench store receipts will be sent to the Adj. as soon as they are signed.

9. Steel helmets will be distributed evenly between Coys. and will be taken up to the trenches to-night.

10. Picks and shovels will be taken up on transport.

11. Relief when complete will be reported by the word "Reliant" by O.C's personally over the telephone

12. Billets to be left scrupously clean. O.C's Coys. will inspect their men's billets before leaving and will send in a certificate to the Adjutant that they did so and left them clean and tidy.

14. In view of severity of weather Coy. Commanders must see that the whale oil issued issued for the feet is used freely by everyone at least once every 24 hours.

Issued by Orderly at 5.30 p.m.
Copy No. 1 Retained
  "   2 A Coy.
  "   3 B "
  "   4 C "
  "   5 D "
       6   Grenadier Officer

B Masseah Palmer
Capt. & Adjutant,
13th. Northd. Fusiliers.

13th. Northd. Fusiliers OPERATION ORDERS No. 44   Copy No. 1.

Ref/ Map & Trench Sketch   HOUPLINES 28/2/16.

1. The Battalion will remain in its present position until it relives the 12th. Northd. Fus. in trench 77 (left portion only) to 82 inclusive.

2. The two Coys. in the Subsidiary line at present will be relieved this afternoon as follows :-
   B Coy. will relieve A Coy. on the right and will use GLOSTER AVENUE.
   D Coy. will relieve C Coy. on the left and will use the HOUPLINES - FRELINGHEIN ROAD
   Not more than half a dozen men are to proceed to or from trenches together during daylight

3. A & C Coys. will take over billets of B & D Coys. respectively in the BRASSERIE. Officers will take over billets at present occupied by Officers of B & D Companies. Company H.Qrs. for both Companies in Subsidiary Line CAMBRIDGE HOUSE.
   The two cookers at present in the Brasserie will be taken over by A & C Companies. Dixies, Braziers etc. in the Subsidiary Line will be handed over and receipts exchanged.

4. Relief will be telephoned through to H.Qrs. by O.C's Companies personally using the code word "Shells"

   Issued by Orderly at 4.45 p.m.

   Copy No. 1 Retained.
    "   "   2 A Coy.
    "   "   3 B "
    "   "   4 C "
    "   "   5 D "
    "   "   6 Grenadier Officer (for information)

                                    Capt. & Adjutant,
                                       13th. Northd. Fusiliers.

12 hath Jay
Vol 7

WAR DIARY
or
INTELLIGENCE SUMMARY
(Erase heading not required.)

Army Form C. 2118

Instructions regarding War Diaries and Intelligence Summaries are contained in F.S. Regs., Part II. and the Staff Manual respectively. Title Pages will be prepared in manuscript.

Place	Date	Hour	Summary of Events and Information	Remarks and references to Appendices
ARMENTIERES	1916 March 1st		Dull weather, wind S.E. Very quiet day up to 4.30 p.m. when the enemy put 10 MINENWERFER Bombs behind 80.5. trench & into PONT BALLOT Farm, no harm done. Wept of snipers shot dead by an enemy sniper while shooting machine guns loor orbis against our communication trenches owing to prompt retaliation upon enemy's front line with rifle grenades, the enemy being found by day. Very heavy firing to the South outside from 3.30 A.M to 5.30 A.M. morning very clear, aeroplanes, our own & those of the enemy active at an early hour. Very quiet day up to 10 o'clock, an our trench mortars, which were then firing at the German front trenches opposite 81 & 82 trenches drew a good deal of retaliation upon 81 trench, 'Consett' avenue communication trench and PONT BALLOT Farm. No damage done except to 81 trench. No casualties. The Battalion was relieved by the 13th (S) Battalion Northumberland Fusiliers 'Consetts'. No casualties. The Battalion returning to the Subsidiary line of the left sector in 77.78.79.80.81 & 82 trenches. The battalion occupying the Subsidiary trenches, C on the right, B on the left, A & D Coys going into billets in C & B Coys occupied the Subsidiary trenches, C on the right, B on the left, A & D Coys going into billets in the Baraque in HOUPLINES, Btn Hqrs CHATEAU LA ROSE. Relief completed at midnight. Lt-Col Warwick went to 64th Field Ambulance. During this tour of duty in trenches one Oman was killed, no other casualties sustained. The Battalion was in Brigade Support in the left Sector of the Subsidiary line (nominally from AUSTRALIA ROAD C.28.A.7.1½ to a point C.16.C.7.4: but as one leg of the 13th S. Btn. was held in reserve on the night of the Line The Battalion held from the Junction of PONT BALLOT Road with the Subsidiary line, to the extreme left.	Ref Map Sheet 36 1/40,000 Edition 6.
	"2nd"			
	3rd 4.5 March		Were being in sufficient accommodation for more than two Coys, B & C Coys were in the line & A & D Coys in reserve in the BRASSERIE in HOUPLINES. On the night of March 5th B & C Coys were relieved in the line, & went into C.21.B.5.3. Battalion Headquarters were at CHATEAU LA ROSE in HOUPLINES; the Headquarters Billets in HOUPLINES. of the 2 Coys in the line at CAMBRIDGE HOUSE (C.22.A.5½.7½). Large working parties were found each day. The weather was very cold & snow fell every day & lay to a depth of a few inches.	

WAR DIARY or INTELLIGENCE SUMMARY

(Erase heading not required.)

Army Form C. 2118

Place	Date 1916	Hour	Summary of Events and Information	Remarks and references to Appendices
ARMENTIERES	March 6 & 7		Battalion remained in Brigade Support; weather dark & snowy; wind ranging from N.E. to N.W.	Ref Map Sheet 36 1/40,000 Edition 6.
	8.		Battalion relieved by 1st Battn East Yorkshire Regiment. 64th Infantry Bde, relief complete at 11.15 p.m.	
	9-13.		In billets in ARMENTIERES, the Battalion supplied working parties daily for the trenches. On March 12th 2 Lt TRENCHMAN joined the Battalion. 2 men were wounded on march 12th on a working party. The Battn occupied were those in the RUE DE LA PAIX.	
	14.		The 62nd Infantry Bde relieved the 64th Infantry Bde in the B/f Divisional Sector viz from Trench 72 to Trench 88: four Battalions being in the front line and finding their own supports, & Coys in the Subsidiary line. The 12th Northumberland Fusiliers were left centre battalion, holding from the right of trench 81 to Bay 14 in trench 85, with one leg in the Subsidiary line between PONT BALLOT Rd and EDMEADS AVENUE & one leg in Reserve in the BRASSERIE at HOUPLINES. The 1st Battn Lincolnshire Regiment were left Battn, the 13th Sheffield Fusiliers right centre Battn & the 10th Yorkshire Regt right battalion. Left Centre Battn. Headquarters were at CHATEAU LA ROSE. Dr. 12th S Battn Sheffield Fusiliers relieved the 15th Durham Light Infantry in trenches 81 and 82, the 10th K.O.Y.LI in trenches 83, 84 & 85 and the 1st East Yorks in the Subsidiary line. The relief was completed at 8.30 p.m.	(C.29.A.0.0 to C.23.A.6.8.)
	15.		Quiet day, wind South East, dry fine. The enemy shelled 84 supports at 8 A M but no damage done. In the evening a German patrol was sighted & a strong patrol was sent out from trench 82 to capture it: but the enemy withdrew to his trenches.	
	16.		Very quiet day, fresh progress made in reclaiming the strong Pt known as FRY PAN on WESSEX AVENUE (C.22.D.5.6½) Two Stokes guns manned by Trench Mortar battery 62/1, fired from 81 fire trench between 6.30 p.m & 10 p.m & succeeded in completely silencing the machine gun in the PONT BALLOT salient.	

WAR DIARY or INTELLIGENCE SUMMARY

Army Form C. 2118

(Erase heading not required.)

Place	Date	Hour	Summary of Events and Information	Remarks and references to Appendices
ARMENTIERES	Mch 17.		Splendid weather, it is now no longer necessary to wear from boots thigh in the trenches. Steel helmets are now available in sufficient numbers for the two coys in the firing line to be completely equipped with them. The enemy put a few shells into HOOPLINES, the trenches were absolutely quiet.	Ref Map Sheet 36 1/40,000 Edition 6.
	18.		At 6.P.m a strong patrol under 2t Gust & 2t Philip went out in order to capture the German patrol, which has been seen in front of trench 82. The patrol remained in close proximity to the German wire for four hours & no Germans came out. The patrol numbered eleven other "knife-nots" from the German wire defences and brought them back into our lines; in this enterprise Pre St Matters was wounded by a stray bullet & died after effects in the Casualty Clearing Station. The Germans shelled trench 81 in the morning, tried to destroy the stolen "knife-nots"; in the afternoon the Battalion Grenadiers carried out a scheme of counter-attack from their position in Werner Avenue against 81 trench. Our patrols were again active but the enemy did not show himself.	
	19.		The Germans opened a very heavy bombardment of the whole Divisional front at 6.30 A.M. The bombardment of 81 trench & the ORCHARD (at (at that being intense 7.7, 10.5 and 15.c.m. guns being used & also against 81 (C.28.B.5.5.) minenwerfer & two or three aerial torpedoes, one of which utterly destroyed two Bays of trench 81, making a hole 18 feet deep & 30 feet in diameter, our casualties, killed 4 two wounded. The Divisional artillery assisted by the Heavy group retaliated with the bombardment ceased at 7.15.A.M. The remainder of the day was very quiet. Very fine warm weather, the 21st Divisional Artillery relieved by the 17th Divisional Artillery; Major Dickson commanding the 12th S. Batt Manchester Regt inspected the trenches prior to taking over. MD shelling by the enemy all day, a few minenwerfer were put into the ORCHARD.	
	20.			
	21.		A very misty day the enemy assisted himself of this to use his minenwerfer with effect against the wire	

WAR DIARY
or
INTELLIGENCE SUMMARY

(Erase heading not required.)

Army Form C. 2118

Instructions regarding War Diaries and Intelligence Summaries are contained in F.S. Regs., Part II. and the Staff Manual respectively. Title Pages will be prepared in manuscript.

Place	Date	Hour	Summary of Events and Information	Remarks and references to Appendices
ARMENTIERES	March 21		and parapet of trench 81. Both were badly breached, in consequence of which application was made to the 62nd Infantry Bde for two Vickers guns, one of which was placed in 80 support trench & the second in (Vancouver), shooting up PONT BALLOT ROAD, & bi-secting the gap. The job was mended by midnight. (C.28.B.2.7)	Ref Map sheet 36 1/40,000 Edition 6
	„ 22		The enemy made no attempt to attack. The 12th S Bn Militia relieved the 9th (S) Bn of the same regiment & the relieving unit took over trench stores etc during the day. The 12th S Battalion of the Manchester Regiment relieved the 12th S Bn Northumberland Fusiliers in trenches (81, 82, 83, 84 & 85) the Subsidiary line in support of their trenches, & also the Coy in the BRASSERIE at HOUPLINES which complete at 8.25 p.m. (C.29.A.0.0. to C.23.A.5.8.) (C.21.B.5.3.5.) The Battalion returned into billets in the Collège des Garçons & Hospice Civile Armentières.	
LA CRECHE	„ 23		The 12th Service Battalion Northumberland Fusiliers & the 1st Batt. Lincolnshire Regiment marched out of Armentières at 9.A.M and reached LA CRECHE (A.5.D.north) at 11.15 A.M (the 12th S Batn marched into ARMENTIERES on October 14th 1915 & have occupied the trenches since, at 23rd 1915 five months in all) these are the next billets of one of the Bdes of the Division in the Battalion went into billets at (A.4.4.0.) These billets having been used by Battalions on the line of march, after our men for one night only were in the second Corps. were found to be in an exceedingly filthy & insanitary condition & large fatigue parties were at once set to work on them.	
	„ 24		Another very quiet day. Officers of the relieving unit took over trench stores etc during the day, the 12th S Battalion (Lt Col Warwick, who had been at the Divisional Rest Station since March 2nd returned to the Battalion & took over command from Major F.J.T. Eckmann).	
	25		General Sir Douglas Haig Commander-in-Chief of the British army in France inspected the Battalion at 2.45 p.m. The Battalion was drawn up along the road from BAILLEUL to STEENE (Map 28.S.27 central). The Commander-in-Chief complimented the Commanding officer on the turn out & appearance of the men on parade.	
	26		2nd Lt Woodhouse & 2nd Lt Burt joined the Battalion from the 15th Reserve Battalion. With officers had served with the 12th (S) Battalion in England	

1875 Wt. W593/826 1,000,000 4/15 J.B.C. & A. A.D.S.S./Forms/C. 2118.

WAR DIARY
or
INTELLIGENCE SUMMARY
(Erase heading not required.)

Army Form C. 2118

Place	Date	Hour	Summary of Events and Information	Remarks and references to Appendices
LA CRECHE	Mch 1916. 27		The Battalion began training, all Coys parading for physical training, arms drill, platoon drill & bayonet fighting under their respective Coy officers.	Ref. Map sheet 36 1/40,000 Edition 6
	28.		General Sir Herbert Plumer, Commander-in-Chief of the Second Army inspected one Coy from each Battn. in the 62nd Infantry Bde: 'A' Coy was sent to represent the 12th (S) Battn. Northumberland Fusiliers; the Commander-in-chief expressed his regret that the Battalion was leaving his command and complimented the Commanding officer on the appearance of the men. Scout-Major Sir Charles Fergusson, Corps Commander of the 2nd Corps in which the Battalion has been since Oct 2nd 1915 also expressed his regret at the approaching transfer of the 21st Division to another part of the front. B, C & D Coys attended a practical exposition of the use of poison gas.	
	29. & 30.		The Battalion continued training at LA CRECHE. Weather very cold, wind South East & very high at times. The ground which had been water logged up to March 27th began to dry rapidly everywhere.	
	31.		The Battalion entrained at BAILLEUL & detrained at 0.8 (12.8 A.M) at LONGEAU (2 East of AMIENS)	Ref. Map Amiens sheet 17 1/100,000
		9.50 A.M	The Battalion then marched into Rest Billets at COISY, six miles NORTH of AMIENS. COISY at this time is in the Third Army Area. Weather is this part of France much drier & warmer than in the area from which the Battalion has come.	
	2/4/16.			

M. Morrack [signature]
Comdg. 12th Northd Fusiliers

Army Form C. 2118

WAR DIARY
or
INTELLIGENCE SUMMARY
(Erase heading not required.)

Instructions regarding War Diaries and Intelligence Summaries are contained in F.S. Regs., Part II. and the Staff Manual respectively. Title Pages will be prepared in manuscript.

Place	Date 1916	Hour	Summary of Events and Information	Remarks and references to Appendices
COISY (6 miles NNE of AMIENS)	Apl 1st		The Battalion in Billets at COISY - Training Continued. Weather Fine and Warm.	R.y. MAP AMIENS Sheet 17 1/100,000
LA NEUVILLE	Apl 8th	12 Noon	The Battalion marched from COISY to LA NEUVILLE via QUERRIEU.	
	9th		The 62nd Infantry Brigade attended Divine Service - The Service was taken by the Chaplain General to the Forces in the Field. Lt.Col. H. B. Warwick proceeded to the Fourth Army School of Instruction (Infantry) and Major F. J. F. Edlmann assumed Command of the Battalion. Training was continued Classes for instruction in Lewis Gun and Grenade Work were commenced -	
	10th		Training was continued until the 12th when 'D' Coy. was inoculated and the remaining Companies employed at the Divisional Grenade School as Digging Parties Major F. J. F. Edlmann proceeded to Hospital with an injured leg and Capt. S. E. Mailer assumed command of the Battalion.	
	13th		Capt. G. NESBIT joined from the 16th Battalion and was posted to 'C' Coy.	
	14th	10.45am	The Battalion marched to VILLE where it remained intact for the night occupying billets vacated by the 4th MIDDLESEX Regt.,	
VILLE	15th	10.45am	Battalion Headquarters, 'A' & 'B' Coys., marched to MEAULTE leaving 'C' & 'D' Coys. under the Command of Capt. A. T. W. Paine at VILLE on arrival, the Battalion, less two Coys., came under the orders of G.O.C. 63rd Infantry Bde. for all purposes except administration; working parties were found from the time the Battalion arrived.	
MEAULTE	16th	4pm	Lt.Col. H. B. Warwick returned from Fourth Army School of Instruction (Infantry) and assumed Command of the Battalion. The Battalion less 'C' & 'D' Coys. in Billets at MEAULTE. 'C' & 'D' Coys. in billets at VILLE.	

1875 Wt. W593/826 1,000,000 4/15 J.B.C. & A. A.D.S.S./Forms/C. 2118.

Army Form C. 2118

WAR DIARY
or
INTELLIGENCE SUMMARY
(Erase heading not required.)

Instructions regarding War Diaries and Intelligence Summaries are contained in F. S. Regs., Part II. and the Staff Manual respectively. Title Pages will be prepared in manuscript.

Place	Date	Hour	Summary of Events and Information	Remarks and references to Appendices
MEAULTE	19-21	12 Noon	The Battalion in Billets at MEAULTE and VILLE. Working Parties supplied daily for trenches &c.	Reference Map AMIENS Sheet 17
MEAULTE	22		The Battalion went into Support of the Two Battalions holding the front line. Headquarters at MEAULTE, 'C' Coy. at BONTE REDOUBT, 'A' & 'B' Coys. at BECORDEL and 'D' Coy. in QUEEN'S REDOUBT. The Battalion relieved was 8th Lincoln Regt. of 63rd Brigade.	
	23-28 /4/1916		The Battalion in BONTE REDOUBT, BECORDEL and QUEEN'S REDOUBT in support of the two Battalions holding the front line. Weather very fine and warm. Working parties were supplied for work on Front line trenches and defences of Becordel. St. George's Day was celebrated quietly owing to the Battalion being in support.	
	29/4/1916		The 12th Northumberland Fusiliers relieved the 13th Northumberland Fusrs. in the Right Sector of the 21st Divisional Front. Relief complete by 3.45.p.m. The disposition of the Companies was as follows :- 'A' Coy. Trench XXX 31.F. 'C' Coy. Trench 32.F. 'D' Coy. 33½F. 'B' Coy. in the Support Line.	
	30/4		At 3.A.M. the enemy heavily bombarded the front and support line trenches. and at 3.30.A.M. a raid was carried out on Trench 32.F. evidently with the intention of blowing up a mine shaft in our trenches. The raid was a complete failure and one of the enemy who entered a sap head was taken prisoner. Prisoner had in his possession a large tin filled with explosive evidently intended for the destruction of the mine sap. He stated he belonged to 6th Bavarian Pioneer Regt. The rest of the day was quiet until 7.30.P.M. when rapid rifle and machine gun fire was heard immediately followed by a heavy	

WAR DIARY or INTELLIGENCE SUMMARY

Army Form C. 2118

Place	Date	Hour	Summary of Events and Information	Remarks and references to Appendices
			Artillery Bombardment of our Trenches by the enemy. This bombardment lasted for an hour during which a great many Lachrymatory Shells were fired. No sign of the enemy trying to leave his trenches during or after the bombardment could be detected. From 9.P.M. onwards everything was quiet. Capt. R. B. Singlehurst of 'D' Coy. was killed durung this bombardment. The following Officers were slightly wounded A - Caotain G. Nesbit. 2/Lt. B. El Bumpus. 2/Lt. C. N. G. Koch., Lt. J. Bailey. 2/Lt. A. P. Harrower received Shell Shock. (Signed0 H. B. Warwick. Lt.Col. Cdg 12th S. Bn. Northumberland Fusiliers.	Ref. Map AMIENS Sht- 17 1/100,000

SECRET.

Copy No. 4

62 Inf. Bde. O.O. No. 62.

30th April 1916.

62 Inf. Bde. will be relieved on 2nd May by 64 Inf. Bde.

1. I/Lincoln R. will be relieved by 9 K.O.Y.L.I. in reserve at 9 p.m. and march to billets in LA NEUVILLE.

2. 13 North'd Fus. will be relieved by I/E. York R. in the intermediate line and take over latters billets in BUIRE.
Relieving Battalion will pass MEAULTE Church at 9-30 a.m.

3. 12 North'd Fus. will be relieved by 15 Durh. L.I. in Right Sector and take over latters billets in BUIRE.
Relieving Battalion will pass MEAULTE Church at 11 a.m.
Billets to be taken over from 9 K.O.Y.L.I.

4. 10 York R. will be relieved by 10 K.O.Y.L.I. in Left Sector and take over latters billets in VILLE.
Relieving Battalion will pass MEAULTE Church at 1 p.m.

5. 62 M. Gun Co. will be relieved at 7 a.m. by 64 M. Gun Co., who will dump their guns etc. at D.I. dump after dark on 1st May.
62 M. Gun Co. will take over billets in VILLE.

6. Relief of Signals to be complete by 12 noon on 2nd.

7. Units will arrange details of reliefs and billets with relieving Units.
I/Lincoln R. will take over billets from 63 Inf. Bde. at LA NEUVILLE.
All Trench Stores, Defence Schemes etc., will be handed over on relief.
STOKES Guns will be handed over to 64/I T.M. Battery.

8. Those parties at present attached to 14 N.F. (Pioneers) will remain with that Unit.

9. H.Q. 62 Inf. Bde. will move to VILLE on relief on 2nd.

Issued at 5 p.m.
by Orderly.

Capt,
Bde. Major,
62 Inf. Bde.

Copy No. 1 & 2 - War Diary and file.
: : 3 - 12 North'd Fus.
: : 4 - 13 North'd Fus.
: : 5 - I/Lincoln R.
: : 6 - 12 York R.
: : 7 - 62 M. Gun Co.
: : 8 - 62/1 T.M. Battery.
: : 9 - 62/2 T.M. Battery.
: : 10 - 63 Inf. Bde.
: : 11 - 64 Inf. Bde.
: : 12 - 178 Tunneling Co.
: : 13 - 97 Fd. Co. R.E.

Copy No. 14 - 126 Fd. CO. R.E.
: : 15 - 15 Durh. L.I.
: : 16 - 94 F.A. Bde.
: : 17 - Bde. Trans. Off.
: : 18 - Bde. Gren. Off.
: : 19 - Bde. Sigs. Off.
: : 20 - 14 N.F. (P)
: : 21 - No.2 Co. Train.
: : 22 - 70 Inf. Bde.
: : 23 - 22 Inf. Bde.
: : 24 - Heavy Group R.G.A. 13 Corps.
: : 25 - Town Major,

Army Form C. 2118.

WAR DIARY
or
INTELLIGENCE SUMMARY
(Erase heading not required.)

vol 4

Place	Date	Hour	Summary of Events and Information	Remarks and references to Appendices
MEAULTE	1/5/16		Weather very fine. A very quiet day.	
MEAULTE	2/5		Very quiet day. The Battalion was relieved by 15th Battn. D.L.I. Relief completed by 2.30.P.M. on which the Battalion proceeded to billets in BUIRE. Capt. R. B. SINGLEHURST was buried at MEAULTE at 3.P.M.	
LA NEUVILLE	3/5/16		The Battalion marched from BUIRE at 7.A.M. to rest billets at LA NEUVILLE, and arrived at 9.45.A.M. Coys. &c., devoted the remainder of day to interior economy.	
	4/5		Companies were placed at the disposal of their Company Commanders - Training and Drill was proceeded with.	
	5/5		2/Lieut. J. C. WRENCH proceeded to the Trench Mortar School for a Course of Instruction. The Battalion carried out an exercise at the practice trenches. LA NEUVILLE. One Coy. attended the Grenade School and a number of men proceeded to the rifle range for practice.	
	6/5		The Battalion carried out route marches by half Battalions - one half Battalion not on the march during the morning attended the baths. Four Officers (one per Company) attended a demonstration in anti-gas measures at BUIRE. All Officers down to and including Officers in Command of Companies attended a Tactical Exercise arranged by 21st Division and held in the village school.	
	7/5		The Battalion attended Divine Service on the Football Ground at 9/A.M.	

Army Form C. 2118.

WAR DIARY
or
INTELLIGENCE SUMMARY

(Erase heading not required.)

Instructions regarding War Diaries and Intelligence Summaries are contained in F. S. Regs., Part II. and the Staff Manual respectively. Title Pages will be prepared in manuscript.

Place	Date	Hour	Summary of Events and Information	Remarks and references to Appendices
LA NEUVILLE	8/5/16		The Battalion carried out an exercise at the practice trenches.	
	9/5/16		The Battalion paraded for a route march. - Route - BONNAY - PONT NOYELLES - BONNAY - LA HOUSSOYE - PONT NOYELLES - Distance about 12 miles.	
	10/5/16		The Battalion carried out training on practice trenches wearing gas helmets. The following memo. was received from G.O.C. Fourth Army. (Copy). "This Battalion acquitted itself well during the action 29th/30th April 1916. Please convey to them my appreciation of their good work and congratulations on their success in defeating the raid." (Signed) H. Rawlinson, General.	
	11/5/16		The Battalion continued training and during the morning Battalion Drill and Manoeuvres was practised	
	12/5/16		Training was proceeded with - One Company attended the Bombing School and a party of one Officer and 30 Other Ranks, proceeded to RIBEMONT for duty as an unloading party.	
	13/5/16		The Battalion marched to BUIRE via BONNAY leaving LA NEUVILLE CHURCH at 8.30.AM and arrived at BUIRE at 11.A.M. Working Parties were found in the evening. Weather was very bad; rain; fell for several hours.	
BUIRE	14/5/16		Men not required for working parties attended Divine Service at 11.AM.	
	15/5/16		Weather very wet. One Company clear of duty for attendance at the Grenade School, for one day Course of Bombing, followed by a lecture in the evening on anti-gas methods.	

Army Form C. 2118.

WAR DIARY
or
INTELLIGENCE SUMMARY
(Erase heading not required.)

Instructions regarding War Diaries and Intelligence Summaries are contained in F. S. Regs., Part II. and the Staff Manual respectively. Title Pages will be prepared in manuscript.

Place	Date	Hour	Summary of Events and Information	Remarks and references to Appendices
BUIRE	16/5/16	10 a.m.	Weather fair. - Wind Light - South-West. The Battalion continued to find working parties by day and night for work on communication trenches, battery positions &c., in rear of the Divisional front.	
	17/5/16	10 a.m.	Weather bright. - Working parties as usual.	
	18/5/16	10 a.m.	Weather bright. - slight North-east wind. Working parties as usual. Six Officers and a number of N.C.Os. and men of the LEWIS GUN DETACHMENTS attended a Lecture on LEWIS and Machine Guns at the old church MORLANCOURT. A. Coy. carried out a one day Course of Bombing	
	19/5/16	9 a.m.	Weather bright. - wind light easterly. Working parties as usual. A Tactical Exercise for all Officers down to Company Commanders was held at the School VILLE at 5.P.M.	
	20/5/16	9 a.m.	Weather - bright with warm sun; Wind - East 3.m.p.h. Three Officers attended a demonstration at the Fourth Army School of Instruction and returned the same day.	
	21/5/16	"	Wind - North East - Lt. Col. H. B. WARWICK proceeded to England on short leave (3 days) and Major. F. J. F. EDLMAN assumed Command - Capt. A. T. W. PAINE returned from the Fourth Army School of Instruction; Officers of the Battalion reconnoitred the left sector of the Divisional Front preparatory to taking over from the 10th YORK & LANCS. R.	

Army Form C. 2118.

WAR DIARY
or
INTELLIGENCE SUMMARY
(Erase heading not required.)

Instructions regarding War Diaries and Intelligence Summaries are contained in F. S. Regs., Part II. and the Staff Manual respectively. Title Pages will be prepared in manuscript.

Place	Date	Hour	Summary of Events and Information	Remarks and references to Appendices
FRICOURT	22/5		The Battalion took over the trenches of the left sector from the 10th YORK & LANCS. R. and moved into the right sector. The relief was complete by 2.30.P.M. the night was unusually quiet but it was thought probable that the enemy was busily engaged on his front line wire.	
	23/5		During the morning the enemy shelled our trenches but not heavily - little damage was done, two men were killed and two others wounded by the explosion of one of the enemy's H.E.Shells. The weather was bright with a very light North Easterly Breeze. Our batteries bombarded SHELTER WOOD from 3.53.P.M. and enemy replied with canisters on our front line.	
	24/5	4am	Wind - North East. Weather - Clear. Some M.G.Fire during night 23/24, which somewhat interfered with wiring. Some rifle grenades were fired into PULPIT between midnight and 2.30.A.M. patrols were out during the night but none of the enemy's patrols were seen although working parties were heard. During the morning the enemy shelled the communication trenches without inflicting any damage or casualties. A large number of canisters were fired into the sector on our right during the afternoon and evening.	
	25/5	4am	Wind - South East. Rain. Dull Light. Enemy fired little during the night and few shells fell during the morning and afternoon but did no damage. 2/Lieut. F.G. HUGHES reported for duty this day.	
	26/5	4am	Wind - North East - There was a considerable amount of firing during the earlier hours of the night 25/26th May and at 10.55.P.M. vibration caused by a mine explosion was distinctly felt.	

Army Form C. 2118.

WAR DIARY
or
INTELLIGENCE SUMMARY
(Erase heading not required.)

Instructions regarding War Diaries and Intelligence Summaries are contained in F.S. Regs., Part II. and the Staff Manual respectively. Title Pages will be prepared in manuscript.

Place	Date	Hour	Summary of Events and Information	Remarks and references to Appendices
FRICOURT.	26/5		Enemy continued to shell both trenches and batteries – no damage was done to trenches. There was little firing during the night 26th/27th. The night was favourable and much work was done to the wire in front of trenches.	
	27/5	7pm	The 13th Northumberland Fusiliers relieved the Battalion in the Front Line and Support Trenches the 10th YORK R. taking over the right sector of the Divisional Front. On relief the Battalion took up positions as follows:– A. Company in BONTE Redoubt. B. Company. in QUEENS Redoubt. C. & D. Companies in BECORDEL Redoubt. Battalion Headquarters in MEAULTE. The Relief was completed by 9.15.A.M. Total Casualties for the period 22nd – 27th – 2 Killed and 4 Wounded. Draft from 3rd Bn. 32. O.R. joined to-day.	
MEAULTE.	28/5	11am	Light – Bright. Wind. Light North East. Detachment in BECORDEL finding Mining Fatigues of 240 per 24 hours.	
	29/5	10am	Light Bright. Wind EAST. moving to South East. Nothing to report.	
	30/5	10am	Dull Wind. North–East. enemy shelled ground East of Meaulte during night of 29th /30th.	
	31/5	10am	Wind North East. Light Bright. Considerable shelling by both sides yesterday and during the earlier part of last night. BONTE Redoubt was shelled this morning at 6.15.A.M. a number of 7.7.c.m. shells striking the parapet – No damaged was done. Casualties one man bruised.	

(Sgd) H. B. Warwick. Lt.-Col.
12th (Service) Bn. Royal Fusiliers
Commdg.

Army Form C. 2118

WAR DIARY
or
INTELLIGENCE SUMMARY
(Erase heading not required.)

Vol 10
12. Northumb.

Place	Date	Hour	Summary of Events and Information	Remarks and references to Appendices
NEUVILLE	June 1916		This Battalion, together with the 1st Battalion Northumberland Fusiliers was mentioned in the despatch by General Sir Douglas Haig G.C.B. Commander-in-Chief of the British Forces in France for excellent work in making and in repelling raids. The total number of units mentioned was less than one hundred.	

WAR DIARY
or
INTELLIGENCE SUMMARY
(Erase heading not required.)

Army Form C. 2118

Instructions regarding War Diaries and Intelligence Summaries are contained in F.S. Regs., Part II. and the Staff Manual respectively. Title Pages will be prepared in manuscript.

Place	Date	Hour	Summary of Events and Information	Remarks and references to Appendices
MEAULTE	JUNE 1-2			
	2		The morning was quieter as regards shelling. The Battalion was relieved in QUEEN'S REDOUBT, BONTE REDOUBT and BECOURT by the 1st S. Bn. Durham Light Infantry. Relief being completed at 2.15.P.M. except for QUEEN'S REDOUBT which was relieved at 4.15.P.M. The Battalion marched by Platoons to BUIRE and went into Billets.	
	3		The Battalion left BUIRE and marched to LA NEUVILLE, where the 62nd Inf. Bde. went into Reserve.	
LA NEUVILLE	4		The Battalion was inspected in full marching order by Brigadier-General WILKINSON Commanding 62nd Inf. Bde. at 2.30.P.M. Formation - Open Mass, with Specialists and Transport drawn up behind.	
	5	8 a.m.	The 62nd Inf. Bde. was drawn up along the LA NEUVILLE - DAOURS Road ready to advance over the Practice Trenches and to keep in touch and communication with an aeroplane. However, the weather proved unsuitable and the operations were postponed till Friday 9th June. The Battalion practised the attack over the trenches.	
	6		The men were bathed in the morning. In the afternoon a detachment consisting of all the Company Officers and 600 Men under Major F. J. F. Edleman moved to BUIRE to act as a permanent working party on the Corps Artillery Cable Trenches.	
	7	8.30 a.m.	The 62nd Inf. Bde. was inspected in full marching order by Major-Gen'l. D. G. M. Campbell Commdg. 21st Div. The Battalion was represented by the LEWIS Gunners, The Signallers, and 30 O.R.	

WAR DIARY
or
INTELLIGENCE SUMMARY

(Erase heading not required.)

Army Form C. 2118

Place	Date	Hour	Summary of Events and Information	Remarks and references to Appendices
LA NEUVILLE	June 8 & 9th		50 Men were inoculated and rested for 48 hours.	
	10th		There was a competition between the various transports of the Bde de the O.C. 21st Divisional Train inspected them, and made the following awards (1) 13th Northd. Fus. (2) 1st Lincolns (3) 12th Northd. Fus. There were also three bombing competitions (a) For the longest throwing (b) For the most accurate throwing (c) For clearing Ten Bays fof .. trench (a) Was won by the 13th Northd. Fus. and (b) & (c) by the 12th Northd. Fus.	
	11th		The Battalion attended Divine Service on the Football Ground at 10.30.AM	
BUIRE	12th		The Battalion marched from LA NEUVILLE at 7.AM. and joined the detachment at BUIRE at 10.AM. Working Parties were found in the evening. Brig-Gen'l. WILKINSON left the 62nd Inf. Bde. to proceed to England and Lt-Col. H. B. Warwick assumed Command of the Brigade until the arrival of Lt-Col. RAWLING. from the SOMERSET L.I.	
	13th 14th 15th 16th 17th		Weather on the whole wet and cold. Large working parties were found every day to dig cable trenches. To carry ammunition and stores, and to work on Redoubts 19 & 20.	
	17th		The Divisional Commander Major-Gen'l D. G. M. CAMPBELL spoke to all Officers of the 62nd Inf. Bde. in the School Room at VILLE on the attack, and on esprit de corps.	
	18/19th		Weather fine -working parties as usual.	

WAR DIARY
or
INTELLIGENCE SUMMARY

(Erase heading not required.)

Army Form C. 2118

Place	Date	Hour	Summary of Events and Information	Remarks and references to Appendices
BUIRE	June 7th?		Battalion marched to BUIRE by Platoons at 4 minutes interval to relieve the 8th Lincoln Regt. in the Right Sector of the Divisional Front. The leading Platoon passed MEAULTE Church at 7.A.M. Relief complete at 11.A.M. The 1/Lincoln Regt. held the left Sector, 10/Yorks regt. held BECORDEL, BONTE & QUEEN'S REDOUBTS. 13th Northd. Fus. were in Reserve in MEAULTE.	
FRICOURT	2/ol		On the whole a very quiet day. Many rifle grenades fell in the TAMBOUR. Casualties :- One man slightly wounded.	
	22 [illegible]	2 p.m.	Our trenches between TAMBOUR & PURFLEET were heavily bombarded with 10.5 cm. Howitzers, 7.7mm. guns, Canisters, and Aerial Torcedoes. Four Bays of the Front Line were blown in — Casualties —Four Killed and Six Wounded. During the afternoon between 2.P.M. and 4.30.P.M. our trenches near CRUCIFIX CORNER were bombarded with canisters. a LEWIS Gun was buried but afterwards recovered undamaged. There were no Casualties. REINFORCEMENTS :- The following Officers joined the Battalion from various Units :- From the 3rd Bn. Northd. Fus. 2/Lt. F. G. Hughes., June 12th., From 15th Northd. Fus. 2/Lt. J.O.B/rne., 2/Lt. J. Findley., 2/Lt. J. L. Griffiths., 2/Lt. W. T. Hindmarsh., 2/Lt. T. W. Cunningham., 2/Lt. J. O. Durham., June 19th., 2/Lt. W. M. Br die., June 20th., 2/Lt. R. D. Smith., June 21st., From 114th Coy., M.G. Corps., 2/Lt. J. E. Borrell., June 16th. From the G.H.Q. Cadet School 2/Lt. S. Marchant., June 6th., From the No.3. I.B.D. 2/Lt. V. M. de Belsbre June 23rd., From 15th Northd. Fus., 2/Lt. H. Oyston., 2/Lt. S. E. H. Anderson., June 25th. On June 19th. 7.O.R. from 21st I.B.D.	

Army Form C. 2118

WAR DIARY
or
INTELLIGENCE SUMMARY
(Erase heading not required.)

Instructions regarding War Diaries and Intelligence Summaries are contained in F. S. Regs., Part II. and the Staff Manual respectively. Title Pages will be prepared in manuscript.

Place	Date	Hour	Summary of Events and Information	Remarks and references to Appendices
FRICOURT	June 23rd		The morning was very quiet. In the afternoon the enemy fired about 3 shrapnel rounds over each of our communication trenches 2/Lt. J. McKINNON., was wounded in the right arm with a shrapnel bullet. KINGSTON AV. where our support Coy. was, was bombarded with 15.c.m. shells. During the night the enemy was very restless. His riflemen and machine gunners were very active.	
	24th		The Bombardment of the German Trenches commenced. Trench Mortars and Field Guns commenced to cut wire. The heavy guns shelled the trenches and other enemy works Retaliation from the enemy was practically nil. Several Lachrymatory shells (20) fell in BECORDEL at 5.30.P.M. Two or three Canisters fell in the Right Company Area and some shrapnel burst over the TAMBOUR. Wind WEST during the day at night there was practically no wind.	
	25th		Second day of the bombardment. Still there was very little retaliation from the enemy. During the morning about 20. 15.cm. shells fell in the centre Coy. area. In the afternoon 10.H.E Shrapnel burst over WILLOW AVENUE. At 10.P.M. a Field Battery fired several rounds into UPPER RONDEL AVENUE. During the night our patrols examined the German wire and reported that several gaps had been made in it. They also reported that the German trenches were strongly held. At 10.30.A.M. 34th Div. on our right launched a gas attack together with the 7th Div. we launched a gas attack at 11.30.A.M. We afterwards learnt that several Germans were killed by it. The enemy formed a barrage behind TANGER and behind FRICOURT STATION & CEMETERY – His Machine Gun and Rifle Fire was quite considerable. The enemy retaliated vigorously on the whole of our area throughout the day. A patrol under Capt. GUSH., went out from the Left Coy., It passed through the enemy's wire and attempted to enter the German Trench, but was met by a shower of bombs. Capt. Gush, unfortunately, was wounded with four others. They, however, found that there were many lanes in the wire, and that the trenches were slightly damaged and were strongly held.	

WAR DIARY
or
INTELLIGENCE SUMMARY

(Erase heading not required.)

Army Form C. 2118

Place	Date	Hour	Summary of Events and Information	Remarks and references to Appendices
FRICOURT	June 26th		Another patrol under Lieut. PHILIP. and 2/Lt. McARTHUR. raided the German Trench at WICKED CORNER and brought back six prisoners. One of our men was slightly wounded. This raid drew heavy artillery retaliation on our trenches for about 10 minutes. CASUALTIES - 2/Lt. F. G. HUGHES -, 2/Lt. J.L. GRIFFITHS. Killed. 2/Lt. G. P. SEELING Wounded Capt. H. W. GUSH Wounded. 4. other ranks killed and 10 wounded.	
	27th		Fourth day of the bombardment. At 5.A.M. a smoke attack was launched on our front and the enemy put up a very heavy barrage on our front line. There were no casualties. During the remainder of the day the enemy was very quiet. The Battalion was relieved by the 7th Bn. Yorkshire Regt. and the 10th Bn. West Yorkshire Regt. both of the 50th Inf. Bde. Relief complete 5.A.M.	
REDOUBTS 19 - 20.	28th		Battalion moved to Redoubts 19 & 20. There was little cover for the men and as the weather was so bad they got very little rest. At 9.30 P.M. orders arrived and the Battalion marched into Billets at RIBEMONT.	
RIBEMONT	29th		The Battalion rested and the Men were bathed.	

E.J A.L.B. Commander
C.g. of the Bn. north of two.

62nd Inf.Bde.
21st Div.

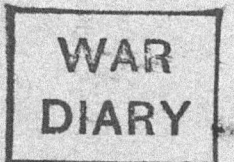

12th BATTN. THE NORTHUMBERLAND FUSILIERS.

J U L Y

1 9 1 6

Army Form C. 2118.

WAR DIARY
or
INTELLIGENCE SUMMARY
(Erase heading not required.)

Vol II

Place	Date	Hour	Summary of Events and Information	Remarks and references to Appendices
RIBEMONT	June 30th 1916	6.40 pm	Notification was received that the operation which had been postponed would commence at 7.30 AM the following day. The Battalion was ordered to move to its place of assembly. Works 19 & 20 immediately north of BECORDEL. At 6.40 P.M. the Battalion less Regimental Transport and a few nucleus officers proceeded to the Assembly Area where it bivouaced for the night.	
FRICOURT	July 1st 1916	7.15 AM	At 7.15 AM the Battalion commenced to move towards the front line. Orders had been issued to carry stores for 63rd Iny Bde.	*Reference Sheet 57d.*
		7.30	At 7.30 A.M. the attack was launched, after an extensive bombardment. That of a coy of the 21st Division with the 50th Brigade attacked. First Objective — FRICOURT FARM — French Junction X 28 c 8.7. CRUCIFIX TRENCH — BIRCH TREE WOOD Second Objective — 63rd Bde X 29 c 5.6. fence along northern edge of BOTTOM WOOD to new trench X 29 a 4.8. along new trench to QUADRANGLE TRENCH X 23 c 4.5. Third Objective — 64th Bde Junction of new trench & southern edge of QUADRANGLE trench to other new Junction X 22 d 6.6.5. The 7th D.L.I. was in ordinary Reserve being in reserve at the disposal of the 21st Div. The Division. The 34th Division from troops were travelling at the disposal was allotted to that of the Division of FRICOURT At 12 noon the 10 Montrose was deployed at front of A.D. and two Platoons D Coy in EMPRESS SUPPORTS. The remainder of the Battalion in QUEENS REDOUBT trenches were disposed of as part of the	

WAR DIARY or INTELLIGENCE SUMMARY

Army Form C. 2118.

(Erase heading not required.)

Instructions regarding War Diaries and Intelligence Summaries are contained in F. S. Regs., Part II. and the Staff Manual respectively. Title Pages will be prepared in manuscript.

Place	Date	Hour	Summary of Events and Information	Remarks and references to Appendices
FRICOURT	July 1st 1916	7.30 P.M.	At 7-30 P.M. the Battalion was ordered to support the 1st London Regt and 10 Yorks Regt who took over the front line, the 13th Royal Fus were of 3rd Brigade, the 64th Bde was withdrawn from the line during the night. At dawn (the Battalion moved into SUNKEN ROAD the northern end of which was occupied by the 1st London Regt and the Southern end by 12th Royal Fus and B Coy occupying advanced post at LOZENGE WOOD. An attack on FRICOURT by the 17th Division cleared the whole of the ground on morning of advance thereto front of this Brigade. By 12 noon. At 7-30 P.M. orders were received to garrison PATCH ALLEY as an attack was considered probable from ROUND WOOD ALLEY where the enemy were known to be massing. No attack took place and the garrison composed of D Coy and Lieut Thompson A Coy were withdrawn to the SUNKEN ROAD.	
	July 2nd 1916	7.A.M.	At about 7 A.M. an attack on SHELTER WOOD was ordered and the following dispositions made 1st 10 [?] Regiment came detached for the Reserve, and would in the northern part of CRUCIFIX TRENCH with A & C Coys in support of the preliminary bombardment commenced at 8.40 A.M. and the attack was launched at 9 A.M. The enemy offered about no resistance and surrendering company surrendered to the 10 [?] the 1st London to follow to [?] lines in rear of the attack being known how. Many officers and men called for to come in and surrender up. About 9-30 A.M. communication	

WAR DIARY

Army Form C. 2118.

Place	Date	Hour	Summary of Events and Information	Remarks and references to Appendices
FRICOURT	July 3rd		Heavy shelling continued throughout the morning and at about 12 noon a Bosche aeroplane flew over 21st Div Head Quarters, that column of German had been observed advancing to the country from CONTALMAISON towards SHELTER WOOD and that it was thought that the enemy were attempting to surround my left. This was considered probable as many prisoners were coming in from the left and the centre of the position. At 1 p.m. (a message from Captain LOCKIE, who was in command of the right portion of the line) was received stating that the objectives had been reached i.e. the Bosche edge of SHELTER WOOD and that the position was being consolidated. The G.O.C. sent the following message to Bgd Head Qrs (by pigeon) "Damned good fight, have not completely disposed of enemy but enemy cannot form counter attack, consolidated, and well held." Considerable fighting took place during the afternoon between the troops holding the newly won position and the enemy in QUADRANGLE trench R.1. Strong hostile bombing operations were carried out by both sides. By 6 p.m. the attackers had consolidated their position and settled down to trench routine as far as was practicable. The G.O.C. 21st Division sent the following message to Col. & G.Q. "G.O.C. sends hearty congratulations to Gen. RAWLIN and all ranks on many splendid fighting qualities shown by 62nd Inf. Bde."

WAR DIARY or INTELLIGENCE SUMMARY

Army Form C. 2118.

Place	Date	Hour	Summary of Events and Information	Remarks and references to Appendices
FRICOURT	July 3rd 1916	6 P.M.	The G.O.C. 62nd Inf. Bde. having inspected the greater part of the line decided to return to Brigade H.Q. and to hand to Col. T.E.D. Warren of the 12th Yorks Regt. the command of the troops holding the position, during the night the July 3/4th the Brigade was relieved by the 32nd Brigade (17th Divn.), the Brigade moved into a field near the Railway crossing DERNANCOURT & about 6 a.m. Rain fell during the greater part of the day. Remainder of the Brigade, 12th & 13th Notts Regts, 13th Royal Fus. 1st Routes Fus. (Pioneers) 10 Yorks Regt and 62nd Divn. S.C. of 4 & D.A.C. DERNANCOURT at 9 P.M. formed billets at AILLY-SUR-SOMME where the Battalion moved into Billets.	
ST SAUVEUR and AILLY-SUR-SOMME	July 5th 1916	9 A.M.	1st to 13th Battalions breakfasted at 9 A.M and spent the day in cleaning and reorganising. Stragglers and prisoners taken by the Brigade was about 450 and a further number who surrendered to the troops on our immediate right was estimated at 400 to Total of 1100; the total enemy casualties during the SHELTER WOOD operations including 2 to be about 2000 total casualties 62nd Inf Bde are not at present known.

During the operations July 1st to 3rd the Battalion Casualties were

3 Officers killed
12 " wounded (includes at duty)
2   " O.R.
142 " killed
197 " wounded
     " missing | 12.50 a.m. orders received of the movement to move at 2 P.M. Particulars to be issued later. |

WAR DIARY
INTELLIGENCE SUMMARY

Army Form C. 2118.

Place	Date	Hour	Summary of Events and Information	Remarks and references to Appendices
ST. SAUVEUR near AILLY-SUR-SOMME	July 6		The Battalion left Billets at St SAUVEUR and marched to the village of MOLLIENS VIDAME distance eleven miles, and went into billets there.	Ref. Map AMIENS 1/100,000
MOLLIENS VIDAME	7-8-9		The Battalion remained in billets, reorganising and carrying out a course of re-equipping, being relieved of all dumping of the movement of being ordered to go to the line. Lieut. Capt. A.T.W. PAINE go to Battalion left Billets at MOLLIENS VIDAME and marched to AILLY-SUR-SOMME where it was boarded from 10 A.M. to 6 P.M. awaiting the arrival of trains. The Regimental transport proceeded by road to MEAULTE. At 6 P.M. 1st & 2nd Battalions entrained as AILLY and alternous three hour train time at CORBIE, travelling to its destination arriving the Battn one mile out of CORBIE on the road to VILLE-SUR-ANCRE and after a meal motor buses conveyed the Battn to VILLE-SUR-ANCRE where companies marched by Platoons to MEAULTE	
MEAULTE	July 11th		& shape of 11.2. O.R. formed there at 11 A.M. July 11/16 The Battalion moved from MEAULTE village to MAMETZ WOOD via BECORDEL & BECOURT this day from the 13th Bn. Battn. FRICOURT and WILLOW AVENUE. In MAMETZ WOOD the Battn relieved a portion of the 11th & 7th Inf. Bde. of the points temporary extended from X.16.c.2.5. to G.13.c.4.4. took up points temporary extended the 13th & Battn. Northumberland Fusiliers held the left of Rd Bd. Line. The Battn front line was composed of B, C, & D, Coys, & Coys. left & Coy on the centre, and D Coy on the right. A Coy was held in reserve just in Pt. Helene. Coys proceeded to dig in immediately upon taking up their respective points while parties penetrated still further into the wood.	MONTAUBAN 1/20,000
MAMETZ WOOD				

WAR DIARY or INTELLIGENCE SUMMARY

Army Form C. 2118.

Place	Date	Hour	Summary of Events and Information	Remarks and references to Appendices
MAMETZ WOOD	July 12th		Entering posts were also put forward. During the night of July 11/12 the ground lying between FRICOURT and MAMETZ WOOD was heavily shelled by the hostile artillery many casualties resulting both during the relief and during the process of getting round wire defences from the 62nd Bde. that the wood was to be cleaned as far north as possible accordingly by patrols were pushed further forward and ultimately reached the northern limit of the wood; thereupon B, C, and D Coys advancing in column and in succession only half cleared much of from enemy groups of the enemy opened fire on whole of the wood using guns from two positions numerous phones and several cannons of large calibre by 5 A.M. Consolidation of the position this gained was entered upon at once. A trench throwing thirty yards from the Northern limit of the wood. At anyway over advanced for two Coys forward for Coy of two which B Coys began work on when Bn were ordered to accommodate loops of FA 6. 110 to 18 to ethers attacks extended to attack and capture BAZANTIN-LE-PETIT WOOD by heavy shell fire through out the day the enemy continued to shell the wood and great portions, the wood being thoroughly searched and all points back particularly long distance and place in high places. Throughout and also gas & shells. In consequence the casualties were very great; in spite of difficulties of removing the wounded down all casualties sickness and walking cases were evacuated by 10 A.M. and of which force was also removed. At 11.10 p.m. the estimated casualties were	

2449 Wt. W14957/M90 750,000 1/16 J.B.C. & A. Forms/C.2118/12.

Place	Date	Hour	Summary of Events and Information	Remarks and references to Appendices
MAMETZ WOOD	July 13th		appeared to be one officer (Lieut E.A. MALCOLM) wounded and 80 O.R. killed and wounded. A draft of 3 O.R. joined the Battn from the 3rd & 5th Seaforths. Parties, the shape & size came up from the Battn transport at MEAULTE at dusk, unmolested, killed and wounded before joining their Coys respectively. During the day the enemy shelling continued and the following casualties were reported:— Capt. H.W. CUSH, Capt. E.H. GRIFFIN, Lieut. J. BRUNTON, Lt. HINDMARSH, and Lt. McARTHUR wounded and 23 O.R. killed and wounded.	
	July 13/14	3.25 AM 4 AM 6 AM	During the night 13/14th Bn assembled in rear of the Battn, ready once more 7th Battn LEICESTER Regt was ordered to prepare for them by being in PHILLIP and the 9th Battn by the 110th Bde. [illegible] had reported to be Brig. the morning the enemy had the programme of the attack was in support and occupation of the centre of BAZENTIN-LE-PETIT WOOD (×B 6.5.h.) Moving from the 13th, no one dreamed that the enemy had been disposed the defences of the 62nd. One of the 62nd to the a.m. on the night of July 13th a large operation was set on foot "Hour" operation in support of with less manner to keep and the enemy boys that the enemy was a... by the... good. It is thought that the enemy already... orders of the map appeared as any little opposition was offered	Read map MONTAUBAN 24000 AREA of MARTINPUICH (parts of) X.A.10.37. × S.E. and 57c. S.W. 1/20,000

War Diary or Intelligence Summary

Army Form C. 2118.

Place	Date	Hour	Summary of Events and Information	Remarks and references to Appendices
MAMETZ WOOD	July 15		and the absence of any hostile machine gun and rifle fire was remarkable. During the morning of July 15th the 12th Battn Sussex Battn Bombers carried up a [?] to the lines supplied by the 110th Bde and formed a dump for that Bde in BAZENTIN-LE-PETIT WOOD. 15th Bn shelling throughout the day and Enemy 3 O.R. casualties. Killed 2/Lt W.E. LIMONT, 2/Lt ANDERSON and 2/Lt OYSTON wounded. 103 O.R. killed and wounded.	
	July 16		During the night 14/15 the enemy shelled spasmodically. The day was spent in consolidation of our position and burying the dead. The 21st Division being in support to the 15th Bn. Somes[?] Suspicion of poison of position [?]	
	July 17		A certain amount of gas shells, the enemy place were dropping apparently [?] and [?] to be fired by the enemy. Bombardment continued at intervals. MAMETZ WOOD. The 2nd Battn WORCESTER REGT were marched to the Bazentin where the transport joined them & later the 2nd Battn was conveyed to BECIRE-SUR-ANCRE where the Battn went into Billets at 11 A.M. July 18th. The total casualties suffered by the 12th (S) Battn Royal Sussex from the commencement of the bombardment on June 24th until finally withdrawn from the trenches of the opposing on July 17th was —	AREA J MARTINPUICH 20,000 map rey 6 Officers 85 1 322 30 O.R. 3 O.R.

Army Form C. 2118.

WAR DIARY
or
INTELLIGENCE SUMMARY

(Erase heading not required.)

Instructions regarding War Diaries and Intelligence Summaries are contained in F. S. Regs., Part II. and the Staff Manual respectively. Title Pages will be prepared in manuscript.

Place	Date	Hour	Summary of Events and Information	Remarks and references to Appendices
BUIRE-SUR-ANCRE	July 18		The enemy exploded 9 mines & artillery of enemy gather increased. Enemy troops put into trenches. Of the Battalion: Lieut. and Killed at BUIRE, Capt. LOCKIE (wounded), Lieut. BRUNTON (wounded) and 2nd Lieut. PHILLIP (wounded) evacuated to England. 10 days sick leave to England. Work in renovation of the Battn continued.	
	19			
	20		Of the Battalion marched to DERNANCOURT. Thence by train to SAILEUX. From there, marching distance being limited at 11 p.m. the Battn marched to MOLLIENS VIDAME, where it arrived at 2.45 am July 21st	
	21		The Battalion rested at MOLLIENS VIDAME	
	22		The Battalion moved by motor bus to the RIFLE RANGE at AMIENS where it bivouacked for the night.	
	23		Battn moved from RIFLE RANGE to LONGEAU entraining here for Battn and afterwards DOULLENS to ST POL. From ST POL where Battn arrived at 7.30 p.m. the Battn marched to billets at AVERDOINGT.	
ST POL				
AVERDOINGT	July 24		The Battalion rest from AVERDOINGT to billets at 12er-LES-HAMEAUX	
	25			
12ER-LES-HAMEAUX	26		Officers proceeded to ARRAS by motor. Other ranks held by rail & no Battn K.O.Y.L.I. commenced training at 12er-LES-HAMEAUX of the Battalion	Ref map ARRAS 57 & N.W.3 Edition 2.B
WANQUETIN	27		to WANQUETIN, where it arrived by motor bus from 12er-LES-HAMEAUX 1/62nd Way Recommenced in barracks until	10. ro.

2449 Wt. W14957/M90 750,000 1/16 J.B.C. & A. Forms/C.2118/12.

WAR DIARY or INTELLIGENCE SUMMARY

Army Form C. 2118.

Place	Date	Hour	Summary of Events and Information	Remarks and references to Appendices
ARRAS	July 28	8-30 p.m.	The Battalion marched by Coys to ARRAS and arrived at ARRAS at 1-15 a.m. on July 29. It was an uneventful relief in the billets of the Bn R. Berks.	
			The Battalion left billets at 2 p.m. and after a short rest by the Colonel had inspection of the front line occupied by the left bank of River SCARPE (B.17.D.8.1) to (G.17.B.9.8.) of the Battalion being stationed on the Railway Embankment. The Battalion Railways D Coy took over the front line from the right of the Battalion front between 81 and 82. 2 Platoons of A Coy took over from 83, 4.87. 2 Platoons of A Coy took over 84, 86 and B Coy likewise reserves at the OIL FACTORY (G.17.C.) Remained Command at G.17.D.M.1 and at a point G.17.D.8.1	
	29		The 10th Bn came known to 67 & more Battn and the left flank of the junction of these Rds 87 and 88. To rear of the Coys was held by A.B. 11th Devons communicating there by day running in from at the Railway. H corner from Extremely well ht. Very little enemy on the part of the Enemy party of his.	
	30		G.17.D. Rolls as a cooking party week. MARCH AVENUE communication trench at 8-40 p.m. No casualties received.	

WAR DIARY or INTELLIGENCE SUMMARY

Army Form C. 2118.

Place	Date	Hour	Summary of Events and Information	Remarks and references to Appendices
	July 31		Spent a very quiet day, our men was worked on supports by a sniper: at 7.30 p.m the enemy fired again 7.70 m. shells into the supports doing no damage. H Whitworth Lieut Col Comdy 12/7(s) Durham Light Infantry	Post Map ARRAS 51 BM.W.B Edward B 1 10,000
	1/8/16			

62nd Brigade.

21st Division.

1/12th BATTALION
6

NORTHUMBERLAND FUSILIERS

AUGUST 1916.

Army Form C. 2118.

Vol 2
12 North Fus

WAR DIARY
or
INTELLIGENCE SUMMARY
(Erase heading not required.)

Place	Date	Hour	Summary of Events and Information	Remarks and references to Appendices
ARRAS	Aug 1st 1916		Weather exceedingly hot, and the enemy absolutely quiet; great progress was made in clearing spoil at trenches.	Ref map ARRAS 51.B.N.W.3. Edition 2.B. 1/10,000
	2.		2nd 12th (S) Battn was relieved in trenches 81-87 by the 13 3 Battalion Northumberland Fusiliers; the Battn HdQrs moved back into billets in ARRAS with A & B Coys, C & D Coys occupied the CANDLE FACTORY and FORESTIER REDOUBT respectively, the Battalion thus being in Brigade Reserve.	
	3.			
	4-8		The Battalion remained in Bde reserve in ARRAS. Working parties were found daily for the trenches. On Aug 7 2/Lt W.H. MORANT joined the Battalion from the 3rd Reserve Battn. on Aug 8 2/Lt J. NOBLE & 2/Lt J. SHERWOOD joined the Battalion from the Cadets School at G.H.Q. on Instruction.	
	9th		2/Lt 12 (S) Battn NORTHUMBERLAND FUSILIERS relieved the 13th Battn in trenches 81-87; C & D Coys being relieved in CANDLE FACTORY & FORESTIER REDOUBTS by the 1st Battn LINCOLN REGT.	
	10th		Weather intensely hot; enemy showed no activity.	
	11th		Between 5pm & 7pm an 60 pounder trench mortar registered the enemy front line, the enemy retaliated on support trenches B2 & B3 with MINENWERFER Bombs & on B4 (fire trench) with small arms torpedoes. No casualties resulted.	
	12th		The Corps Commander of the VIth Corps Lieut-Gen HALDANE inspected the trenches. The enemy was again very quiet. There was a certain amount of snipinf activity in which we felt the upper hand. Lt-Col NORWICK went to England on special leave, Major J.J.J. Saltmann assumed command.	

2449 Wt. W14957/M90 750,000 1/16 J.B.C. & A. Forms/C.2118/12.

Army Form C.2118.

WAR DIARY
or
INTELLIGENCE SUMMARY
(Erase heading not required.)

Instructions regarding War Diaries and Intelligence Summaries are contained in F. S. Regs., Part II. and the Staff Manual respectively. Title Pages will be prepared in manuscript.

Place	Date	Hour	Summary of Events and Information	Remarks and references to Appendices
ARRAS	Aug 13th		The morning was very quiet; at 2 p.m however our 60 pounders & trench mortars opened on the enemy's front line trenches, in retaliation for the activity of the enemy's MINENWERFER on the left of the Divisional front. The enemy replied with medium MINENWERFER bombs, small aerial torpedoes and 7.7 cm shells. The enemy's wire was destroyed & no hostile patrols in several places: one line kept in trench 82 was destroyed, otherwise we suffered no material damage & no casualties. Our patrols were very active but had "No mans land" to themselves.	Ref. Map ARRAS 51 B.N.W.3 Edition 2.17 1/10.000
	Aug 14th		A very quiet day; much work done repairing damage done to trenches by previous days bombardments.	
	15.		A draft of 30 O.R. joined the Battalion and were posted to Coys. A very quiet day. 2nd Lt Hasley wounded on patrol.	
	16.		At 7.30 pm the enemy began trench mortaring our support trenches 83 & 84 & enfilading FEBRUARY AVENUE with 7.7 cm shells; we retaliated with 60 lb bomb mortars, & STOKES GUN; at 8.45 p.m a bomb aeroplane flying from S. to N. dropped 4 bombs near 82 support trench. Casualties 1m day 1 man wounded.	
	17		A quiet day; some trench mortar activity at 8.30 p.m, no damage or casualties. Both Bombers & Signallers & Lewis guns relieved by those of the 9" (S) Batt. LEICESTER REGT.	
	18		The 12R (S) Batt. Northumberland Fusiliers relieved in J.1. Right sector by the 9"(S) Bath LEICESTERSHIRE REGT 1110.17.13 & the Batt proceeding to Billets in ARRAS by platoons. The relief was completed at 11.45 A.M; the Batts proceeding to Billets in ARRAS by platoons. At 8.30 P.M the Battalion moved by Coys to AGNEY-LEZ-DUISANS, where it went into Batt. & Divisional Reserve Billets.	
AGNES-LEZ-DUISANS	19-26		The battalion remained eight days in Divisional Reserve and much reorganisation and training was accomplished during this period. This was the first real opportunity which the Battalion had since	

WAR DIARY or INTELLIGENCE SUMMARY

Army Form C. 2118.

Place	Date	Hour	Summary of Events and Information	Remarks and references to Appendices
	1916			Ref Map ARRAS 51.B.N.W.3 Edition 2.B. 1/10,000
ARRAS	Aug 27		The Battalion was withdrawn from the SOMME & went for rest, training & refitting. Lt Col Warwick returned from leave and assumed command of the Battalion. The Battalion relieved the 13th Batln. Northumberland Fusiliers in the I.1 sector ; this sector extends northwards from the river SCARPE at a point G.35.B.8.0, the right half of the sector — from G.35.B.8.0 to G.30.A.7.4. was held by the 12th Batln Northumberland Fusiliers, the left half sector by the 10th S. Batln Yorkshire Regt. The Batln holding the next sector to the Right (the H. sector) was the 5th Batln Berkshire Regt. & the 12th Division. The front line of I.1 sector was held by A Coy on the right, B Coy in the Centre and D Coy on the Left, C Coy being in reserve at a point G.29.C.7.8.	
	28		A very quiet three days in which the enemy showed no initiative. Our patrols were very active but could not locate any enemy patrols; the enemy seems very busy strengthening his line	
	29			
	30		Weather turned very wet & colder, but the trenches are on the whole very good. A day of very heavy rain with West wind ; very little military activity.	
	31		Weather cleared, situation remained very quiet	

[signature]
Army 13th September 1916

62nd Brigade.
21st Division.

1/12th BATTALION

NORTHUMBERLAND FUSILIERS

SEPTEMBER 1916.

Army Form C. 2118.

WAR DIARY
or
INTELLIGENCE SUMMARY
(Erase heading not required.)

12th Bn Northumberland Fusiliers **VOL 13**

13-9

Place	Date 1916	Hour	Summary of Events and Information	Remarks and references to Appendices
ARRAS	Sept 1st		Quiet day, our aeroplanes shewed great activity over the enemy's lines. 24 - 12th Battn. Northumberland Fusiliers was relieved by the 13th Battn. Northumberland Fus. the relief was completed by 8.45 p.m. On relief "A" Coy went into the St SAUVEUR defences (G.29.D.5.5.); "B" Coy into the Cemetery Defences (G.29.B.5.5); "C" and "D" Coys into Billets at ARRAS, Headquarters to RUE DE LA PAIX ARRAS, the Battn. Hdqrs in Btn reserve.	Ref Map ARRAS 51.B.N.W. Edition 2.13 1/10,000
	Sept 2		A Reinforcement of one officer (2nd Lieut BRIANCE) from the 31st R. Battn. and 137 other ranks from the 15th, 18th, 19th & 20th R. Battns joined the 12th Battn. from the ETAPLES BASE.	
	3		2nd Battn. Rev. A & B Coys in Billets in ARRAS; special attention paid to boots & equipment in view of probable move of the Division to the SOMME. 12th Northumberland Fusiliers relieved by the 23rd Battn. Manchester Regt. (Bantams) of the 35th Division; A & B Coys were relieved in St SAUVEUR Defences & the CEMETERY Defences by 3 p.m. & returned to Billets in ARRAS. At 8.30 p.m. the Battalion marched by Coys to WANQUETIN & billeted there.	
	4		2nd Battalion marched from WANQUETIN to GRAND ROLLECOURT via HAUTEVILLE and AVESNES-LE-COMTE arriving at GRAND ROLLECOURT at midday. The Battalion went into Billets a little last named place.	Ref LENS map 1/100,000
	5		A Reinforcement arrived consisting of 30 N.C.O's & men from 2nd Battn., 5 from 12th Battn., 11 from Territorial Battalions.	
GRAND ROLLECOURT	6		Reinforcements of 63 N.C.O's & men arrived from the Territorial Reinforcement Depot. The Battalion continued training for active operations.	

WAR DIARY
or
INTELLIGENCE SUMMARY

(Erase heading not required.)

Army Form C. 2118.

Place	Date	Hour	Summary of Events and Information	Remarks and references to Appendices
GRAND RULLECOURT	1916. Sept 7		Lt. Col. WARWICK was evacuated sick to England. Major F.J.F. EDLMANN assumed command. 2/Lts. M.J. PIPER and F.A. JENKYN joined the Battn. from the 32nd Battn. Hon. Lieut & Quartermaster T. BAMFORD reported himself for duty and was taken on the strength of the Battn.	Ref map LENS 1/100,000
	8.		A Reinforcement of 27 NCOs & men arrived from the 24th Battn.	
	9.		A Reinforcement of 50 NCOs & men joined the Battn. from the 2nd Entrenching Battn. The Battn. continued training, particular attention being paid to Route marching and Bayonet fighting.	
	10.		A Reinforcement of 30 N.C.Os & men arrived from the 1/4 Territorial Battn. Norfolk Fusiliers. The Battn. continued its training at GRAND RULLECOURT. 2/Lts B.P. BENNETT, T.H. McLEAN, B. READING, L. SINCLAIR and E.R. PERSON joined the Battn. from the Cadet School near St. OMER.	
	11 – 12		The Battn. marched to PETIT BOURET via LE CAUROY and WAMIN; Cadres accompanied the Battn. The Battn. billeted at PETIT BOURET. Remainder of the Battn. transport moved by road to the XV Corps area and entrained at FREVENT Ry. station.	
	12.		The Battalion marched out of billet at PETIT BOURET at 5.30 A.M and entrained about ten hours.	
DERNANCOURT	13.		at 7 A.M. Train journey via DOULLENS, AMIENS, CORBIE the ALBERT occupied about ten hours. The station at ALBERT was being shelled by a high velocity gun from the direction of THIEPVAL during the detraining; The Battalion marched into bivouac between ALBERT & DERNANCOURT (about E.14.B.5.5.) where the transport had already arrived.	Ref map ALBERT (combined sheet)
	14.		The Battalion remained in bivouac; in the afternoon the bivouac was shelled from the direction of THIEPVAL by a high velocity naval gun; no casualties resulted.	
BECORDEL	15.		A general attack was launched on the SOMME front; the 21st Division in XV Corps reserve moved up in support; the 12" Battn. Norfolk Fusiliers moved into bivouac at BECORDEL camp E.12 central.	

Army Form C. 2118.

WAR DIARY
or
INTELLIGENCE SUMMARY
(Erase heading not required.)

Place	Date	Hour	Summary of Events and Information	Remarks and references to Appendices
BECORDEL	1916. Sept 16		The Battalion moved from BECORDEL CAMP at 7 A.M. and with 62nd Infy (5 Bde.) Battalions at 440 yds interval Coys at 100 yds via FRICOURT to POMMIERS REDOUBT. (F.6.B.6.3); the Bde remained at POMMIERS REDOUBT until 9 p.m. when battalions moved up to relieve battalions of the 43rd Infy Bde. to positions between FLERS and GUEUDECOURT. The Battalion moved via MONTAUBAN, BOIS de DELVILLE which had been enjoyed in the attack on the German positions EAST OF DELVILLE WOOD and had advanced to SWITCH TRENCH where A.B. & C. Coys relieved 2 Coys of SHROPSHIRE LIGHT INFANTRY & 2 Coys of OXFORD and BUCKS LIGHT INFANTRY; D Coy was left in reserve at S.22.5.3. The transport remained at POMMIERS REDOUBT, except SAA carts & tool cart which moved up to S.22.5.3.	Ref. map ALBERT coloured sheet 1/40,000
FLERS	17.		The relief of the 43rd Infy Bde. 14th Division was not complete until about 6 A.M.; no casualties were suffered during the relief. The position of the 62nd Infy Bde. was then as follows: front line 13th Yorks pushed on night (11pm N.32.c.6.7 to T.2.B.5.1½) Left 10 Batt. YORKSHIRE REGT (front N31.B.2.5 to N.32.c.6.7); 1st Batt. LINCOLNSHIRE REGT in CENTRE 2 Coys in GAP TRENCH and 2 Coys in SWITCH TRENCH (old German main trench at S.22. central. 12th Batt. Northumberland Fusiliers 3 Coys in SWITCH TRENCH (old German main trench Line) from T.B.A.5.5 to T.I.C.8.3. A detachment of the 62nd machine gun company was allotted to Batt. and communication established with 1st Batt. Coldstream Guards on the right. 2nd Lieut. E. Every stilled to rocket. Whythe Battalion Throughout the day but did little damage. 2nd Lt. C. H. CORKE was killed by a shell.	Ralph of British Front from HIGH WOOD to GINCHY 1/10,000
	18.		Battalion Hqrs were at T.8.A.5.2. A and B Coys relieved the 2 Coys of the 1st Batt. LINCOLNSHIRE REGT in GAP TRENCH and took up a position from T.2.C.3.7½ to T.1.B.2.1. Hostile shelling of GAP & SWITCH TRENCH continued all day.	

WAR DIARY or INTELLIGENCE SUMMARY

Army Form C. 2118.

Place	Date	Hour	Summary of Events and Information	Remarks and references to Appendices
near FLERS	Sept 18th		Considerable difficulty was experienced on the night of the 18th in getting rations to the troops, owing to the bad state of all roads and tracks. A party brought rations to DELVILLE WOOD but were so exhausted that they had to dump rations. Owing to hostile fire rations could not be sent to Coys until nightfall.	Ref Map "HIGH WOOD to GINCHY" 1/10,000
	19.		During the 24 hours ending 6 p.m. 19.9.16 great difficulty was experienced in keeping rifles and ammunition serviceable owing to the bad weather conditions. A fair number of men were sick. Several men were sent to hospital with rheumatism. 2nd Lt A. McArthur M.C. and 2nd Lt B.D. BENNETT received head wounds from enemy shrapnel, the latter officer remained at duty.	
	20 & 21		Enemy shelling continued & some casualties were suffered each day; all dead in and near our trenches were buried. Work of consolidation was continued night & day on SWITCH & GAP TRENCHES.	
	22.		On the evening of Sept 22nd the 62nd Infantry Bde was relieved by the 64th Bde; the 12th (S) Battn Northumberland Fusiliers were relieved by the 9th Battn K.O.Y.L.I. The relief was completed by 8.30 p.m., the Battn moved to S.22. Central & bivouacked for the night.	
	23.		D/c Battn moved before dawn via MONTAUBAN and MAMETZ to "FRICOURT" CAMP (F.B.C. central) the Battn remained in FRICOURT camp resting and cleaning up.	
	24.			
	25.		D/c Battalion marched back to S.22. Central to act on reserve to 64th & 110th infantry Bdes, the Bdes were to attack GIRD TRENCH and Re village of GUEUDECOURT respectively at 11.30 A.M. on this day.	
	26.		At 3 p.m. orders were received that the 12th Battn Northumberland Fusiliers was attached to the 64th infantry Bde, & orders from that Bde arrived simultaneously ordering the Battn to move up to the original position - front line in N.32. without delay; the Battn moved by platoons at 400 yds interval into DELVILLE WOOD SWITCH & GAP TRENCHES and the SUNKEN ROAD in S.32.C.	

WAR DIARY or INTELLIGENCE SUMMARY

Army Form C. 2118.

Place	Date	Hour	Summary of Events and Information	Remarks and references to Appendices
EUCEDECOURT	1916 Sept 26		On arrival at 64th Bde HQrs at N.32.c.5.0 Major Edmann received verbal instructions from Brig General HEADLAM commanding 64th Infantry Bde to move up the 12th Battn Northumberland Fusiliers and take up a line of platoon posts along the line of the road from N.34.A.1.9 (Pt 13) to N.27.A.4.1, to which line units of the 64th Infantry Bde were supposed to have advanced; orders were issued accordingly - A Coy moved across the fair in artillery formation. B Coy on the right, D Coy right centre, C Coy left centre, A Coy on the left : units of the 64th Bde however had not attained their objective and it was necessary to form A Coy on the left : units of the 9th and 15th D.L.I in order to reach the proper alignment which though scattered units of the 9th and 10th R.Y.L.I and 15th D.L.I were encountered in advance of the previously most advanced positions, in most cases from 250 to 350 yards in advance of the previously most advanced positions. B Coy made contact with the 1st Battalion Scots Guards at about 6.30 pm at N.34.A.2.5 and at the same time on the left A Coy patrols went with the 110th Bde at N.27.A; all four Coys proceeded to dig in under heavy artillery fire, a system of platoon posts being established, 2nd Coy having 2 platoons in the front line & two platoons in support. Strong hostile were fired apparently to ease the digging parties, and a German patrol of eight men was encountered and captured by 2nd Lieut McLEAN & a patrol from B Coy at the same road; at Pt 13. the 126th Coy R.E. constructed a strong point at 34.A.5.2. Battn Headquarters were established in a shell hole at N.33.A. Central. At 9 p.m. orders were received that the 62nd Infantry Bde was relieving the 64th Infantry Bde & that patrols were to lead up the 10th Battn Yorkshire Regt to hold over the line held by the 12th Scottish Fusiliers : by midnight the 10th Battn Yorkshire Regt had taken over the line held by C and A Coys, & these Coys moved , C Coy to relieve D Coy, D Coy to fill in the gap between B & C Coys of A Coy Coys to be in Battn reserve at N.33. Central. all Coys	Ref Map "HIGH WOOD" to "GINCHY" 1/10,000

Army Form C. 2118.

WAR DIARY
or
INTELLIGENCE SUMMARY
(Erase heading not required.)

Instructions regarding War Diaries and Intelligence Summaries are contained in F. S. Regs., Part II and the Staff Manual respectively. Title Pages will be prepared in manuscript.

Place	Date	Hour	Summary of Events and Information	Remarks and references to Appendices
GUEUDECOURT.	1916 Sept 27th		Men commenced to dig a continuous trench & before dawn a continuous trench five to six feet deep had been dug from the left of the Guards at 34.A.5.2 to the right of the 10th Batln up to the Buff battery position at N.33. at 27.C.10.0. Battalion Headquarters were then moved to the old German battery position at B.4.4 when there was good accommodation. A contact aeroplane flew over our lines & dropped a copy of Ref map of area and photograph of position; an aeroplane photograph was obtained early in the morning of own position & trenches on a numbered whirl. G.O.C. 21st Division telegraphed "well done 12th". During the day construction of position continued, a straight fall the 14th Batln started further (Pioneers) sent up two coys to wire in front of the line. The enemy shelled twenty all day with shrapnel but caused very few casualties.	Ref map "HIGH WOOD" to "GINCHY" 1/10,000
	28.		Heavy shelling all day. 2nd Lt L. SINCLAIR was half wounded and died on the way to the clearing station. A very misty day, the enemy shelled at random, causing few casualties; at dusk the Battalion was relieved by the 7th Batln. Somerset Light Infantry and marched by platoons to S.22 Central where the 62nd Infantry	
BERNAFAY WOOD	29. 30.		Bde. remained in Divisional Reserve until October 1st. The following casualties were suffered during the operations – Officers Killed 2, wounded 5, Other ranks killed 17, wounded 76, missing 15; the trench strength of Batln on going into action on Sept 15th was 850; on coming out of action on Sept 29 trench strength 694.	

J M McIlwaine Major.
Commanding 12(S) Batln
Northumberland Fusiliers

Army Form C. 2118.

WAR DIARY or INTELLIGENCE SUMMARY

(Erase heading not required.)

19th Northumberland Fusiliers

Vol 14

Place	Date	Hour	Summary of Events and Information	Remarks and references to Appendices
BUIRE	1916 Oct 1st		The Battalion marched from BERNAFAY camp via MONTAUBAN, MAMETZ, FRICOURT, MEAULTE and DERNANCOURT to BUIRE; tanks were picked up at POMMIER'S REDOUBT en route. Reballt went into Billet at BUIRE.	Ref Maps ABBEVILLE 14. / 100,000 and LENS 11 / 100,000
	" 2.		Battalion remained at BUIRE resting and cleaning up; transport proceeded by road to FLIXECOURT.	
	" 3.		At 2 p.m the Battalion entrained at DERNANCOURT SIDING (EDGE HILL) and arrived at LONG PRE' at 10.30 p.m & marched to L'ETOILE & went into Billet there.	
L'ETOILE	" 4.5 6. 7.		Battalion in Billets at L'ETOILE reorganizing and refitting. The Battalion entrained at LONG PRE' at 4.30 p.m & travelling via DOULLENS & ST POL detrained at midnight at FOUQUEREUIL and marched into Billets at LAPUGNOY; Bde Headquarters being at MARLES-LEZ-MINES.	HAZEBROUCK 5A / 100,000
LAPUGNOY	8.		Billet former dirty & better than any in which the Battn has been since commencement of the offensive; the 21st Division is now in reserve in the 10th Corps area, 1st Army.	
	9.		Battalion in Billets at LAPUGNOY	
FOUQUIERES	10.		Von officers, including the Commanding officer & all Coy Commanders proceeded by motor omnibus to VERMELLES and reconnoitred the QUARRY SECTOR thereto, returning in the afternoon to FOUQUIERES, to which place the Battalion had been moved during the afternoon from LAPUGNOY. Battalion billeted for one night at FOUQUIERES.	
VERMELLES QUARRY SECTOR	11.		The Battalion marched from FOUQUIERES at 11 A.M, halted at 1 p.m at SAILLY LABOURSE for dinner, reached VERMELLES at 2.45 p.m where guides from 1st Batt: NOTTS & DERBY Regt conducted coys into support trenches left by that Battalion. The relief was completed by 4.45 p.m. The 62nd Bde took over trenches from the 24th Bde of the 8th Division.	

Army Form C. 2118.

WAR DIARY
or
INTELLIGENCE SUMMARY
(Erase heading not required.)

Instructions regarding War Diaries and Intelligence Summaries are contained in F. S. Regs., Part II. and the Staff Manual respectively. Title Pages will be prepared in manuscript.

Place	Date	Hour	Summary of Events and Information	Remarks and references to Appendices
TRENCHES	12/12/16		The Battalion remained in trenches the 62nd Inf Bde was disposed as follows 13th Yorks in leading the right of the Brigade sector, 1 Queens Rt to the left, 12 Yorks due in support and 10 York R in reserve.	
QUARRIES	ditto		Capt. H.W. GUSH returned from sick leave	
HULLOCH	ditto		2 officers and 8 O.R. proceeded to the Divisional school of Instruction	
	ditto		On the 14th several inter Battalion changes took place to allow of two companies of the Battalion in Reserve moving into the trenches.	
	13		Lieut Colonel F.T. FEDMANN proceeded on 10 days leave and Captain H.W. GUSH assumed command of the Battalion	
	14		2 Lieu W.M. BARBER and 1 O.R. proceeded to the hampois line to attend a course at the I CORPS sniping School	
	15		and Lieut. JONES D Coy for a musketry Instructors course at the Machine Gun School CAMIERS	
	16		A squad of Battalion bombers left for the Brigade Bombing School	
	17		Nothing to report	
	18th		do	
	19 "		do	
	20			

WAR DIARY
or
INTELLIGENCE SUMMARY

(Erase heading not required.)

Army Form C. 2118.

Place	Date	Hour	Summary of Events and Information	Remarks and references to Appendices
TRENCHES HULLUCH	21/10/16		The Battalion relieved the 13 London's too in the front line and was disposed as follows. Right D Coy Boys 44 to 82 Centre B " 82 - between Boys 86 + 84 Left A " between Boys 84 - 94 Reserve C " Each Company with 3 Platoons in the front line and one Platoon in support, Battalion HQ remained	
	22/10/16		Two casualties occurred from rifle fire (snipers) 1 killed, 1 wounded.	
	23/10/16 24/10/16		Day nothing unusual to report	
	25/10/16		2nd Lieut W.H. MORANT was killed (sniper) and 3 O.R. wounded	
	26/10/16		The remains of the late 2/Lt MORANT were interred at VERMELLES cemetery, Capt. NESBIT attended.	

WAR DIARY or INTELLIGENCE SUMMARY

Army Form C. 2118.

Place	Date	Hour	Summary of Events and Information	Remarks and references to Appendices
	27/4/16	—	Lieut: C.D. OWNE and 1 O.R. proceeded to the Numbers School ABBEVILLE to-day for a course of instruction in Rapid Transport duties. 75 O.R. N.C.O.'s joined the Battalion from the Pioneer Battalion	
	28/4/16		Lieut T. McLEAN assumed command of "B" Coy vice CAPT J. BRUNTON who with Lieut BROCKLEHURST left Battalion to proceed to the Army School of Instruction	
	29/4/16		Lieut-Col COFFIN (C.R.E. 21 Div) assumed command of the 62nd Inf Bde Captain J. BRUNTON and Lieut J. BROCKLEHURST proceeded to the 1st Army School of Instruction and four O.R. to the 2nd Div School of Instn. 1 O.R. proceeded to the 1st Corps School of Sniping	
	30/4/16		The Battalion was relieved in front line trenches by the 13 Royals Yor. the 10 YORK'R. round out support being relieved by 1 LINCOLN 'R.' in relief the 19 hauled Lewises move into Brigade Reserve A and D Coys going into billets at NOYELLES LES VERMELLES B and C Coys remained in Reserve Trenches with Battalion H.Q. at CURLY CRESCENT Lieut J. McKINNON reported himself from 3rd I.B.D on transfer from 5th Ian Rifles	
	31/4/16		Nothing unusual has occurred	

W.P.Oliver
Lieut Colonel
Cmdg 12 Royals Fus.

WAR DIARY or INTELLIGENCE SUMMARY

12th N.F. Fus Army Form C. 2118.
Vol 15

Place	Date	Hour	Summary of Events and Information	Remarks and references to Appendices
RESERVE (BDE)	1/7/16		The Battalion was in Brigade Reserve trenches. The Commanding Officer inspected the detachment at NOYELLES les VERMELLES and visited the Quartermasters Stores and Transport.	LOOS 36c. N.W.3. Edition 7.c 1/10,000
	2/7/16		The detachment (A and D Coys) moved into trenches at 10 a.m. and were replaced in billets by B and C. Coys.	
	3/7/16		Battalion in reserve. Captain G. Kerlin proceed to England on 10 days leave.	
	4/7/16		2nd Lieut N. McLARE reported from 3rd I.B.D. for duty and was posted to B Company. The Battalion provided a guard of honour of 2 officers and 100 R+F on the occasion of the presentation of medal ribbons by the G.O.C. I CORPS. 4 N.C.Os. and men of the Battalion were decorated	
	6/7/16		Battalion in reserve	

Army Form C. 2118.

WAR DIARY
or
INTELLIGENCE SUMMARY
(Erase heading not required.)

Place	Date	Hour	Summary of Events and Information	Remarks and references to Appendices
QUARRIES SECTOR	4/11/16		The Battalion relieved 1 Bn. Royal Irish in the right sub-section, the front was held as follows:- A Coy Left B " Centre C " Right D " Reserve The relief was completed by 1am	Rf/map LOOS 36ᵉ.M.W.3. 1/10,000
	8/11/16		4114.5 Coy Sergt Major I Robinson of A Coy was awarded a bar to the Distinguished Conduct Medal	
	9/11/16		14 men of the Battalion proceeded to the 62nd Coy R.M.G. Corps to complete the Coy to its establishment	
	10/11/16		Major M. HAY. A.V. Coto. was attached to the Battalion from this date. A Conference was held at Battalion H.Q. at 9.30 a.m. the O.C. 62nd Bn. presiding and our C.O. of the Brigade attended.	
	11/11/16		Three men proceeded to the 251st Tunnelling Company were stationed at CHICORY FARM near BETHUNE. Lieut G.M. PHILIP reported the shooting of two GERMANS during the night 10/11 whilst attempting to strengthen their wire.	

Army Form C. 2118.

WAR DIARY
or
INTELLIGENCE SUMMARY

(Erase heading not required.)

Place	Date	Hour	Summary of Events and Information	Remarks and references to Appendices
QUARRIES SECTOR.	12/1/16		Five O.R. proceeded to the 33rd Divisional School of Instruction	Ref/Map LOOS 36c.N.W.3 1/10,000
	13/1/16		Nothing to report. 2nd Lieut W.T. HINDMARCH joined for duty from 31.I.B.D.	
	14/1/16		The Battalion was relieved by 12 minute Fus in front line trenches and went into support replacing the 1st LINCOLN R. who relieved the 10th Y & R.R. in the left Battalion area of the Quarries Sector. Working parties were provided according to programme and Companies were accommodated as follows:- A & B Coys O.G.1 Line C " " O.B.4 D " " O.G.1 & Devon Lane H.Q. as before	
	15/1/16 16/1/16 17/1/16 18/1/16		Nothing unusual to report	

WAR DIARY or INTELLIGENCE SUMMARY

Army Form C. 2118.

Place	Date	Hour	Summary of Events and Information	Remarks and references to Appendices
HARRIS'S SECTOR	19/4/16		One Officer and four O.R. proceeded to the 31st Division School of Instruction.	Ref Map LOOS 36.C. N.W.3 1/10,000
	20.		2 men killed & 2 wounded on a working party in DUDLEY LANE by a MINENWERFER BOMB.	
	21.		Quiet day, during the night Nov 21/22 after a brisk mortar bombardment, the enemy raided the trenches held by the 13th Battn. Notts Fusiliers, causing 28 casualties.	
	22.		The 12th Battn took over the trenches of the 13th Battn; the left Coy area from BOYAU 73 to BOYAU 80 was very badly damaged; all the wire cut and communication along the front line impossible, it was decided not to hold the front line between BRECON SAP (G.12.D.50.65) and BOYAU 78 G.12.D.7.1 until the wire had been repaired and the trenches cleared. During the night the whole frontline patrolled and strongposts were established at G.12.D.55.40 (BOYAU 79) and in the SPOIL HEAP at G.12.D.40.55.	
	23.		No work was possible by day on the damaged trenches, so work proceeded slowly; the attitude of the enemy was on the whole quiet, and no hostile patrols were encountered in NoMansLand; our patrols raided the enemy's wire for gaps but without success. One patrol brought back the body of 14. J.R. used by the patrolling party; a dig was also brought into our lines with a collar marked 14. J.R.	
	24.		The trenches were cut through the debris left after the recent mortar bombardment, and though communication established along the frontline; the frontline between BOYAU 79 and BRECON SAP was not held as there was no wire in front; no mans land was therefore kept thoroughly	

WAR DIARY
or
INTELLIGENCE SUMMARY

Army Form C. 2118.

Place	Date	Hour	Summary of Events and Information	Remarks and references to Appendices
QUARRIES SECTOR	1916 Nov 24.		Patrols and Lewis gun posts were kept at G.12.D.55.40 and G.12.D.40.55 until covered the whole portion of the line.	Ref Map LOOS 36.c. N.W.3 1/10,000
	25.		2nd Lt BERESFORD was wounded by a sniper. Our bomb throwers a Stokes guns very active, the enemy did not retaliate.	
	26.		Our patrols again very active; one Lt Ran[?]six officers patrols examining the enemy's wire for hostile gaps; 2 Lt M.M. BRODIE and a patrol of 1 NCO & 3 men successfully bombed an enemy sap head at G.12.c.70.85. The wire however was so thick that it was impossible to get through it to secure an identification.	
	27.		In retaliation for recent raid the 1st Corps heavy artillery & No 21st Divisional artillery shelled the enemy trenches opposite STELLA CRATERS, also Northedge of CITÉ ST ELIE and enemy organisations in rear. The enemy did not retaliate; much damage was done to the enemy's works in spite of the front. Not a very large percentage of our heavy shells were "duds". At night our patrols were again very active, but the enemy was very alert & scared the expectation of our bombardment, the enemy's wire was not however cut through in any place.	
	28.		The 15th Battn relieved the 12th Battn in front line trenches, the relief being completed by midday; the H.dqrs 12 Battn moved back to CURLEY CRESCENT G.10.D.5.6, 1 Coy into O.B.5, 1 Coy to CURLEY CRESCENT and 2 Coys to billets in MAZINGARBE.	

Army Form C. 2118.

INTELLIGENCE SUMMARY

(Erase heading not required.)

Place	Date	Hour	Summary of Events and Information	Remarks and references to Appendices
1916 QUARRIES	1916 Nov 29 30		Weather cold but dry. There has been very little rain during the month of November and the trenches are everywhere dry; pumps hosts scarcely being necessary in the worst places. The health of the men has in consequence been very good during the month, in spite of the fact that 21 days out of 24 are spent in trenches.	Ref/Map LOOS 36c. N.W.3 Edition 7. 1/10.000

J.P. Elhuran Lt Col
Commanding 12" (S) Battn
Northumberland Fusiliers

WAR DIARY
or
INTELLIGENCE SUMMARY

(Erase heading not required.)

Army Form C. 2118.

12th North'd Fus

9/7/16

Place	Date	Hour	Summary of Events and Information	Remarks and references to Appendices
HULLOCH QUARRIES. SECTOR	1916 Dec 1st		The Battalion was in Brigade reserve, nothing of importance occurred.	
	2nd 3rd			
	4th		The Battalion took over trenches of the right subsector from 13 North Fus, the relief was completed by 12.20 p.m. Companies were disposed as follows:- Left: A Coy — Commanded by Lieut W.T. HINDMARCH Right: C Coy — Captain F.W. SHANN Centre: B Coy — Captain J. BRUNTON Reserve: D Coy — Lieut T.H. McLEAN	
	5th		Wind much West, fine by day and at night rain. During the day the enemy shelled the sector with 5.9 and lachrymatory shells, LeBoy mnenwerfer bombs were used	
	6th		A fairly quiet day, wind West — So dew., considerably less shelling than on 5th.	
	7th		Wind — East, overcast dull a very quiet day followed an unusually quiet night. Capt F.W. SHANN reported sick	

Army Form C. 2118.

12th North'd Fus

WAR DIARY
or
INTELLIGENCE SUMMARY
(Erase heading not required.)

Place	Date	Hour	Summary of Events and Information	Remarks and references to Appendices
HULLOCH'S QUARRIES SECTOR	8th		There was very little T.M. activity during the morning. One man was sniped during the early morning. Enemy T.M. fire damaged the front line trench continually.	
	9th		Kind hard to-So alive on, a few shells fell near Company HQ centre Coy at 2.30pm and large minenwerfer bomb 6 night of NEWPORT crater on the right Company front	
	10th		The 13th North. Fusiliers relieved the Battalion in the front line trenches and this Battalion took over the Support Battalion trenches. The relief was completed by 12.30pm which toured, weather dull. Lieut. Colonel P.H. STEVENSON joined from 2nd Bn K.O.S. Borderers this day and assumed command of the Battalion. Major F.J.F. KBL MANN was wounded. Major H.W. GUSH, M.C. took over the command of C Coy during the absence of Captain SHANN sick.	
	11th to 15th		The Battalion remained in Support, working parties were found according to programme. There is nothing to report.	

2449 Wt. W14957/M90 750,000 1/16 J.B.C. & A. Forms/C.2118/12.

WAR DIARY or INTELLIGENCE SUMMARY

Army Form C. 2118.

Place	Date	Hour	Summary of Events and Information	Remarks and references to Appendices
HULLUCH QUARRIES SECTOR	16/7		The Battalion relieved the 13th Battalion in the front line trenches. The relief was complete by 11.30am. From 12 noon till 1.30pm the Divisional Artillery bombarded the enemy salient at G.12.d.58. Troops were withdrawn from all posts within 300 yards of this point. Major F.J.F.EDLMANN proceeded to the First Army School to attend a Commanding Officers Conference.	
	17/7		Wind South-West. Enemy fired little during the night. Considerable rifle fire during the early morning. Three O.R. were wounded.	
	18/7		Wind South-West – A mine was exploded by the Brigade on our left at 9.30am. No casualties.	
	19/7 10am		Wind South – No casualties. Capt J.BRUNTON proceeded to England on 30 days leave.	
	20/7		Wind South-West – Snow a little on our left. No casualties. 1 NCO and 4 men proceeded to the Brigade Bomb School.	

Army Form C. 2118.

WAR DIARY
or
INTELLIGENCE SUMMARY
(Erase heading not required.)

Place	Date	Hour	Summary of Events and Information	Remarks and references to Appendices
HULLUCH QUARRIES SECTOR	20/7/16		The Heavy Artillery bombarded the enemy's defences from H.4.c.0.3 to G.12.a.80.64 from 1.15 pm to 2.30 pm the STOKES Gun co-operated and fired on the bombarded area also to prevent the enemy working.	
	21a		Wind South West — Dull. A draft of 215 untrained men joined from 31 I B D but were billeted at FOUQUERES.	
	22nd		The Battalion was relieved by 1 Brack'd'n in front line and proceeded to MAZINGARBE trenches in relief. A and D Coys proceeded to Battalion trenches. B and C moved into the reserve Battalion trenches. The enemy shelled O.B.1 during the day	
	23rd		The enemy shelled the Divisional sector freely. Wire was cut and trenches badly damaged. Lachrymatory shells were used. The enemy's T.Ms fired heavily during the bombardment. 4.4 cm, 10 cm and 15 cm shells were fired into front line, support, communication trenches and Batt. H.Q. VERMELLES was shelled by a high velocity gun	
	24th		Shelling by the enemy commenced at about 8 am and continued throughout the day. Lachrymatory shells were used in the	

WAR DIARY or INTELLIGENCE SUMMARY

Army Form C. 2118.

Place	Date	Hour	Summary of Events and Information	Remarks and references to Appendices
HULLOCH	24/7/16		Vicinity of O.B.1. T.M. bombs were fired into the enemy trenches by the Battn in the front line.	
	25/7/16		Considerable shelling on the Divisional front, so casualties were caused to the Battn. Telegrams were received from the Army and Brigade Commanders. A letter was received from the G.O.C. 2nd Division in which he thanked the Battalion for all it had done during the time he (Major Gen. Cuthbert) had commanded the Division.	
	26/7/16		B and C Coys marched to HOUCHIN under Major F.J.FIEDLMANN, on being relieved by the 9th Northampton.R.	
	27/7/16		The 62 Inf Bde was relieved by the 41 Inf Bde. Bn. H.Q. and two Companies (A and D) were relieved by the 2nd Sherwood Foresters, on relief the Companies marched to HOUCHIN where they billeted for the night. B and C Coys marched from HOUCHIN to ALLOUAGNE.	
	28/7/16		The remainder of the Battalion marched from HOUCHIN to ALLOUAGNE the village allotted to the Battalion for the final part of the rest period.	

Army Form C. 2118.

WAR DIARY
or
INTELLIGENCE SUMMARY
(Erase heading not required.)

Instructions regarding War Diaries and Intelligence Summaries are contained in F. S. Regs., Part II. and the Staff Manual respectively. Title Pages will be prepared in manuscript.

Place	Date	Hour	Summary of Events and Information	Remarks and references to Appendices
ALLOUAGNE	28/7/16		The detachment of 215 other ranks with a staff of NCO's marched from FOUQUIERS under Lieut G. SHERWOOD and joined the Battalion in billets, the turnover and details from SAILLY LABOURSE reported during the evening thus completing the move.	
	29/7/16		A draft of 15 O.R. from 31 Inf Base Depot joined the Battalion. Companies were placed at the disposal of Company Commanders and the day spent in cleaning clothing and equipment.	
	30/7/16		Training and reorganization, a draft of 50 O.R. from the 31 I.B.D joined the Battalion.	
	31/7/16		Divine Service.	

G.W.Kerr, Captain Adjt.
for O.C. 12 Border Regt.

Army Form C. 2118.

12th North'n Fusiliers

Vol 17

WAR DIARY or INTELLIGENCE SUMMARY

(Erase heading not required.)

Place	Date 1916 Jan.	Hour	Summary of Events and Information	Remarks and references to Appendices
ALLOUAGNE	1st		Training and walking was proceeded with. Major F.J.E. EDLMANN proceeded on 30 days leave and Major H.W.GUSH, M.C. proceeded to England for a course of instruction for senior officers. Training. Capt. W.LOCKE returned to duty after 30 days leave to England.	
	2nd		Training	
	3rd		Training	
	4th		Training	
	5th		Training	
	6th		Training	
	7th		Divine Service	
	8th		The Brigade carried out a route march distance about 6 miles on return the Army Commander inspected the Brigade pass.	
	9th		Training	
	10th		Training	
	11th		Training	
	12th		Training	
	13th		Training	
	14th		The Battalion Cross country run took place at 11 am. and was won by "C" Company.	
	15th		The Battalion was inspected by the Brigade Commander.	
	16th		Training	
	17th		Training	
	18th		Training	
	19th		Training took place in the BOIS de REVEILLON, dinners were eaten in the open.	

17-2

Army Form C. 2118.

WAR DIARY
or
INTELLIGENCE SUMMARY
(Erase heading not required.)

Place	Date	Hour	Summary of Events and Information	Remarks and references to Appendices
ALLOUAGNE	1917 Jan 20th		Training in the afternoon a section Competition was held for all officers N.O.'s and Lewis Gunners armed with revolvers.	
	21st		100 men took part in a Brigade Cross country run from the Aerodrome at AUCHEL to Brigade Headquarters the rest who won by Second NORTON "A" Company the second & third places also being to the Battalion 2nd Lieut. R.C. ALFORD and N.H. SISTERTON joined 2nd Battalion from 31 I.B.D. A Platoon of "B" Company were awarded 2nd prize in a Brigade Competition for the best turned out platoon, the Competition was won by 1 LINCOLN REGIMENT by 5 points. 2nd Lieut. E.G. PASSINGHAM joined from 31 T.B.D.	
	22nd		The Battalion carried out a route march and halted in the afternoon.	
	23rd		Training in Billeting Area.	
	24th		Training in Billeting Area. 2nd Lieut. E.C. PASSINGHAM proceeded to join the 1st Battalion on reporting.	
	25th			
	26th		Officers of the Battalion proceeded to reconnoitre the trenches held by the 9th E. SURREY REGIMENT, the remainder of the Battalion carried out training. During the evening a message was received from Brigade stating that the Brigade would be ready to move off at short notice early the following day.	
	27th	3 am.	O.O. was received from Brigade ordering the Battalion to parade at 8.14 am. to entrain at CHOCQUES. The Battalion entrained at CHOCQUES	

Army Form C. 2118.

WAR DIARY
or
INTELLIGENCE SUMMARY

(Erase heading not required.)

Instructions regarding War Diaries and Intelligence Summaries are contained in F. S. Regs., Part II. and the Staff Manual respectively. Title Pages will be prepared in manuscript.

Place	Date	Hour	Summary of Events and Information	Remarks and references to Appendices
	1914 Dec			
	28th		and arrived at POPERINGHE at 3 p.m. marched to "G" Camp and remained in readiness to support BELGIAN troops should it be necessary to do so.	
	29th		The Battalion remained at "G" Camp training and furnishing working parties	
	30th		ditto	
	31st		ditto	
			Positions in rear of the BELGIAN line and our own left were reconnoitred by all officers of the Battalion.	

G. White. Capt. for. Lieut. Col.
Cmdg. 12th (S) Bn. Northumberland Fusiliers.

WAR DIARY
or
INTELLIGENCE SUMMARY

Army Form C. 2118.

12th Northumberland Fusiliers
21st Division

Vol 18

Place	Date	Hour	Summary of Events and Information	Remarks and references to Appendices
'G' Camp (A.16.b.)	1/2/17		"P" system of defence was reconnoitred by all officers	YPRES 28 N.W. 1/20000
POPERINGHE	2/2/17 3/2/17		"P" system of defence was reconnoitred by all officers. Capt SHANN Evac. & 2/Lt WILLIAMS reported sick. Training at 'G' Camp & furnishing working parties. 2/Lt McLEAN & 2/Lt Finlay returned from 10 days leave in England.	
	4/2/17		The battalion carried out a route march in the morning distance 7 miles — Route: POPERINGHE — cross roads A 18 d 38 — cross roads A 11.c.32 — Camp. 2/Lt A.P. HORROWER joined the battalion from 31 IBD.	
	5/2/17 6/2/17		Training — A "Test Turnout" was practiced by battalion in the morning	
	8/2/17 9/2/17		2/Lt BENNETT & 3 OR proceeded to England on leave Capt. J. BRUNTON rejoined the battalion from C.C.S (HAZEBROUCK) and resumed command of "B" Coy	
	11/2/17		'A' & 'B' Coys carried out a 'practice attack' on farm SE of COUVENT St SIXTE.	

WAR DIARY
or
INTELLIGENCE SUMMARY
(Erase heading not required.)

Army Form C. 2118.

Place	Date	Hour	Summary of Events and Information	Remarks and references to Appendices
POPPERINGHE	12/2/17		A tactical scheme under Brigade arrangements was carried out by all company & platoon commanders. Major F.T. EDLMANN D.S.O. assumed command of the battalion from 1 P.M. — Lt.Col. P.H. STEVENSON assumed command of the 62nd Inf. Bde. during the absence of Brig.Gen. RAWLINS. Capt. SHANN E.N. rejoined the battalion from hospital and resumed command of 'C' Coy.	Ref. L/20000 28 N
	13/2/17		Lt. C.N.G. KOCH & billeting party proceeded to BÉTHUNE. The battalion carried out a route march - distance about 6 miles. Training —	
	14/2/17			
	15/2/17		The battalion marched off from 'G' Camp at 6 A.M. & proceeded to POPPERINGHE Station where it entrained for BÉTHUNE, at 7 A.M — Detrained at BÉTHUNE at 12 noon and marched to billets in the MONTMORENCY BARRACKS. Billets were good.	
BETHUNE	16/2/19		Commanding Officer, Company Cmdrs & L.C.O. left at 9.30 A.M. for trenches to take over from the 9th SUFFOLK REGT in the right subsection of the QUARRIES SECTOR, returning in the afternoon to SAILLY LABOURSE, to	

Army Form C. 2118.

WAR DIARY
or
INTELLIGENCE SUMMARY
(Erase heading not required.)

Instructions regarding War Diaries and Intelligence Summaries are contained in F. S. Regs., Part II. and the Staff Manual respectively. Title Pages will be prepared in manuscript.

Place	Date	Hour	Summary of Events and Information	Remarks and references to Appendices
SAILLY LX	16/2/17		which place the battalion had been moved during the afternoon from BETHUNE. The Bn. billeted in SAILLY LABOURSE for one night. Billets were bad.	Ref. 100000 HAZEBROUCK 5A
QUARRIES	17/2/17		The Bn. marched from SAILLY at 12 noon, & reached VERMELLES at 1.15 pm where Guides conducted Coys to the front line trenches. The 62nd Inf. Brigade took over from 91st Inf. Bde. (6th Div.) The Bn. relieved the 9th SUFFOLK REGT. Relief complete at 6 p.m. Disposition of Coys — 'A' Coy — Left — Capt. LOCKIE. T. 'B' Coy — Centre — Capt. BRUNTON J. 'C' Coy — Right — " SHANN E.W. 'D' Coy — Support — 2/Lt. McLEAN.	Ref. 10000 LOOS. 36c NW.
	18/2/17		Weather: dull and cold — Wind S.W. Trenches in a very bad state — front line from G.12 d 7.3 to G.12 d 45.60 being obliterated. Most of the communication trenches were badly damaged.	
	19/2/17		Wind — SW. Weather: misty in early morning, bright for rest of the day. — Much work was done during previous night on DEVON LANE. Enemy MG + rifle fire active. 2/Lt. BARBER + 30 O.R. returned to duty from 21 Divnl School at FERFAIX. 2/Lt. JACKSON joined the battalion from 31 I.B.D. & was posted to 'B' Coy.	

2449 Wt. W14957/M90 750,000 1/16 J.B.C. & A. Forms/C.2118/12.

Army Form C. 2118.

WAR DIARY
or
INTELLIGENCE SUMMARY.
(Erase heading not required.)

Instructions regarding War Diaries and Intelligence Summaries are contained in F. S. Regs., Part II. and the Staff Manual respectively. Title pages will be prepared in manuscript.

Place	Date	Hour	Summary of Events and Information	Remarks and references to Appendices
QUARRIES.	20/2/17		Raining in the morning. Afterwards proceeded to WIMEREUX for 2 days course at the Special Works Park — Ref. map. LOOS 36.E. N.W.3 Casualties 1 man killed by T.M. 1.O.R. wounded. — Lt. C.N.G KOCH.	
	21/2/17		Enemy artillery active. Casualties 2 O.R. killed — 1 O.R. wounded.	Edition Y.C.
	22/2/17		At about 5.25 a.m. the enemy put a barrage of High Explosive and Shrapnel from 5"9, 4"2, and 77 mm guns and trench mortars on the entire length of the close support trenches from G.18.B.58 to G.12.C.0.75. also of down BOYEAUX 76, 84, & 85 and along St GEORGES trench and on DEVON LANE, half way between O.G.1. and St GEORGES trench. Almost immediately the enemy appears to have entered the unoccupied portions of the front line at G.12.D.65.25 and G.12.D.05.75. From information gathered from a prisoner captured near the eastern point of the raiding party totalled 2 Officers and 40 other ranks, but nothing with these numbers were seen by the garrison of the strong points on which counter attacking platoons. At the hour of the attack there was a mist and a man would not be visible about 20 yds; the Battalion was "standing to" at the time	

Army Form C. 2118.

WAR DIARY
or
INTELLIGENCE SUMMARY.
(Erase heading not required.)

Place	Date	Hour	Summary of Events and Information	Remarks and references to Appendices
Vermelles QUARRIES SECTOR	21-7-16		the front line-platoons in the strong points and the counter attacking platoons in the close support line. One strong point however which is only held by a single platoon by day, but by two platoons during the hours of darkness (the Strong point at G.12.D.B.D.75.) was being vacated by one platoon when the relieve was put in - this is a necessary precaution as no movement is available to and from the position in daylight - the officer in command 2nd Lt. M.M. BRODIE was moving this platoon in single file towards the junction of the close support line and DEVON LANE, and promptly making the situation requires the front line to the left of the strong point in time to capture an enemy mischief. Unless the enemy mischief which drop to a home and the strong counter attack and abandoned this part after surprise. On question of mylomine stick bombs were thrown away by them even at the point which further action followed. A few minutes later the Coy Commander of the Coy which showed the repulse fire from the strong point and reporting that all eight Signallers were to advance in the front line with immediate platoons (which they were) arrived in the front line with immediate counter attack platoons.	

WAR DIARY or INTELLIGENCE SUMMARY

Army Form C. 2118.

Place	Date	Hour	Summary of Events and Information	Remarks and references to Appendices
Vermelles QUARRIES SECTOR	Jan 22		All trenches in what area were reported but no trace of the enemy could be found except the remains of one or two Lyddens who had been blown to pieces by their own barrage. The fact that our own men were all wearing "gum boots" made our advance rather slow owing to the nature of much whittled our front line. Meanwhile the raiding party which entered the trenches of the right Coy at G.12.D.65.25 had divided into two parties, one of which moved south along the mocupied portion of the front line until it encountered the traverse wire gate on the left flank of the post at the head of BOYEAU.78, (G.12.D.70.15) where a few bombs had been thrown by each sides, the raiders turned & withdrew across "No Man's Land", they were however caught by the fire of the Lewis Gun in their point, for which mine cleared a little at mid-day, a Lyddens was seen lying in front of the enemies wire at G.12.D.94. The other party which entered at G.12.D.65.25 were defined on them by a Squad of Battalion Bombers posted in DUDLEY DUMP, and bombs were thrown at them by a Squad of Battalion Bombers posted at the junction of DUDLEY LANE and the loose support line, this LEWIS GUN was unfortunately out of action owing a line of jam of an assist dust which somehow amassed the mechanism while it was firing at the raiders. This party also withdrew too quickly for the counterattack platoon to intercept, but was sounded by the counterattack platoon as there of enemy the night Coy area was at once scoured by the counterattack platoon but no trace of enemy	

WAR DIARY
INTELLIGENCE SUMMARY

Army Form C. 2118.

Place	Date	Hour	Summary of Events and Information	Remarks and references to Appendices
Vermelles	Feb 23rd		except abandoned equipment could be found. The counter attack Coy was not called upon. The prisoner captured belonged to the STORME TRUPPE of the 26th I.R. (Prussian).	
QUARRIES SECTOR			Our casualties were 1 Sergt and one man killed by shell fire, 10 wounded or missing. The S.O.S. was not sent in, but the enemy's artillery was asked to retaliate and did so. The Battalion was relieved by the 13th Battn Northumberland Fusiliers in night sectors of the Bde front. The Relief being complete at 5.30 p.m., the Batt went into support trenches, its headquarters being at CURLEY CRESCENT.	
	Feb 25th–26th		The Battalion was in support and formed working parties to clear communication trenches, also almost immediately the action of the chase. Casualties in Support 3 killed, 6 wounded.	
	Feb 27th		On Feb 25th 2nd Lieut QUEEN returned for duty from the Cadre School at BLENDECQUES. Feb 27th the 12th Battn Royal Fusiliers relieved the 13th Battn. in the front line system of the QUARRIES night sector. Dispositions as follows:—	
			"A" Coy .... left Company	
			"B" Coy .... centre Company	
			"C" Coy .... right Company	
			"D" Coy .... reserve.	

Army Form C. 2118.

WAR DIARY
or
INTELLIGENCE SUMMARY.
(Erase heading not required.)

Place	Date	Hour	Summary of Events and Information	Remarks and references to Appendices
VERMELLS	4/2/17		The relief was completed by 1 A.m. (except for 2 platoons of "A" Coy which relieved after dark owing to bad state of trenches.) 2/Lt READING rejoined the Battalion from hospital. 2/Lt G.H. BRAMWELL returned from 3rd I.B.D. 2/Lt M.M. BRODIE proceeded to 1st Army School for 5 weeks general course.	
	5/2/17		Activity normal.	

J. M. Oliver Major.
Comdg. 12th (S) Bn. Northumberland Fusiliers.

Army Form C. 2118.

WAR DIARY
or
INTELLIGENCE SUMMARY.
(Erase heading not required.)

R.B. Oxford & Bucks Light Infantry

Vol 19

Place	Date	Hour	Summary of Events and Information	Remarks and references to Appendices
QUARRIES	1/9/17		Weather mild. Wind S.W. The Battalion was relieved by the 9th NORFOLK REGT. Relief being completed by 2.30 a.m., except for one platoon in NEWPORT CRATER which was relieved after dark. The Battalion billeted for the night in SAILLY LABOURSE. Billets were fair.	1 of map 10,000 LOOS 36c N.W.3
ANNEZIN	2/9/17		Marched off from SAILLY at 10.30 A.M. through BEUVRY & BETHUNE	1 of map HAZEBROUCK 57g 1/100,000
	3/9/17		to ANNEZIN where the night was spent. Very good billets. Companies were billeted at BETHUNE often which they marched to LA PIERRIÈRE, a little village north of BUSNES. Billets were good.	
LA PIERRIÈRE	4/9/17		Divine Service at 10.30 A.M. The Commanding Officer inspected billets and dinners.	
	5/9/17		The day was spent reorganising the battalion in accordance with the new scheme. Competition paid out in the afternoon.	
	6/9/17		The Battalion was inspected by the Brigadier Commander who was accompanied by Officers of the 13th Rocket Jus	

WAR DIARY or INTELLIGENCE SUMMARY.

Army Form C. 2118.

Place	Date	Hour	Summary of Events and Information	Remarks and references to Appendices
LA PIERRIERE	6/7		10th YORKS and 1st LINCOLNS. The Battalion was drawn up and accompanied the two Kitchens. Weather changeable, rain fell during the night and early morning, weather from noon E strong.	10 Bat map HAZEBROUCK S.A. 1/100,000
	7/7		Enemy - splendid hirried in the afternoon. Bearers - Billeting Party proceeded to RELY to arrange for Billets.	
	8/7		Weather - Rain fell in the morning - Wind strong E - Training continued.	
RELY	9/7		The Battalion marched past 1/7 at 12.15 p.m. and proceeded to RELY via LA MIQUEALERIE - LILLERS - BOURECQ - ST HILAIRE - distance 10 miles, billets were good.	
HESTRUS	10/7		Marched to HESTRUS via AUCHY-AU-BOIS - NÉDONCHELLE - FIEFS - SAINS-lès-PERNÉS - TANGRY and HESTRUS where the night was spent distance about 10 miles - Bde H.Q. at ANTIGNEUR CHATEAU, 1 mile S.W. of DIÉVAL.	1 Bat map LENS 1/100,000
	11/7		Left Hestrus at 4-30 P.M. & marched to HERICOURT via GUERNONVAL -	

Army Form C. 2118.

WAR DIARY
or
INTELLIGENCE SUMMARY.
(Erase heading not required.)

Instructions regarding War Diaries and Intelligence Summaries are contained in F. S. Regs., Part II. and the Staff Manual respectively. Title pages will be prepared in manuscript.

Place	Date	Hour	Summary of Events and Information	Remarks and references to Appendices
HERICOURT	11th		- HUCLIER - ST. POL - RAMECOURT - CROISETTE - distance about 11½ miles. The road between HESTRUS and GUERNONVAL was very bad causing slight delay. The transport was unable to continue by the route the battalion followed and had to proceed by a different route to HERICOURT. Billets were good.	Ref. map LENS 11 100,000
	12th		Left HERICOURT at 7-30 A.M. in order to pass the Brigade starting point at NUNCQ at 10-25 A.M. - Route cross roads S.E. of 2nd E in CROISETTE - ECOIVRES - NUNCQ - SERICOURT - SIBBIVILLE - HONVAL - REBREUVE - REBREUVIETTE - LE SOUICH - BREVILLERS - LUCHEUX - HALLOY - distance about 19½ miles. The Battalions was billeted in "C" Camp.	
HALLOY	13th		Rest. Companies found out in the afternoon.	
	14th		Battalion was inspected in the morning by the Commanding Officer - afterwards companies paraded under company arrangements	
	15th		Training - specialists trained in the afternoon.	

WAR DIARY
or
INTELLIGENCE SUMMARY.
(Erase heading not required.)

Place	Date	Hour	Summary of Events and Information	Remarks and references to Appendices
HALLOY	16th		Training in the morning – "A" Coy Sports were held in the afternoon.	Ref map LENS 11 1/100,000
	18th		Divine Service at 11 AM – "B" Coy, "C" Coy, & "D" Coy Sports held in the afternoon. In all cases the Sports were a great success.	
	19th		Training under Company arrangements – We understand expected night operations. Afternoon 'A' & 'B' Coys tested Box respirators.	
	20th		Training – 'C' & 'D' & HQ Coys tested Box respirators.	
	21st		A Battalion attack was rehearsed.	
	24th		The Battalion made practice assault in the new formation according to Scheme D. The Brigadier and officers of the 21st Divnl Staff and officers of the other units and the Brigade attended. The Brigadier expressed his satisfaction of the assault.	
			2/Lieut FORSYTH. T.T. from 4. H. Q Coeur de but reported for duty. 2 Lieut ESKDALE. J.R. 2/Lieut B. READING and C.S.M. BYRON proceeded to 3rd Army School of Instruction	
	25th		Left HALLOY at 8.30 AM and marched to POMMIER – Distance 9 miles – Route taken – HALLOY – PAS – MENU – ST AMAND – POMMIER. Billets were comparatively good. Route Capt Griffith R.A.M.C. proceeded on	

WAR DIARY or INTELLIGENCE SUMMARY

Army Form C. 2118.

Place	Date	Hour	Summary of Events and Information	Remarks and references to Appendices
HALLOY	25/7		10 days leave.	Ref Map LENS 11 1/100,000
	26/7		The Commanding Officer & Company Commanders proceeded to inspect the line at 8.30 A.M. The Battalion under Capt. D.E. WRIGHT marched to BOIRY ST MARTIN, where the night was spent as routed. Route taken — BIENVILLERS — MONCHY-AU-BOIS — ADINFER — BOIRY STE RICTRUDE, and BOIRY ST MARTIN. The route from MONCHY-AU-BOIS was across land just evacuated by the enemy. A draft of 44 men joined the Battalion from 31 I.B.D.	
	27/7		The Commanding Officer & Coy Commrs proceeded to BOISLEUX ST MARC to take over from the 2/5th London Regt, 58th Division. At 6 P.M. the battalion moved up & relieved the 2/5 LONDON REGT. Disposed as follows:— Front line "B" Coy on the right holding BOYELLES "D" " " " Left " BOIRY BECQUERELLE "A" Coy supporting "D" Coy in railway cutting (S.18.a.) "C" Coy " " " " in BOISLEUX ST MARC.	Ref Map 1/20,000 57B SW3

WAR DIARY
or
INTELLIGENCE SUMMARY.
(Erase heading not required.)

Army Form C. 2118.

Place	Date	Hour	Summary of Events and Information	Remarks and references to Appendices
BOISLEUX ST MARC	28		H.Q Company in BOISLEUX ST MARC. H.Q at S.11.d.3.4. WIND Westerly. fair weather - rain at intervals. An advance was made by B & D Coys - the line taken up from BOIRY BECQUERELLE (Left to 1200 yards E by N. of BOYELLES. Capt W'Ried returned from 20 days leave.	B.F. Map 1/20 57 B.S.W.3
	29		B Coy moved up remainder of company to some disused German trenches S.E. of BOIRY BECQUERELLE. D Coy advanced their left & took up a line running N & about 800 E of BOIRY BECQUERELLE. A Coy moved into B Coys previous position "C" into D Coys previous position. There is good footholding was done. Lgt MARTIN & 9 O.R. entered CEMETERY 800 yards in advance of our position, 10 of the enemy were encountered, after a sharp fight he fled leaving 3 dead behind. These men belonged to 207 R.I.R.	

Army Form C. 2118.

WAR DIARY
or
INTELLIGENCE SUMMARY.
(Erase heading not required.)

Instructions regarding War Diaries and Intelligence Summaries are contained in F.S. Regs., Part II. and the Staff Manual respectively. Title pages will be prepared in manuscript.

Place	Date	Hour	Summary of Events and Information	Remarks and references to Appendices
BOISLEUX ST MARC			Enemy artillery very active. Another large patrol encountered 2 German groups - one of 8 men the other of 20 to 30 men. After a brief fight the Germans were put to flight and were pursued up to the village of HENIN. 2/Lt G. NOBLE was wounded, 2 prisoners of the 99th R.I.R. were captured.	Ref. Map 10,000 512.S.W.3.
BOYELLES.80³			Bn H.Q. moved up to a dug out near main ARRAS-BAPAUME road (400 yards N of BOYELLES) "B" Coy moved up to sunken road running S.E. from BOIRY BECQUERELLE. "B" and "D" Coys maintained their positions but dug a trench running through CEMETERY parallel with main HENIN-CROISILLES Road. They were assisted by working parties from 10th Yorks. One of our patrols encountered a German patrol which was put to flight. 2/Lt T.T. FORSYTH proceeded on signalling course.	
	31/3/17		In conjunction with the 6th Dismounted bde. it intended to	

Army Form C. 2118.

WAR DIARY
or
INTELLIGENCE SUMMARY.
(Erase heading not required.)

Instructions regarding War Diaries and Intelligence Summaries are contained in F. S. Regs., Part II. and the Staff Manual respectively. Title pages will be prepared in manuscript.

Place	Date	Hour	Summary of Events and Information	Remarks and references to Appendices
BOYELLES			capture HENIN. Orders were received to occupy town HENIN-CROISILLES road. D Coy succeeded in reaching the wood after a sharp fight but was counter attacked on both flanks. After one hours fight the enemy were beaten off. Later, the road was exploded by machine gun fire from HENIN rendered untenable. The left division was not successful in capturing HENIN with the result that D Coy moved back to its previous position - We suffered 10 casualties & it is estimated that we inflicted at least 20 casualties to the enemy. BOIRY BECQUERELLE and BOYELLES were heavily bombarded. We suffered 10 casualties in the first named village. Work was continued on new trenches - a working party from the 14th R.N.F. assisted.	Ref map 1 10,000 51.B.S.W.3

M Milner Major

Commanding 12th (Sv) Bn Royal Fusiliers

WAR DIARY or INTELLIGENCE SUMMARY

Army Form C. 2118.

12th Northumberland Fusiliers

Vol 20

Place	Date	Hour	Summary of Events and Information	Remarks and references to Appendices
BOYY ECOUST	1917		Quiet – Battalion Boundaries moved from the BOYELLES – BOIRY-BECQUERELLE to T.8.c.3.3.	Ref Maps 51.B.S.W. 1 20,000
	2nd		Information was received that the operations which had been postponed for 24 hours, would take place on the morning of April 2. The objectives for the 34th Division were as follows:- First Objective: Main CROISILLES-HENIN road from T.4.c.4 to T.3.a.3.2. Second Objective: to establish posts on the road N.E. of CROISILLES-HENIN road from T.iy.a.y0.65 to T.3.6.1.9. The 34 Division was on the right attacked CROISILLES. The 21st By Bde (30th D.) attacked HENIN. The 12th Northumberland Fusiliers attacked on the left of Brigade front. 1st Objective: Main CROISILLES – HENIN road from T.9.6.7.4 to T.3.a.3.2. 2nd Objective: to establish strong posts on road N.E. of first objective from T.4.c.4.3 to T.3.6.1.9. Dispositions: 'B' Company on the right 'D' Coy on the left, 'A' Coy in Support 'C' Company in reserve – Battalion H.Q. at T.8.c.3.3.

Army Form C. 2118.

WAR DIARY
or
INTELLIGENCE SUMMARY
(Erase heading not required.)

Instructions regarding War Diaries and Intelligence Summaries are contained in F. S. Regs., Part II. and the Staff Manual respectively. Title Pages will be prepared in manuscript.

Place	Date	Hour	Summary of Events and Information	Remarks and references to Appendices
BOTH? BECOURELLE	1st/July		At 4 a.m. "B" Company and "D" Company moved up to a forward position 180 yards from the first objective. At 5 a.m. the dispositions of the companies were as follows:- "B" Company and "D" Company in the open on a line roughly from T.10.a.0.8 to T.3.a.8.7. "A" Company in recently dug trench from T.9.c.4.4 to T.9.a.0.8. "C" Company in old German practice trenches in T.8.a. ZERO 5.15 a.m. Zero was the hour at which the artillery bombardment commenced. ZERO + 10 - Barrage lifted and our troops advanced. Considerable resistance was met with on our left whilst enemy had a strong post at T.3.c.8.8. The resistance was overcome after a tanks execution and 1 Machine gun silenced. The right company did not meet with much resistance and succeeded in reaching its objective without casualties. Nine prisoners belonging to the 99 R.I.R. (Prussians) 220 R. Reserve Division were captured and it is estimated that about 40 Germans were killed.	

WAR DIARY or INTELLIGENCE SUMMARY

Army Form C. 2118.

Place	Date	Hour	Summary of Events and Information	Remarks and references to Appendices
BOIRY BECQUERELLE	2nd /4		Meanwhile 2 platoons from the Reserve Company were pushed forward to establish posts at forts marked S. of HENIN at T.3.d.4.5. and on HENIN-ST LEGER Road at T.3.c.6.5. The captured position on the HENIN-CROISILLES Road was consolidated. T. Sgts were dug from the N.E. side of the road and strong points constructed at T.3.c.9.8. and T.3.d.2.0. There were now pushed forward unmolested. After capturing position and consolidated 150 yards in advance of position. Enemy barrage was poor. It was erected in CEMETERY in T.2.d. and ground between CEMETERY and Sunken Road running from T.2.b. and T.8.b. The barrage consisted of roughly 60% 15 c.m. shells and 40% 4.4" shrapnel. Casualties were slight and mostly to system from HENIN. The battalion was relieved in the M.O.F.K.O.Y.L.I. Relief complete at 1 am. (2nd 4/7) Companies moved independently to BOIRY ST MARTIN.	
	3rd	A.M.	Advance resulting part unit went forward in the morning to BERLES au BOIS. Companies followed in the afternoon the cars company reaching BERLES at 6.30 p.m. Billets were good.	Rel. Lloyd's LENS M 1/100 000
	5th		Lieut T.F. FORSYTH returned from Signalling course	

WAR DIARY or INTELLIGENCE SUMMARY

Army Form C. 2118.

Place	Date	Hour	Summary of Events and Information	Remarks and references to Appendices
BERLES AU-BOIS.	5th		Party under Capt. D.E. WRIGHT proceeded to ADINFER. Reorganization.	
	6th 7th 8th			
	9th		The battalion moved by companies to ADINFER, first company leaving BERLES at 4.30 a.m. Route BERNVILLERS AU-BOIS — MONCHY-AU-BOIS — ADINFER, whole battalion assembled for the night.	
	9th		Moved in the afternoon first to BOISLEUX-AU-MONT. Route: BOIRY ST. RICTRUDE and BOIRY ST. MARTIN. Later in the evening moved to BOISLEUX ST. MARC.	Ref. Map. J51 B S.W. 20,000
	10th		The battalion moved east in the morning to BOIRY BECQUERELLE. "A" Coy on sunken road immediately S.E. from outskirts (in T.8.c.) "B" Coy along main BOYELLES — BECQUERELLE road. "C" and "D" Coys in the village. Headquarters were in S.18.D.9.4. At dusk another move took place, the Battalion moving up to the main CROISILLES — HENIN road in support to 1st LINCOLN REGIMENT, and 10th YORKSHIRE REGIMENT, who relieved units of the 61st Brigade. Coys all west of 1st LINCS and 10th YORKS, who began East tunnels in HINDENBURG trench system. 1 Company remained carrying parties to the 10th LINCS REGT.	
	11th			
	12th		Relieved as the operations carried out by 1st LINCS, + 10th YORKS on the previous day, the Battalion relieved the 1st LINCS on the night	

Army Form C. 2118.

WAR DIARY or INTELLIGENCE SUMMARY

Army Form C. 2118.

Place	Date	Hour	Summary of Events and Information	Remarks and references to Appendices
	12th April		of the 11th/12th and took up the following dispositions:- Two companies held the newly dug trenches in front of the HINDENBURG LINE with right flank at T.4.b.5.2 and left flank at T.10.a.85.95. One company in support in trenches from T.11.a.8.0.0. to T.4.a.3.6. One company in reserve in trench from T.10.b.0.9 to T.4.c.3.5. During night the support trench was prolonged to T.5.E. and N.W. to allow the two companies in front line to withdraw to an assembly trench which was to take place at 5 a.m. in the morning. The enemy trenches were reconnoitred by an enemy bombardment ceased at 10.30 a.m. Patrols were immediately sent out to ascertain whether the enemy had withdrawn from his position. As signs of withdrawal had been observed earlier in the morning. The trenches were found unoccupied. Up to approximately T.5, 6, 5, 4. The C.O. (Capt. RICKIE) immediately gave orders to 2 companies to occupy the front and support trenches and at 2 p.m. the dispositions were as follows:- Two companies plus 2 platoons in HINDENBURG original support line with right flank at 6.a.10.46 - left flank N.35.c.2.4. Remain: two platoons of B company formed a defensive flank	

2449 Wt. W14957/M90 750,000 1/16 J.B.C. & A. Forms/C.2118/12.

WAR DIARY
or
INTELLIGENCE SUMMARY

(Erase heading not required.)

Army Form C. 2118.

Place	Date	Hour	Summary of Events and Information	Remarks and references to Appendices
	12th		along C.T. running from T.6.a.10.46 to T.6.a.0.3. with strong points 50 yards E. along both lines. One Company in support using front line Battalion H.Q. at T.5.a.10.55. In a line connects northward from Kahr Bokaros HQ moved to Canal Station in enemy original support line at N.36.c.4.3. Orders were received to continue to advance in conjunction with 56th Division on our left. The objective, three.	
	13th		1st Objective Sunken road from T.6.c.3.6. through V.1.c. — V.1.d. C.V.1.d.S.9.
2nd Objective. Q dig in on a line running from V.13.b.4.5. through U.Y.d. — U.S.c. — U.R.a. — East of FONTAINE-LES-CROISILLE — line north to cross the SENSEE RIVER at U.2.6.33. — N.E. of wood to sunken road at U.2.a.6.8.
Dispositions. A Coy with 2 platoons of B Coy continue leading attack down railway support line. D Coy with remaining 2 platoons Combed down railway front line.	

Place	Date	Hour	Summary of Events and Information	Remarks and references to Appendices
	13th		"C" Coy were to attack across the open jumping off from a mick dug trench running from T.5.a.9.5 to N.35 central. The attack was held up by M.G. fire and company withdrew to support A Company. Bombing attack was held up at sunken road N. from T.5.b.6.4 after 1000 yards advance. The enemy were holding trench strongly and further progress was impossible without support from Northern flank. Dispositions at 6 p.m. were as follows:- A Coy in support post at T.5. b. 5.4. D " " do T.5.6.20.15 B " in G.T. mound from T.5.b.4.3 & T.5.b.25.15. C " in trench N. from T.5.b.25.15. Casualties occurred during operations on April 2nd and April 13th so far as known. The battalion was relieved by the 1st CAMERONIANS and went back to trenches in T.3.b. and T.4.c.	[illeg] M/g. 51 B S.W. Killed: 33 O.R. wounded: 98 O.R. 2 officers
	14th			
	15th		Moved to BUSIEUX ST MARC. Marched to BELLACOURT. Route: BUSIEUX M.MONT – FICHEUX – BLAIRVILLE and BRETENCOURT.	

Army Form C. 2118.

WAR DIARY
or
INTELLIGENCE SUMMARY
(Erase heading not required.)

Place	Date	Hour	Summary of Events and Information	Remarks and references to Appendices
BELLACOURT	18th to 23rd		Resting in BELLACOURT. Reorganisation and training of battalion. The following reinforcement joined 70 officers and 3 O.R. from Corps Reinforcement Camp. Lieut. M.M. BRODIE, M.C. rejoined from Army School. Lieut. A. QUEEN in hospital with slight wounds received when Battalion went A.P. HARROWER and Lieut. JACKSON sick to hospital (Corps Rest Station).	2/Lt. WHITWORTH " FIELD " CUNDY " DIVISION " DICKINSON " JENKYN " DIGWRT
	24th		C.O.B. BELLACOURT at 9 am for MERCATEL Roads. BRETENCOURT – BLAIRVILLE – FIC HEUX – MERCATEL. The battalion bivouacked in a field N.E. of the village and remained in camp for 48 hours.	
	29th/28th		Moved to companies at V.3.b in 6 BOYELLES. Remained in BOYELLES. 2/Lt. J. QUEEN and 2/Lt JACKSON returned from hospital.	
	29th		The battalion moved to ST LEGER. Headquarters were situated in the QUARRY N.W. of the village (T.28.a.3.) – C and D Companies were near H.Q. – "A" and "B" Companies in field S.E. of JUDAS FME (T.34.d.5.8)	
	30th		In ST LEGER the Brigade were in Divisional Reserve.	

Mahnann Major
2nd/5th 15th Northumberland Fusiliers

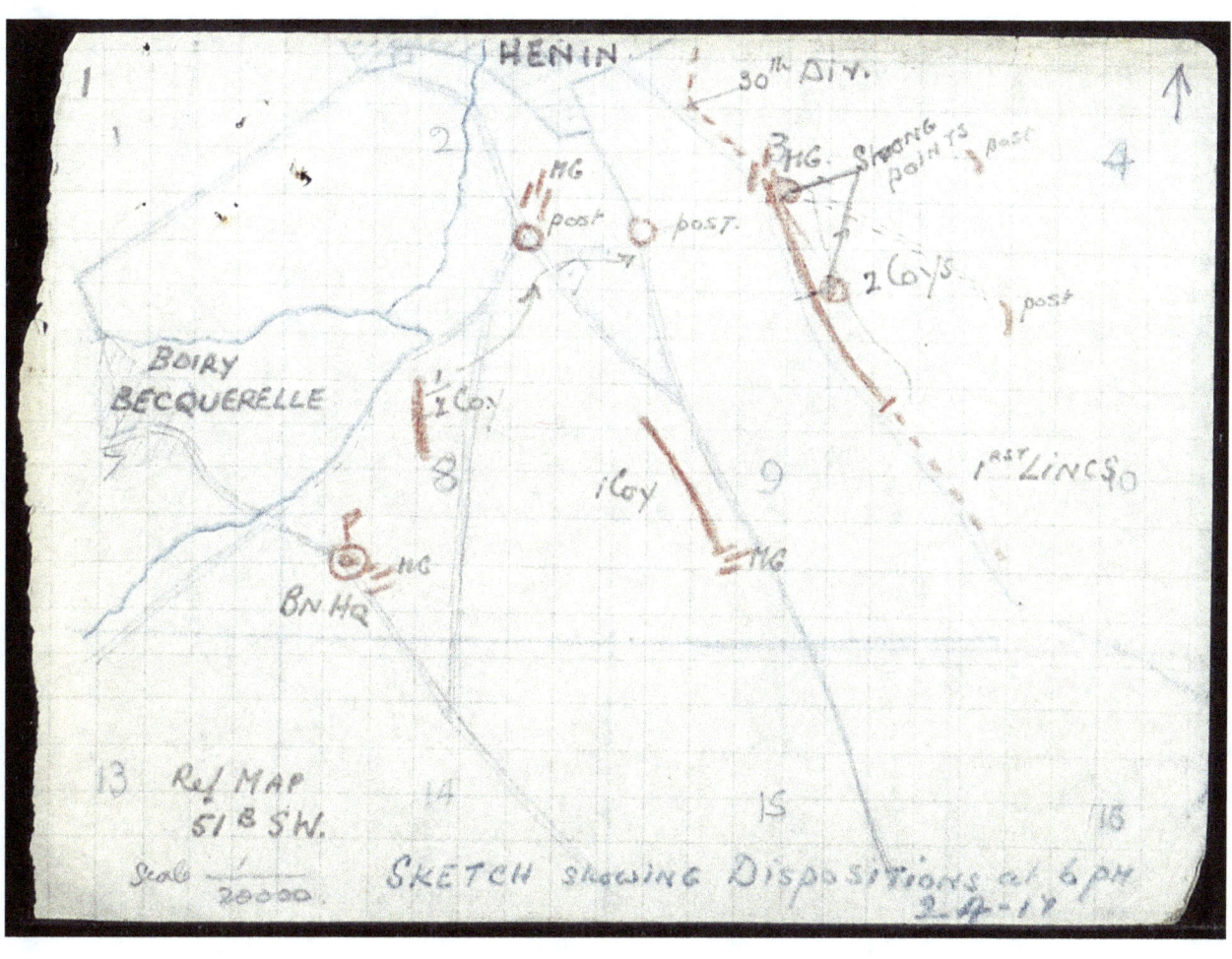

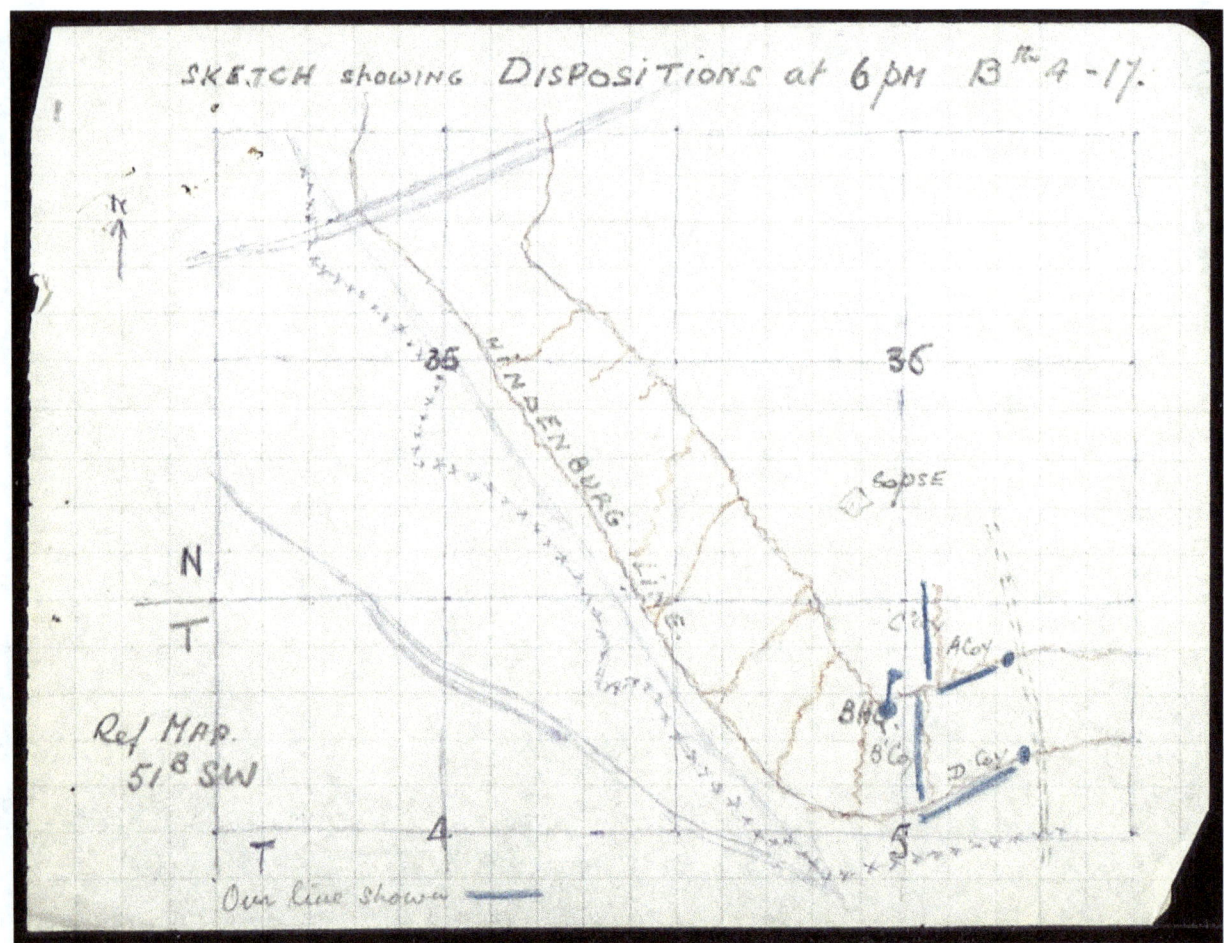

WAR DIARY
or
INTELLIGENCE SUMMARY
(Erase heading not required.)

Army Form C. 2118.

12th North Fus Vol 21

Place	Date	Hour	Summary of Events and Information	Remarks and references to Appendices
ST LEGER	MAY 1st & 2nd		Still in Divisional Reserve in Quarry at St Leger. The following NCOs & men were awarded the Military Medal for gallantry and devotion to duty during the operations of the 2nd April and 13th April: 5339 Pte D Ainsworth (SB) 14572 LCpl D. Moody D Coy 35184 Sgt A. Dobson 'B' Coy 38359 LCpl T. Clark D Coy 5889 Cpl G.T. Jackson B Coy 38361 Pte W. Cooper D Coy Pte W. Richardson 'B' Coy (S.B)	Ref Map 57BSW 1/20000
	2nd		The Battalion moved to Post 5 (T.16.c.4.5.) The Nucleus party and Transport moved from T.20.d to T2.c, S.W of Henin-sur-Cojeul.	
	4th		The 62nd Inf Bde relieved the 110th Inf Bde in the evening. The Battalion relieved 9th Leicestershire Regt and took up the following dispositions A Coy in Pug Lane, Cable Trench and The Gun Pits. B Coy along the original Hindenburg Support Line C Coy and D Coy in Concrete Trench Bn HQ was at T6.a.1.8.	
	5th		Patrols were sent out under Lt GM Phillips to reconnoitre Bush Trench.	

WAR DIARY
or
INTELLIGENCE SUMMARY

(Erase heading not required.)

Army Form C. 2118.

Place	Date	Hour	Summary of Events and Information	Remarks and references to Appendices
	6th to 9th May		Normal — Good patrol work was done during this period. The object of these patrols were to reconnoitre YORK SAP, YORK TRENCH, ROTTEN ROW & WOOD TRENCH, and in all cases very good results were obtained. A local relief took place on the 6th May. 'B' Coy relieving 'A' Coy in PUG LANE and the "Gun pits" — 'C' Coy moved from CONCRETE TRENCH to GREY TRENCH. On the 9th May. — 'B' Coy was relieved by 1 Company 1st LINCOLNS in PUG LANE and moved to CONCRETE TRENCH	
	10th		The enemy showed unwonted activity today. Our front line trenches & support line, were shelled heavily at intervals and increased aerial activity was noticeable.	
	11th		The Battalion was relieved at 2AM by the 6th ROYAL BERKSHIRE Regt. — 'C' Coy in GREY TRENCH was relieved by 2 Coys of the 8th SUFFOLK REGT. (18th Division) On completion of relief Companies marched to T2.C. (SW of HENIN). Marched to BLAIRVILLE in the evening, via BOIRY-BECQUERELLE — BOISLEUX ST MARC — BOISLEUX-AU-MONT and FICHEUX.	

Army Form C. 2118.

WAR DIARY
or
INTELLIGENCE SUMMARY

(Erase heading not required.)

Instructions regarding War Diaries and Intelligence Summaries are contained in F.S. Regs., Part II. and the Staff Manual respectively. Title Pages will be prepared in manuscript.

Place	Date	Hour	Summary of Events and Information	Remarks and references to Appendices
BLAIRVILLE	12th MAR to 30th		Resting at BLAIRVILLE. During this period, officers & men were sent to Musketry and training for the offensive.	Ref map 51c 1/40000
	18th		The Battalion was inspected on the 19th by the Divisional Commander and on the 25th by the Corps Commander.	
			2/Lieut. H.W. Dickinson and 20 O.R. joined from the Corps reinforcement camp.	
	22nd		2/Lt. C.H. Williams rejoined the Battalion 3rd Northumberland Fusiliers, and was posted to 'C' Coy.	
	23rd		The following officers left the battalion to reinforce 29th North'd Fus.	
			2/Lt. T. Cunningham 2/Lt. T.T. Forsyth	
			2/Lt. W. McLane " A.G. Whitworth	
			2/Lt. O.D. Bennett " Conway	
			2/Lt. Davison " H.W. Dickinson	
	24th		The following names appeared in Field Marshall Sir Douglas Haig's Dispatches:	
			Captain T.H. McLean R.S.M. H. Ransom	
			Lieut. R.C. Nolson Sergeant E. Brockhurst	
			2/Lieut. G. Sherwood	

WAR DIARY or INTELLIGENCE SUMMARY

Army Form C. 2118.

Place	Date	Hour	Summary of Events and Information	Remarks and references to Appendices
	30th		Coys BAPIRVILLE and MORY Red and FICHEUX - BOYELLES - JUDAS COPSE N.W. of LE LEGER. The Battalion relieved the 5th Cameronians and sent the 11th R.S. and transport (less a party at MOYENVILLE) Bn Nd back. Commanders went early in the morning to reconnoitre trenches	
E. NE. of CROISILLES	31/5		The Battalion moved up at 9 p.m and relieved the 2nd WORCESTERSHIRE REGT (133rd Am.) The following were the dispositions 22/1/99 "B" Coy, "A" Coy, & "C" Coy in the original HINDENBURG front line. "D" Coy on the night working the form[ation] on U.19.c.10.95. "A" Coy on the Flanks. "C" Coy on the left and left flank in NERRY KANE inclusive. "D" Coy H.Q. at U.19.a.1.5. 13th Bn attd. Inn on our left and the 58th Division on our right. Reliefs for the month were light - in O.R. were wounded during the period 5th may to 10th may	

J McIlwain Major
12th (S) Batt. Royal Scots Fusiliers

WAR DIARY
or
INTELLIGENCE SUMMARY

Army Form C. 2118.

Btn North Fusiliers Vol 2.2

Place	Date	Hour	Summary of Events and Information	Remarks and references to Appendices
CROISILLES	June 1st		During night June 1st/2nd two new trenches were dug, one by "A" Coy. connecting HUMP LANE and BURG TRENCH from U13.d.75.60 (in HUMP LANE) to U13.b.9.1. (50 yards NE of our block in BURG TRENCH). The other trench was dug by the 1st LINCOLN Regt connecting FACTORY AV. and NELLY AVENUE from U13.b.35.0 to U13.a.9.5.	Ref. to 1/50000 S/B S.W.
	2nd		"A" Coy. moved to LINCOLN TRENCH, thus relieving the congestion in the front line	
	3rd		There was a slight change in our dispositions "A" Coy relieved the right company of the 15th North. Fusiliers and took over a portion of BURG TRENCH from NELLY AVENUE exclusive to the Machine Gun emplacement in GUM TRENCH. The division on our left carried out a heavy bombardment of the HUMP, during the night in retaliation for which the enemy shelled our positions and caused a number of casualties	
	4th		One Coy 2/4 ROYAL FUSILIERS (58th DIVISION) relieved "D" Coy in Lone trench. "D" Coy moved to LINCOLN TRENCH	

WAR DIARY
or
INTELLIGENCE SUMMARY
(Erase heading not required.)

Army Form C. 2118.

Place	Date	Hour	Summary of Events and Information	Remarks and references to Appendices
TRENCHES CROISILLES	5th and 6th		The battalion was relieved in the evening by the 1st Lincoln Regt. and moved into Brigade Reserve West of CROISILLES. The disposition of the companies were as follows. "A" + "B" Coys on CROISILLES-BOYELLES road 500 yards west of CROISILLES. "C" + "D" Coys in trench running North and South from 723 c 8.6. HQ at 723 c 0.9. During the period spent in the trenches, the battalion did much good work in consolidating Burg. Lone, Lincoln and Hump trenches; a considerable amount of wiring was also done. Our snipers were very active and claimed 17 kills. The enemy was fairly active, shelling our back areas and CROISILLES. The front line was only shelled occasionally.	CASUALTIES 2nd Lt M.M. Brook 2nd Lt Esedale wounded. O.R. 5 wounded. 1 killed.
	7th		Marched to MOYENVILLE and took over "F" Camp from the 9th Leicestershire Regt. 2nd Lt Reading and Lt McKinnon proceeded on 10 days leave to England	

WAR DIARY or INTELLIGENCE SUMMARY

Army Form C. 2118.

Place	Date	Hour	Summary of Events and Information	Remarks and references to Appendices
MOYENVILLE	8th		Resting at MOYENVILLE. During this period, the companies were reorganized, equipped, etc. Attacks were practiced on broken trenches, and on two occasions in conjunction with the 13th North'd Fus.	
	10th 15th		Lt. C.N.G. KOCH proceeded on leave to England (13th June).	
	15th		The Battalion left F camp at MOYENVILLE by companies at 8 P.M. and marched by the entrainment of the STEEGER - BOYELLES railway, at T.20.D, where the Battalion remained until 8 P.M. At 8 P.M. the Battalion marched up by platoon to BURE trench, where an attack was to be made, Coy of the 7th Batn LEICESTER REGT occupying BURE trench withdrawing into LINCOLN trench upon which. During this march to trenches, Platoons passed through heavy shelling in the village of CROISILLES and in the SENSEE VALLEY, and a few casualties were sustained. By midnight all Coys had taken up their positions for the attack in BURE trench. D Coy being on the right with C Coy in the right and A Coy on the left. 2nd Lt. "B" D Coy was 200 yds to the left of the HUMP (U.14.c.2.9) and the left of A Coy at a point 150 yards left of NELLY AVENUE (U.13.b.3.8.). A Coy was commanded by Lt. BYRNE, B Coy by 2 Lt. FINDLAY, C Coy by 2 Lt. WILLIAMS, D Coy by Capt. McCLEAN. Upon arrival in BURE trench, all Coys proceeded to lay tapes from the jumps which had been previously constructed in BURE trench in the division after to be followed by the attack. Between midnight and	

WAR DIARY or INTELLIGENCE SUMMARY

Army Form C. 2118.

Place	Date	Hour	Summary of Events and Information	Remarks and references to Appendices
CROISILLES	June 16th		3.10 A.M. BURG TRENCH was subjected to heavy trench mortar bombardment and casualties were suffered by all Coys. C Coy in particular most. At 3.10 A.M. after a windlia barr of an artillery barrage the Battalion attacked with the 13th Middlx Front line on the left and the 2nd/2nd London Regt (58 Division) on the right; the objective of the 12th Batln mostly being was TUNNEL TRENCH from U.14.A.35.SD to U.7.D.80.20; the attack was made on a front of four Companies in two lines of small Columns, the average distance from the jumping off trench to the objective was 300 yds. The attack was met by the enemy with heavy barrage fire, who commanded a machine gun & rifle fire, while on a main approach to the enemy trenches which were very strongly manned, the attackers were met with showers of stick grenades; inspite of this 2 Lt QUEEN with a party of D Coy & Coy Sgt Major BYRON with some men of C Coy effected an entry into TUNNEL TRENCH where after a desperate hand to hand fight, then wounds being exhausted the party was overwhelmed by superior numbers & all became casualties. Of the other officers of D Coy Capt MCCLEAN was mortally wounded & 2Lt FIELD killed before reaching the parapet of TUNNEL TRENCH. Meanwhile parties to the left B Coy party (or the Coy Commander 2Lt FINDLAY killed & 2Lt MOWATT & 2Lt JACKSON wounded were mostly occupying still kills from 200 to 300 yards in front of the enemy trench: A Coy having been frustrated in their attempt to capture Tunnel trench by rifle fire & hand grenades, had consolidated a small German & Wormed trench some 80 yards in front of TUNNEL trench when 2Lt Byrne fell on until it became dark enough on the evening of June 16th to withdraw to BURG trench. Of the 10 officers and 391 O.R. who made the attack, 6 officers and 208	51.B.S.W. / 20.000

WAR DIARY or INTELLIGENCE SUMMARY

Army Form C. 2118.

Place	Date	Hour	Summary of Events and Information	Remarks and references to Appendices
ROISELLES	April 16th		Other ranks became casualties. As soon as it was dark enough "No man's land" was thoroughly searched and all the wounded who could be found were brought in; meanwhile the 7th Bath. of the Leicestershire Regt. had relieved the 12" Northd. Fusiliers in BURG trench, and the 12" Batth. moved out in small parties to ST LEGER & were emerged thence to 7 camp at MOYENVILLE on main Lawis.	
	June 17-19		The Battalion remained at 7 camp MOYENVILLE; Captain A.J. White was appointed 2nd in command. He 2nd Batch. of Royal Welsh Fusiliers being informed of Capt. J. Lowte's M.C. The Battalion marched to BASSEUX via ADINFER and went into rest billets, the Division having been relieved by the 33rd Division.	
BASSEUX	June 19-30		The Battalion remained at BASSEUX; training & reorganization being carried out there. On June 25th the following officers reported for duty from the 3rd I.B.D and were taken onto strength. 2nd Lieut. E. WAISTELL, W.S. HUTCHINSON, F.A. URWIN, J.W. ELLIOTT, C. TOLKIEN, L. CHAPMAN. On June 27, 2/Lts. P.J. GREGORY and E. THOMAS reported from the ARTISTS RIFLES O.T.C and were taken onto strength. On June 28 a Reinforcement of 60 O.R. arrived from ETAPLES. The Battalion left BASSEUX, & proceeded by train from BEAUMETZ to BOYELLES by train & went into bivouac at BOYELLES.	
At	June 30		The fighting strength on June 30, actually with the Battn. 22 officers and 467 O.R. P. Stuteron Lieut-Col. Commdg. 12th Bn. Northumberland Fusiliers	

62 Inf. Bde. O.O.119.　　　　　　　　　　SECRET.
Ref. Map HAZEBROUCK &A.　　　　　　　　　Copy No. 4
1/100,000　　　　　　　　　11th February 1917.
----

1. The 21 Division has been ordered to return to the I Corps Area.

2. (a) The dismounted portions of the 62 Inf. Bde. Group (less the 65 Field Amb.) will move by train on the 13th February from HOPOUTRE. { Personnel Trains POPERINGHE reads.　Omnibus Trains HOPOUTRE

   (b) Times for departure of trains are as follows :-

1st Personnel Train.	...	9.18 a.m. reads 8-23 AM
2nd Personnel Train.	...	10.18 a.m. 9-27 AM
1st Omnibus Train.	...	1.20 p.m. 10-14 AM
2nd Omnibus Train.	...	4.30 p.m. 1-46 p.m.

   (c) The 12 Northd Fus. and 10 York R. will proceed by the 1st Personnel Train, detraining at BETHUNE - due 11.30 a.m.

   The 13 Northd Fus. and 1 Lincoln R. will proceed by 2nd Personnel Train, detraining at FOUQUEREIL and CHOCQUES. - due 12.2 p.m.

   (d) The amount of 1st line transport going by rail and carried on the Omnibus trains is shewn on the tables marked 'B' already circulated to units.
   The Omnibus Trains will detrain at CHOCQUES and are due there at 2.52 p.m. and 6.2 p.m.

   (e) Personnel will be at the Station one hour before time of departure of train. Transport and loading parties three hours before departure of train.

3. Billeting Parties from each unit will proceed by train leaving PROVEN at 9.18 a.m. on 13th February and will report to Staff Captain, 62 Inf. Bde. at PROVEN Station at 8.15 a.m. on that day. [Cancelled]

4. The Starting Point and Times on the 13 February will be as follows :-
   'A'. Personnel Trains. Troops only without Transport.

Unit.	Starting Point.	Time.
10 York R.	Rd. Jnc. PEZELHOEK ¾ mile east of K in HAHHOEK.	7.33 a.m. 6-53 AM
12 Northd Fus.	do.	7.43 a.m. 6-58 AM
1 Lincoln R.	do.	8.33 a.m. 7-57 AM
13 Northd Fus.	do.	8.43 a.m. 8-02 AM

'B'. Omnibus Trains. 1st Line Transport etc. proceeding by rail.

                                            S.P.   Time.

(i) 1st Omnibus Train.

	S.P.	Time
Bde. H.Q. and Transport.	Rd. Jnc. PESELHOEK ¼ mile East of K in HALHOEK.	9.35 a.m.
4 Lewis Gun Limbered Wagons per battn.	do. 10 York R.	9.35 a.m. 6-29 AM
	do. 12 N.F.	9.37 a.m. 6-31 AM
2 Cookers & 1 Mess Cart. per bn.	do. 1 Lincs.	9.39 a.m. 6-33 AM
Chargers and Pack Animals. 20.	do. 13 N.F.	9.41 a.m. 6-35 AM
1 Maltese Cart. "		
97 Fd. Coy. R.E. (dismounted personnel)	do.	~~12.35 p.m.~~ 11.35 am 8-29 AM

(ii) 2nd Omnibus Train.

	S.P.	Time
62 M.G.Coy. (Troops and transport).	do.	12.45 p.m. 10-01
Tools 2 Limbered Wagons. per bn.	10 Yorks.	12.50 p.m. 10-06
	12 N.F.	12.52 p.m. 10-08
2 Cookers. " "	do. 1 Lincs.	12.54 p.m. 10-10
	13 N.F.	12.56 p.m. 10-12 AM
2 Water Carts. " "		
62 T.M.Battery. (Troops and handcarts).	do.	2.45 p.m. 11-30 AM
H.Q. Platoon.	do.	2.45 p.m. 12.0 PM

5. Loading Parties. 1 Officer and 100 men will load and unload each Omnibus train.
   97 Field Coy. R.E. will detail the party for the 1st Omnibus Train to be at HOPOUTRE Station at 10.20 a.m. 7-14 AM.
   62 M.G.Coy. will detail 1 Officer and 50 men and the 1st Lincoln R. 1 Officer and 50 men to act as the loading party for the 2nd Omnibus train, to be at HOPOUTRE Station at 1.30 p.m. 10-46 am

6. Orders for the move by road of the mounted portions of the Bde. Group (including the whole of the 65 Fd. Amb.) have been issued separately.

7. Blankets. One blanket per man will be taken in Personnel Trains in the carriages with the men.
   The second blanket per man will be carried in the 2nd Omnibus Train.
   Endeavours are being made to obtain lorries. Arrangements as to these will be notified later.

-2-

8. Instructions as to the relief by this Brigade of a Brigade of the 6th Division in the trenches (QUARRIES Sector) will be issued in BETHUNE as soon as received from Division.
   Arrangements will be made for officers to visit the trenches on the 13th February.

9. Brigade H.Q. will close at 'K' Camp at 8 a.m. on the 15th February and open in new area on arrival.

[signed] Capt,
Bde. Major,
62 Infantry Bde.

Issued at 7 p.m.
by orderly.

```
Copy No. 1 & 2 - War Diary & File.
     "    "   3    - 12 Northd Fus.
     "    "   4    - 13 Northd Fus.
     "    "   5    -  1 Lincoln R.
     "    "   6    - 10 York R.
     "    "   7    - 62 Coy. M.G.C.
     "    "   8    - 62 T.M.Bty.
     "    "   9    - H.Q. Platoon.
     "    "  10    - 97 Field Coy. R.E.
     "    "  11    - 65 Field Amb.
     "    "  12    - No. 2 Cpy. Train.
     "    "  13    - 21 Division.
     "    "  14    - Signals.
```

62 Infantry Bde. O.O.130.   SECRET.

                                                Copy No. 4

Ref. Map HAZEBROUCK 5A.   11th February 1917.
     1/100,000

1. No. 2 Coy. Train and the portions of 1st Line transport not proceeding by rail will move from present billeting area on the 15th February by road to HAZEBROUCK.

2. Lieut. DARGIE, Bde. Transport Officer, will be in charge of the transport of this Brigade which will move independently to the meeting point ¼ mile beyond STEENVOORDE.
   O.C. No. 2 Coy. Train will be in charge of the column after STEENVOORDE.

3. Route :- POPERINGHE - HILLEHOEK - ABEELE - STEENVOORDE - ST. SYLVESTRE CAPPEL - HAZEBROUCK.

4. Starting Point. Rd. Jnc. PESELHOEK ¼ mile East of K in HAHHOEK.   Time :-   8 a.m.
   This party will join on to No. 2 Coy. Train at 11 a.m. at a bend on the STEENVOORDE - ST. SYLVESTRE CAPPEL Road ½ mile due south of last E in STEENVOORDE.

5. Billets in HAZEBROUCK will be arranged by O.C. No. 2 Coy. Train.

6. O.C. No. 2 Coy. Train will arrange to send baggage wagons to units by night of the 14/15th February. These wagons will march under Bde. Transport Officer.

7. 2 days' rations of forage will be carried.

                                    A.R. Gallally
                                            Capt,
                                            Bde. Major,
                                            62. Infantry Bde.

Issued at 7 p.m.
by orderly.

           Copy No. 1 & 2 - War Diary & File.
              "   "   3 - 12 Northd Fus.
              "   "   4 - 13 Northd Fus.
              "   "   5 -   1 Lincoln R.
              "   "   6 - 10 York R.
              "   "   7 - 62 Coy. M.G.C.
              "   "   8 - No. 2 Coy. Train.
              "   "   9 - Bde. Transport Officer.
              "   "   10 - 21 Division.
              "   "   11 - Signals.

To:- 13 North'd Fus

B.M.530 – 12th February 1917.

1. Entraining and detraining stations and times given in Bde. O.O.119 of the 11th February are cancelled and the following amendments should be substituted.

   In para. 2 (a) for HOPOUTRE read Personnel Trains POPERINGHE.
                                           Omnibus Trains HOPOUTRE.

"	"	2 (b)	" 9.18 a.m.	" 8.25 a.m.
			" 10.18 a.m.	" 9.27 a.m.
			" 1.20 p.m.	" 10.14 a.m.
			" 4.30 p.m.	" 1.46 p.m.
"	"	4 (a)	" 7.37 a.m.	" 6.53 a.m.
			" 7.42 a.m.	" 6.58 a.m.
			" 8.33 a.m.	" 7.57 a.m.
			" 8.42 a.m.	" 8.02 a.m.
"	"	4 (b)(i)	" 9.35 a.m.	" 6.29 a.m.
			" 9.35 a.m.	" 6.29 a.m.
			" 9.37 a.m.	" 6.31 a.m.
			" 9.39 a.m.	" 6.33 a.m.
			" 9.41 a.m.	" 6.35 a.m.
			" 11.35 a.m.	" 8.29 a.m.
"	"	4 (b)(ii)	" 12.45 p.m.	" 10.01 a.m.
			" 12.50 p.m.	" 10.06 a.m.
			" 12.52 p.m.	" 10.08 a.m.
			" 12.54 p.m.	" 10.10 a.m.
			" 12.56 p.m.	" 10.12 a.m.
			" 2.45 p.m.	" 11.30 a.m.
			" 2.45 p.m.	" 12.01 p.m.
"	"	5	" 10.20 a.m.	" 7.14 a.m.
			" 1.30 p.m.	" 10.46 a.m.
"	"	9	" 9.00 a.m.	" 8.00 a.m.

2. Para. 3 is cancelled. Revised orders as to billeting parties are being issued in a separate memorandum.

                                                  Capt,
                                          for Bde. Major,
                                          62 Infantry Bde.

SECOND OMNIBUS TRAIN.

1 coach, 30 covered wagons, 17 flat trucks.

U N I T.	Personnel Off.	Personnel O.R.	Horses	G.S. Wagons.	G.S. Limbered.	2-wheeled carts.
Brigade Machine Gun Co. (less train transport & 2 G.S.L.Wagon)	10	149	52	-	10	2.
Tools (2 limbered wagons per Battalion)	-	8	16	-	8	-
Two cookers and two water carts or) per One cooker, one G.S. wagon and) or two water carts) Battalion	- -	16 16	32 32	- 4	8 4	8 8
Field Co., R.E.	-	1	2	-	1	-
	10 10	174 174	102 122	- 4	27 23	10 10

64 Axles.

16 Handcarts and 8 Mortars of Light T.M.Battery will be carried on this train.

  64 Axles = 16 flats
  100 Horses = 12½ covered wagons.
  173 O.R. = 4 : :
  Balance spare = (13½ : :
         (1 flat.

B

FIRST OMNIBUS TRAIN.

1 coach, 30 covered wagons, 17 flats.

Unit.	Personnel Offrs.	O.R.	Horses	G.S. Wagons.	G.S. Limbered	2-wheeled carts.
Brigade Headquarters and L.G.S.Wagon for cooks. (A.P.S., A.S.C., & A.O.D. Personnel are not included).	6	25	11	1	1	-
Signal Section.	1	27	9	-	1	1
Lewis Gun Detachments; 4 Limbered G.S.Wagons per Battn. Transport 4 Battalions.	-	32	32	-	16	-
(If only 2 L.G.S.Wagons for Lewis Guns are in possession one L.G.S.Wagon for S.A.A. should be taken.)		12				
Two Cookers and one Mess Cart per Battalion.	-	27	20	-	8	-
Chargers and Pack Animals: 11 & 9 - 20 per Battalion.	-	80	80	-	-	-
Medical Personnel (Part personnel with one Maltese Cart per Battalion.)	4	6	4	-	-	4
Field Ambulance	-	1	2	-	-	-
Divisional Hd. Qrs.						
H.Q.Platoons				1	1	-
	11	175	158	1	27	9

65 Axles.

65 Axles = 16½ flats.
156 Horses = 20 covered wagons.
175 Personnel = 4 : : (part personnel travels with horses)
Balance spare = { 6½ flat
                  { ½ flat

SECRET.

To:-
A.1337.

13 Nthd Inf

INSTRUCTIONS FOR MOVE TO I CORPS AREA.

1. ENTRAINING.

   (a) Field Coys R.E.
   The dismounted personnel of Field Coys will proceed by the first Omnibus Train.

   (b) Trench Mortar Bde.
   The Trench Mortar Bde will proceed by the Second Omnibus Train from ESQUELBECQ.

   (c) Personnel will be at the Station one hour before the time of departure of Train, transport will be at the Station three hours before departure of Train. *and loading parties*

2. STAFF CAPTAINS & BILLETING PARTIES.

   Staff Captain & Billeting party of 62nd Inf.Bde will proceed by first train from PROVEN on Feb.13th.

   Billeting parties of 64th Inf.Bde will proceed by first train on Feb.11th.

   Staff Captain & Billeting party of 110th Inf.Bde will proceed by first train from ESQUELBECQ on Feb.11th.

3. FIELD AMBULANCES.

   Field Ambulances including dismounted personnel will proceed by road on Feb.12th.

4. BLANKETS.

   One blanket per man will be taken in Personnel Train in carriage with the men. The second blanket per man will be sent in the First Omnibus Train.

   new carry in M.O.

5. LOADING PARTIES.

   Parties of 100 men will be told off as loading and unloading parties for each Omnibus Train. Loading parties for First Omnibus Train will be supplied as under :-

62nd Inf.Bde.	by	97th Field Co.R.E.	
64th "	by	126th "	
110th "	by	98th "	

   Loading parties for the Second Omnibus Train will be supplied by the Machine Gun Coys.

6. ROAD PARTIES.

   The Officer Commanding each Road Party will arrange with Town Major, HAZEBROUCK, for billets. The O.C. of the party proceeding on Feb.12th, loading parties will report to the Staff Captain R.E., at the Town Major's Office, HAZEBROUCK, at 11 a.m.

P.T.O.

7. Tables showing the accommodation on each Omnibus Train are attached.
   Each Personnel Train carries the personnel of two Battalions.

   Time of departure of trains will be notified as soon as received.

G Acland Troyte
Lt.Colonel.
A.A. & Q.M.G.,
21st Division.

H.Q., 21st Div.
10th Feb.1917.

13th. (S) BATTALION NORTHUMBERLAND FUSILIERS.

SECRET

PRELIMINARY ORDER.

The Battalion will be ready to move off about 7-20 a.m. on THURSDAY morning to be at starting point, Road Junction PESELHOEX half mile EAST of K in HANOEK.   Time:- 8.02. a.m. PERSONNEL Train departs from POPERINGHE at 9-27 a.m. and will detrain at FOUQUEREIL or CHOCQUES.

BLANKETS   One Blanket on the man will be taken in Personnel Train and carried on the Train.

The other Blanket per man will be loaded on lorries and taken on the Omnibus Train.

LORRIES.   Two lorries for the Battalion will report three hours before the time of loading trains on the 15th. inst. These lorries will carry One Blanket per man.

TRANSPORT.   Four Lewis Gun Limbered Wagons.

Two Cookers and Mess Cart

Chargers and Pack Animals,   Twenty.

Maltese Cart.

Will be loaded on First Omnibus Train leaving Road Junction PESELHOEX half mile EAST of K. in HANOEK at 6-35 a.m.

Two Limbered Tool Wagons.

Two Cookers.

Two Water Carts.

Will travel on Second Omnibus Train and leave Road Junction PESELHOEX half mile EAST of K in HANOEK at 10-12 a.m.

BILLETING PARTY.   The Billeting Party will breakfast at 4-0 a.m. at H.Q.s. Company CookHouse.   Party will parade under Lieut. S.M.HERBERT on the road opposite Headquarters Mess at 5-0 a.m.

Capt. & Adjt.,
13th. Northd. Fusrs.,

12.2.17.

13th Northumberland Fusrs.   Copy No...1...

           OPERATION ORDER   No 3   14th Feb 1917
     Ref Map HAZEBROUCK   5 A. 1/100090

1.   The 21st Division is ordered to return to First Corps area.

2.   The 62nd Inf Bde will move by train on the 15th Feby from POPERINGHE.

3.   The Battalion will parade on the Rad facing N.W. and be ready to move off at 7.15 a.m.
ORDER OF MARCH   STARTING POINT   TIME
     Pioneers   Road Junc.PESELHOEK
     Signallers   ¼ mile East of K   8.02
     "A" Co   in HANHOEK
     "B" "
     "C" "
     "D" "
     Remainder of HQ. Co

     Battalion marches to POPERINGHE Station.
     Train departs 9.27.a.m
     Detraining Station BETHUNE
DRESS. Marching Order.

4.   BLANKETS   One Blanket will be carried on the man and will be folded neatly on the back of the Pack under the Cross Straps.
     All other Blankets will be rolled carefully, and tied up in bundles of ten and piled on the edge of the Road where path crosses to the Guard Room, by 5.15.a.m
     A Sentry from the Guard will be posted in charge of them.
     The Duty Company will furnish a loading party for each lorry of one N.C.O. and eight Men to load the two lorries at 5.30 a.m

5.   BREAKFASTS will be at 4.30 a.m. The Mess Cart and Cookers etc will be ready to move off by 5.45.a.m.

6.   OFFICERS KITS will be piled close to the Wagons at the back of H.Q. Cookhouse at 6 a.m.
     "C" Company will furnish one N.C.O. and six men to load them at 6.15 a.m
     The Orderly Officer will superintend all loading.

7.   The whole camp must be left spotlessly clean, and will be inspected at 6.45 a.m.

8.   RATIONS. Unconsumed portion of the day's Rations for the 15th inst. will be carried on the man.
     Rations for the 16th inst will be carried on the Cookers and Wagons.

9.   CAMP FURNITURE All tables, chairs. washing bowls, latrine buckets etc will be taken to the Sergts Mess Hut at 5 a.m where they will be carefully checked by 2nd Lieut RUTHERFORD and handed over to the Camp Caretaker, and a receipt obtained and handed in to the Adjutant.

10 WORKING PARTY   The Battalion will find one Officer and 100 O.R's as a working Party, to be attached to 170th Tunnelling Coyv Lieut H. W. JACKSON will be in charge, and each Coy will detail one N.C.O. and 24 O.R's. This party will parade in Marching Order outside Battalion H.Q's at BETHUNE at 10 a.m on the 16th inst, and be taken by lorries (if available) to VERMELLES. Guides have been asked for to meet party at the Cross Roads in VERMELLES, by the Dressing Station.

11. Lieut G.B. RIDDELL is detailed to proceed with Transport travelling by Rail and will be responsible for seeing all Wagons and horses etc loaded on to the Omnibus train. He will report to the Adjutant for instructions.

12. Reports to head of Column after 7.15 a.m.

Issued by Orderly at 1 p.m
```
Copy No 1    Retained
 "    2    "A" Co
 "    3    "B"  "
 "    4    "C"  "
 "    5    "D"  "
 "    6    L.G.O and B.O.
 "    7    T.O.
 "    8    A/Q.M.
```

Captn & Adjt
13th North Fusrs.

12th Northd. Fus.
13th Northd. Fus.
1st Lincoln R.
10th Yorks R.
62nd Coy M. G. Corps.
62nd Trench Mortar Bty.
97th Field Coy R.E.
Forty Thieves.

SECRET.

S.C. 313 - 13th February 1917.

1. The attached table showing times etc. that lorries (if available) will arrive on the 15th instant is forwarded for your information.

2. All Units will arrange to send guides to meet the lorries at the times and places mentioned. The map reference A.16.c.1.9 Sheet 28 is the cross roads where Chemin Militaire crosses Poperinghe-Woesten Road by 'X' Camp.

3. Poperinghe Station is given as the destination of the lorries for the four battalions, but the lorry drivers should be instructed to go to HOPOUTRE Station as the second blanket is to be carried on the Omnibus Train.

4. Units must see that lorry drivers understand the destination and that they arrive at HOPOUTRE Siding three hours before the train departs.

5. "Times of Entraining" Col. 6 should read "Time of departure of train", and in the case of the 62nd T.M. Bty. this should be 13.46 instead of 10.14 as stated.

Captain.
for Staff Captain.
62nd Infantry Bde.

To:- 62nd Inf. Bde. (for information) A. 1237.

May lorries be sent to places mentioned below at the times stated, where they will be met by Guides from each Unit :-

15th February 1917.   62nd Infantry Brigade.

Unit.	No. of Lorries.	Time.	From.	To.	Time of entraining.
97th Field Coy R.E.	1	4.15 a.m.	"X" Camp	HOPOUTRE siding.	10.14 a.m.
62nd Inf. Brigade H.Q.	1	4.15 a.m.	(A.16.c.1.9. Sheet 28) "	"	10.14 a.m.
12th Northd. Fus.	2	4.50 a.m.	"	POPERINGHE station.	8.23 a.m.
13th Northd. Fus.	2	5.30 a.m.	"	"	9.27 a.m.
1st Lincoln R.	2	5.30 a.m.	"	"	9.27 a.m.
10th Yorks R.	2	4.30 a.m.	"	"	8.23 a.m.
62nd Coy M. G. Corps.	1	7.45 a.m.	"	HOPOUTRE siding.	13.46
62nd Trench Mortar Bty.	1	4.30 a.m.	"	"	10.14
Divisional H.Q.	1	9.0 a.m.	WORMHOUDT Church.	"	13.46

(Signed) G. ACLAND TROYTE,
Lt. Colonel,
A.A. & Q.M.G.,
21st Division.

H.Q. 21st Div.
13/2/17.

PROPOSED MOVEMENTS OF 62nd INFANTRY BRIGADE

Dates	Unit.	From.	To.
15th Feb.	12th Northd. Fus.	Detraining Stn. BETHUNE.	BETHUNE.
	10th Yorks R.	do	do
	13th Northd. Fus.	do	do
	1st Lincoln R.	Detraining Stn. CHOCQUES.	CHOCQUES.
	62nd Coy M.G.C.	do	BETHUNE.
	62nd Trench Mor. Bty.	do	do
16th Feb.	12th Northd. Fus.	BETHUNE.	MAZINGARBE.
	10th Yorks R.	do	SAILLY LABOURSE.
	13th Northd. Fus.	do	LABOURSE.
	1st Lincoln R.	CHOCQUES.	BETHUNE.
	62nd Coy M.G.C.	BETHUNE.	TRENCHES.
	62nd T.M. Bty.	do	do.
17th Feb.	12th Northd. Fus.	MAZINGARBE	TRENCHES.
	10th Yorks R.	SAILLY LABOURSE.	do.
	13th Northd. Fus.	LABOURSE.	do.
	1st Lincoln R.	BETHUNE.	MAZINGARBE.

21st Division.
All Units - for information.

B.M. 547 - 14th February 1917.

May lorries be supplied for this Brigade on the 16th inst. as under, please, and may this Brigade be informed whether lorries will be supplied for the personnel mentioned, as well as for the blankets?

(sgd) M. IBBETSON, Captain.
for Brigadier Lt. Colonel,
comdg: 62nd Infantry Bde.

Unit.	Personnel. Offrs.	O.R.	Material to be carried.	Time.	From.	To.	Remarks.
62nd M.G. Coy.	10	170	Blankets etc.	8.30 a.m.	BETHUNE X roads E.11.c.8.5.	PHILOSOPHE X Roads.	To relieve 71 M.G. Coy.
62nd T.M. Bty.	4	75	Blankets, guns etc.	do.	do.	do.	To relieve 71 T.M. Bty.
13th Northd. Fus.	1	100	Blankets etc.	11.30 a.m.	do.	VERMELLES.	To report 174 Tunnelling Co R.E.
10th Yorks R.	1	75	do.	do.	do.	do.	To report 253 Tunnelling Co R.E.
1st Lincoln R.	1	75	do.	11.0 a.m.	CHOCQUES Church.	do.	To report 253 Tunnelling Co R.E.

SECRET.

DISPOSITION OF 62nd INFANTRY BRIGADE.

Unit.	Detrain at.	Feb.15th.	16th.	17th.
A. Battn 12th N.F.	Bethune 11-0 a.m.	Bethune Montmorency Bks. relieve 9th Leic.	Sailly	Trenches.
B. Battn. 10th Yorks.	Bethune 11-0 a.m.	Bethune Orphanage, relieve 8th Leic.	Mazingarbe	Trenches.
C. Battn 13th N.F.	Bethune 12.2 p.m.	Bethune Tobacco Factory	Labourse relieve 7th Leic.	Trenches Support.
D. Battn 1st Lincs	Chocques 12.2 p.m.	Chocques relieve 6th Leic.	Bethune Montmorency Bks. relieve 12th N.F.	Mazingarbe.
Bde. H.Q. Office	Chocques 12.52 p.m.	Bethune 7 Grand Place.	same as 15th Feb.	Trenches.
97th Fld Co. R.E. Dismounted portion	Chocques 12.52 p.m.	Bethune Montmorency Bks.	same as 15th Feb.	Noyelles.
Mounted portion	By Road.	-	-	Noyelles.
62nd M.G.Co.	Chocques 15.52	Bethune 33 Faubourg D'Arras	Trenches	Trenches.
62nd T.M.B.	Chocques 15.52	Bethune Avenue de Bruay	Trenches	Trenches.
No.2 Co.Train	By Road	~~Annequin~~ Hazebrouck	Relieve No.2 Co. 6th Div. Train. Noeux les Mines	same as 16th Feb.

    Transport proceeding by Omnibus Trains will remain with Units at above places.
Transport proceeding by Road will proceed direct to their old lines at SAILLY LABOURSE and LABOURSE and double up with transport of Units now there until relief of latter is complete, when the whole of the transport will take over their old lines.
    The Old Q.M. Stores at SAILLY LABOURSE & LABOURSE will be taken over by Units of this Brigade when vacated by Units now there.
    Each Unit will send a cyclist to Brigade H.Q. No. 7, Grand Place, BETHUNE as soon as possible after arrival in billets on 15th and 16th Feb.
    The runners will remain at Brigade H.Q. for any outgoing messages.
    Until further orders Railhead will be at BETHUNE. Refilling Point will probably be at NOEUX LES MINES, but this will be confirmed later.
    Baggage wagons will arrive at the old Transport Lines sometime on the 16th Feb. Units will send a representative there to guide the baggage wagons to where they are required.
    O.C. billeting parties will send a guide to meet their Units at Detraining Stations. They will also send guides to meet the Omnibus Trains arriving at Chocques at 12.52 and 15.52 respectively to guide transport. Blanket Lorries will be at Detraining Stations and will also report to Units on mornings of 16th and 17th Feb

14th February, 1917.

C.P. Gibson Captain.
Staff Capt., 62nd Inf. Bde.

21st DIVISION.

Location of Units on 15th February 1917.

UNIT	LOCATION
H.Q. 21st Division. (G. & Q. Offices)	7 Rue de College, BETHUNE.
G.O.C., 21st Div.	1 rue Poterne, BETHUNE.
H.Q. 21st Div. Art.	28 & 30 Bde Frederic de Georges, BETHUNE.
C.R.E. 21st Div.	17 Rue Buridan, BETHUNE.
A.D.M.S.)	
A.D.V.S.)	53 Bde. Victor Hugo.
A.P.M.)	
Camp Commandant.	50 Grand Place, BETHUNE.
Div. Signal Coy.	11 Rue de College, BETHUNE.
D.A.D.O.S.	Rue Faidherbe.
Salvage Coy.	LABEUVRIERE.
Compo. Coy.)	Cinema, Rue de Deux Moulins,
Band.)	BETHUNE.

62nd Infantry Brigade.
Bde. H.Q.	7 Grand Place, BETHUNE.
12th North. Fus.	Montmorency Bks, BETHUNE.
13th North. Fus.	Orphanage, BETHUNE.
1st Lincoln Rgt.	Chocques.
10th Yorks Regt.	Tobacco Factory, BETHUNE.
62nd M.G. Coy.	33 Faubourg d'Arras, BETHUNE.
62nd T.M. Batty.	Avenue de Bruay, BETHUNE.

64th Infantry Brigade.
Bde. H.Q.	Annequin.
1st East Yorks Rgt.	Trenches (Right Sector)
9th K.O.Y.L.I.	Annequin (Reserve)
10th K.O.Y.L.I.	Trenches (Left Sector)
15th Durham. L.I.	Trenches (Support)
64th M.G. Coy.	Trenches.
64th T.M. Batty.	Trenches.

110th Infantry Brigade.
Bde. H.Q.	Hulluch Alley (Trenches)
6th Leicester Regt.	Noyelles (Reserve)
7th ; ;	Trenches (Support)
8th ; ;	Trenches.
9th ; ;	Trenches.
110th M.G. Coy.	Trenches.
110th T.M. Batty.	Trenches.

97th Field Coy. R.E.	GONNEHEM.
98th Field Coy. R.E.	NOYELLES.
126th Field Coy. R.E.	BEUVRY.

Divisional Train.
Headquarters	45 Rue St Py / Billet 59, Faubourg St Py (Main Bethune - Bruay Road)
No. 1 Coy. (Div. Troops)	BELLERIVE.
No. 2 Coy. (62nd Inf. Bde.)	HAZEBROUCK
No. 3 Coy. (110th Inf. Bde)	Nocux-les-Mines.
No. 4 Coy. (64th Inf. Bde)	Annezin.

UNIT.	LOCATION.
63rd Field Ambulance.	Ecole Jules Ferry. BETHUNE.
64th Field Ambulance.	Ede; Frederic de George. BETHUNE, and Avenue Bruay. BETHUNE.
65th Field Ambulance.	Archives Library. BETHUNE. (Place Barthelmy)
38th Sanitary Section.	Cinema. Rue de Deux Moulins, BETHUNE.
33rd Mob. Vet. Section.	NOEUX-LES-MINES.
94th Brigade. R.F.A.	Mt. BERENCHON.
95th Brigade. R.F.A.	LES HARISOIES.
Div. Amn. Column.	RIEZ DU VINAGE.
Railhead.	NOEUX-LES-MINES.

----

62 Infantry Bde. O.C.121.   SECRET.

Map Reference Sheet   Copy No. 4
Nos. 1/40,000.

15th February 1916.

1. Units will move tomorrow 16th instant as follows :-

Unit.	C.P.	Time.	To.	Route.	Remarks.
62 M.G.Coy.	BETHUNE Cross Roads. H.11.c.6.5.	9.00 a.m.	Trenches.	Via Beuvry & Sailly Labourse.	Guides from 71 Inf. Bde. will be at PHILOSOPHE X Rds. at 11 a.m.
62 T.M.Bty.	do.	9.05 a.m.	do.	do.	
10 York R.	do.	8.30 a.m.	Mazingarbe.	X Rds, N.29.b. - NOEUX LES MINES - Level Crossing L.29.b. - Mazingarbe.	
13 Northd Fus.	do.	2.30 p.m.	Labourse.	Beuvry - Cross Roads P.N.6 - Labourse.	
12 Northd Fus.	do.	3.00 p.m.	Sailly Labourse.	via Beuvry.	
1 Lincoln R.	Chocques Cross Rds. D.6.a.C.9.	2.30 p.m.	Bethune.	Via X Rds. E.5.a.	

2. All movement of troops by daylight east of Bethune will be by Companies at 200 yds. interval, and East of a line drawn through F.21 central - Sailly Labourse, or East of Noeux-les-Mines by platoons at 200 yds. interval.

3. On arrival at Mazingarbe the 10 York R. will come under the orders of the G.O.C. 71 Inf. Bde.

4. The 71 Inf. Bde. have been asked to leave one man in each M.G. and T.M.emplacement, with the 62 Inf. Bde. for 24 hours after relief.

5. LORRIES. One lorry will pick up the blankets of the 62 M.G.Coy. and 62 T.M.Bty. at 8.30 a.m. at X Rds. H.11.c.6.5. These units will arrange to have their blankets at this place at the time stated, with loading parties.

     Lorries have also been asked for to take each battalions blankets tomorrow. In any case where they have not arrived when the units move off a sufficient loading party must be left.

6. ACKNOWLEDGE.

                                Capt,
                         Acting Brigade Major,
Issued by orderly   62 Infantry Brigade.
   at 9 p.m.

           Copy No. 1 & 2 - War Diary & File.
              "   "   3 - 12 Northd Fus.
              "   "   4 - 13 Northd Fus.
              "   "   5 - 1 Lincoln R.
              "   "   6 - 10 York R.
              "   "   7 - 62 Coy. M.G.Corps.
              "   "   8 - 62 T.M.Bty.
              "   "   9 - 71 Inf. Bde.
              "   "   10 - 21 Division.
              "   "   11 - No. 2 Coy. Train.

12 Northd Fus.
13 Northd Fus.
 1 Lincoln R.
10 York R.
62 Coy. M.G.Corps.
62 T.M.Battery.
No 2 Coy. Train.

B.M.548 - 14th February 1917.
----

1. Please note following alterations in the table of proposed movements of units sent with B.M.541 dated 13th.

2. On the 16th February the 10 York R. moves from BETHUNE to MAZINGARBE instead of the 12 Northd Fus. and the 12 Northd Fus. moves from BETHUNE to SAILLY LABOURSE instead of to MAZINGARBE.

3. Similarly on the 17th the 10 York R. moves from MAZINGARBE to trenches, and the 12 Northd Fus. from SAILLY LABOURSE.

4. The ~~proposed~~ other moves stand as in table.

5. Billets have been arranged accordingly.

Capt,
Acting Bde. Major,
62 Infantry Brigade.

Copy No....6

13th. Nrthd. Fusrs. Operation Order. No. 5., 15.2.17.

1. The Battalion will be ready to move off at 2.15 p.m. tomorrow the 16th. inst. to proceed to LABOURSE. Starting Point:- BETHUNE Cross Roads E.11.c.8.5. and pass the starting point at 2-30 p.m.
ROUTE:- BEUVRY - Cross Roads F.21.c. - LABOURSE.
ORDER of MARCH:- "B" Coy.
"C" "
"D" "
"A" "
"H.Q.s. Cot.

There will be an interval of Two hundred yards between Companies which must be maintained throughout the march to LABOURSE. Dress, Marching Order.

All Blankets will be rolled in bundles of Ten and piled in the Billet Yard by 12 noon. Duty Company will furnish a loading party of Two N.C.O's and Twenty Men. If the lorries have not arrived before the Battalion moves off this loading party must be remain behind to load lorries when they arrive.

All Billets and their vicinity must be left scrupulously clean before moving off.

Dinners will be served before the Battalion leaves.

2. WORKING PARTY. (Ref: O.O. No. 3. para 10 a/- 14.2.17.)

This party will parade at 10-0 a.m. tomorrow under Lieut. H.W. JACKSON and be marched to PHILOSOPHE and will meet guides of the 41st. Inf. Bde. at the PHILOSOPHE CROSS ROADS at 1-15 p.m. tomorrow the 16th. inst.

One N.C.O. and Twenty four men of this party will report independently at Headquarters XXXXX INF.XBXX 170th. Tunnelling Company at NOEUX les MINES.

3. TRENCHES - TOUR of. A Bus to convey Officers to reconnoitre the Line will leave BETHUNE Cross Roads E.11.c.5.8 at 9-30 a.m. tomorrow 16th. inst. Ref: Map Sheet 36.B.1/40.000
Guides will meet party at 1st. Inf. Bde. H.Q.s at G.9.c.10.75 at 10-15 a.m.
Bus will return in the afternoon to SAILLY LABOURSE

Issued by Orderly at 1-20 a.m.
Copy No.1. Retained.
" " 2. "A" Coy.
" " 3. "B" "
" " 4. "C" "
" " 5. "D" "
L.G.O. & B.O. (No.6.)
" " 7. A/ Q.M.
" " 8. T.O.

Capt. & Adjt.,
13th. Northd. Fusrs.,

SECRET.

62 Infantry Brigade O.O. No. 122.

Copy No. 4

Ref. Sheets
36B. 1/40.000
36C. 1/40.000

16th February 1917.

---

1. (a) The 62 Inf. Bde. (less 62 M.G.Coy. and 62 T..Bty) will relieve the 71 Inf. Bde. in the QUARRIES Sector on the 17th instant (tomorrow).

   (b) The relief will be complete by 5.30 p.m. 17th instant.

   (c) On completion of relief 62 Inf. Bde. will come under orders of G.O.C. 6th Division.

2. (a) The 10 York R. will relieve the 1 Leic. R. in the Left Sub-sector, leaving Cross Rds. VERMELLES G.8.c.5.6 (Sheet 36C.) at 9 a.m.

   (b) The 13 Northd Fus. will relieve the 2 S. Foresters in Support leaving above Cross Rds. VERMELLES at 9.45 a.m.

   (c) The 12 Northd Fus. will relieve the 9 Suffolks in the Right Subsector, leaving above Cross Roads, VERMELLES at 1.30 p.m. (less one platoon in Centre Company to be relieved after dusk)

   (d) The 1 Lincoln R. will be in Brigade Reserve at MAZINGARBE.

3. Units will march to trenches &c. in accordance with attached table.

4. Attention is drawn to para 2 of 62 Inf. Bde. O.O.No. 121 of 15th instant.

5. Guides will be provided as under for the three trench battalions-
   1 guide for each platoon.
   1 guide for each Battn. H.Q.
   All guides will be at Cross Rds. VERMELLES G.8.c.5.6 (Sheet 36C.) at times mentioned above.

6. Communication trenches to be used for relief are as follows :-

Unit.	Subsector.	In	Out.	Remarks.
10 York R.	Left.	(Right Coy.) Chapel Alley. (Remaining 3 Coys. Stansfield Rd.	Chapel Alley. Stansfield Rd.	Right Coy. to lead.
13 Northd Fus.	Support.	Chapel Alley & Foose Way.	Chapel Aley & Foose Way.	Front Coy. to lead.
12 Northd Fus.	Right.	Chapel Alley and Devon Lane.	Chapel Alley & Devon Lane.	

7. The relief of Signals will be complete by 1 p.m. 17th instant.

8. H.Q. Platoon will march independently to MAZINGARBE, tomorrow morning (17th inst.) arriving by 12 noon.
   Billets have been allotted to them by the Town Major, to whom they will report.

9. Two lorries for each battalion and one each for 97 Field Coy. R.E. and 62 Inf. Bde. H.Q. have been asked for, to report at 10 a.m. in each case.

10. A list will be made of Trench Stores taken over and receipts given. A duplicate of the list, which will include log books, aeroplane photographs, maps etc., will be sent to Staff Captain, 62 Inf. Bde. by 12 noon on the 18th instant.

11. The command of the QUARRIES Sector will pass to Brigade Comdr. 62 Inf. Bde. on completion of relief.

12. Completion of relief will be notified to Bde. H.Q. by BAB Trench Code.

13. The 12 Northd Fus. will report completion of relief, when they have relieved the 9 Suffolks, less the one platoon to be relieved after dusk. A further report by runner will be sent as soon as this platoon has been relieved.

14. 62 Inf. Bde. H.Q. will close at BETHUNE at 2.30 p.m. on the 17th instant. and open at G.9.c.10.75 (Sheet 36C) at the same hour.

15. ACKNOWLEDGE.

Issued by orderly
at 7 p.m.

Capt,
Actg. Bde. Major,
62 Infantry Brigade.

```
Copy No. 1 & 2 - War Diary & File.
  "     "   3   - 12 Northd Fus.
  "     "   4   - 13 Northd Fus.
  "     "   5   -  1 Lincoln R.
  "     "   6   - 10 York R.
  "     "   7   - 62 M.G.Coy.
  "     "   8   - 62 T.M.Bty.
  "     "   9   - H.Q. Platoon.
  "     "  10   - Signals.
  "     "  11   - 71 Inf. Bde.
  "     "  12   - 110  "    "
  "     "  13   - 21 Division.
  "     "  14   - 97 Field Coy. R.E.
  "     "  15   - No 2 Coy. Train.
  "     "  16   - 21 Div. Train.
  "     "  17   - 170 Tunnelling Coy. R.E.
  "     "  18   - 253     "      "    "
```

MARCH TABLE.

17th February 1917.

Unit.	Starting Point. (Map Ref. Sheet 36B.)	Time.	To (Map Ref. Sheet 36C).	Route.
10 York R.	MAZINGARBE Rd. Jnc. L.23.b.2.8.	8.30 a.m.	Trenches, X Rds. VERMELLES G.8.c.5.8 at 9 a.m.	via PHILOSOPHE X Rds.
13 Northd Fus. LABOURSE Rd. Jnc. L.2.d.7.3.		8.30 a.m.	Trenches Leads VERMELLES at 9.45 a.m.	via SAILLY LABOURSE and X Rds. PHILOSOPHE.
12 Northd Fus. SAILLY LABOURSE. X Rds. L.3.b.4.5.		12.27 p.m.	Trenches Cross Roads VERMELLES at 1.30 p.m.	via PHILOSOPHE X Rds.
1 Lincoln R. BETHUNE X Rds. E.11.c.8.5.		8.30 a.m.	Mazingarbe by 11 a.m. X Rds E.29.b. – NOEUX LES MINES – Level Crossing L.20.b (Map Sheet 36B.)	

62 Infantry Brigade O.O. No. 123.　　　　　　　　SECRET.

　　　　　　　　　　　　　　　　　　　　　　　Copy No. 4

　　　　　　　　　　　　　　　　　　　18th February 1917.

1. The 2nd Machine Gun Squadron, strength 5 Officers 86 O.R., 12 guns, are due to arrive at LABOURSE today, 18th inst. They will be billeted in LABOURSE tonight.

2. On Monday, 19th February, Officers and N.C.Os of 2nd M.G. Squadron will reconnoitre the line in the QUARRIES Sector.

3. O.C. 62 M.G.Coy. will arrange for two guides to meet the party at PHILOSOPHE X Rds at 9.30 a.m. (19th instant) to conduct them to 62 M.G.Coy. H.Q., and will make the necessary arrangements for the party to be shown round the line.

4. On Tuesday, 20th February, 2nd M.G.Squadron will relieve the 62 M.G.Coy. (less one section) in QUARRIES Sector. Relief to be completed by 4.30 p.m.
　One section 62 M.G.Coy. will remain in QUARRIES Sector and will be attached to 2nd M.G.Squadron.

5. Arrangements for above relief will be made direct between O.C. 62 M.G.Coy. and O.C. 2nd M.G.Squadron.

6. A list will be made of Trench Stores handed over, which will include Log books, aeroplane photographs, trench maps and S.A.A. receipts being taken.
　Duplicate lists will be sent to Staff Captain, 62 Inf. Bde. by 12 noon 21st instant.

7. On completion of relief 62 M.G.Coy. (less one section) will move to LABOURSE and will be in Divisional Reserve.

8. O.C. 62 M.G.Coy. will send an advance billeting party on Monday 19th inst. to report to Town Major, SAILLY LABOURSE, at 10.30 a.m. for the purpose of arranging billets in LABOURSE.

9. Completion of relief will be wired to Bde. H.Q. in DAB Trench Code.

　　　　　　　　　　　　　　　　　　　　　　Capt,
　　　　　　　　　　　　　　　　　　Acting Bde. Major,
　　　　　　　　　　　　　　　　　　62 Infantry Brigade.

Issued by orderly
at 2 p.m.

```
Copy No. 1 & 2 - War Diary & File.   Copy No. 15 - No. 2 Coy.
   "    "    3  - 12 Northd Fus.                    Train.
   "    "    4  - 13 Northd Fus.      "    "   16 - 2 M.G.Squ d.
   "    "    5  - 1 Lincoln R.        "    "   17 - QUARRIES
   "    "    6  - 10 York R.                        Group F.A.
   "    "    7  - 62 M.G.Coy.         "    "   18 - 97 Field
   "    "    8  - 62 T.M.Bty.                       Coy. R.E.
   "    "    9  - H.Q. Platoon.
   "    "   10  - Signals.
   "    "   11  - 111 Inf. Bde.
   "    "   12  - 110 Inf. Bde.
   "    "   13  - 21 Division.
   "    "   14  - C Division.
```

SECRET   Copy No....

13th. Northd. Fusrs. Operation Order. No. 1.   16-2-17

Ref: Sheets 36B. 1/40.000
        36C. 1/40.000.

1 (a) The 62nd. Inf. Bde. (less 62. M.G. Coy and 62. T.M.B.)
     will relieve 71. Inf. Bde. in the QUARRIES SECTOR on the
     17th. inst. (tomorrow)
  (b) The relief will be complete by 6-30 p.m. on the 17th. inst.
  (c) On completion of relief 62nd. Inf. Bde. will come under
     orders of G.O.C., 6th. Division.

2. The 13th. Northd. Fusrs., will relieve the 2nd. Sherwood
   Forresters in SUPPORT leaving Cross Roads VERMELLES G.8.c.5.6.
   (Sheet 36 C.) at 9-45 a.m.
      The Battalion will proceed to the Trenches by Platoons
   with Two Hundred yards distance between platoons, strict march
   discipline being maintained.
      ORDER of MARCH:- "C" Coy.
                        "B" "
                        "A" "
                        "D" "
                        "H.Q.s.Coy.
      The leading Platoon of "C" Coy. will leave LABOURSE Road
   Junction L.2.d.7.3. at 8-30 a.m. ROUTE:- via SAILLY LABOURSE,
   and Cross Roads PHILOSOPHE.
      Companies will relieve Companies of 2nd. Sherwood Forresters
   as arranged today.

3. One Guide for each Platoon) will be at Cross Roads VERMELLES
   One Guide for Battn. H.Q.s.)- G.8.c.5.6.(Sheet 36.C.)at 9-45 a.m.

4. Communication Trenches to be used for Relief will be CHAPEL ALLEY
   and FOSSE WAY.

5. Advanced parties will consist of One Officer and One N.C.O. per
   Coy. which will leave LABOURSE at 7-30 a.m. and proceed to
   71st. Inf. Bde. H.Q., where a Guide will conduct them to
   2nd. Sherwood Forresters H.Q., Great care must be exercised
   in the taking over of all Trench Stores and the usual triplicate
   receipts signed and countersigned. All receipts must be sent in
   to the Adjutant by 7-0 p.m.

6. Breakfasts will be at 6-30 a.m.

7. One Blanket per man will be carried on the man to the Trenches.
   All oher blankets will be carefully rolled and tied in bundles
   of Ten in the yard adjoining the Orderly Room by 7.30 a.m.
   A Guard of One N.C.O. and Six men being left in charge of them
   from the Regtl. Drums. The Transport Officer will arrange
   as soon as possible, to convey these Blankets to the Q.M.Stores.

8. The Regtl. Drums will not proceed to the Trenches. They will
   report to the Q.M. and will practice daily.

9. Six men per Coy. are to report 2nd. Lt. T.H.ARMSTRONG at Q.M.
   Stores SAILLY LABOURSE at 10-0 a.m. tomorrow for training as
   Lewis Gunners: These men will return to their Coys. when the
   Battalion goes into the Front Line.

10. Water can be obtained when in the Trenches from Pump in
    GORDON ALLEY and from Tanks in O.B.4.

11. Companies will immediately notify the Adjutant by Runner when
    relief is complete.

12. BAB Code up to Midnight Feby. 17/18 should read, code letter
    AFC Minus 20.

13. Reports to Battn. H.Q.,s CURLY CRESCENT after 10-0 a.m.
    Issued by Orderly at 11-50 a.m.
    Copy.No.1.Retained. Copy No.2. "A"Coy. Copy No.3. "B"Coy.
      "   " 4 "C" Coy.   " " 5. "D" "
      "   " 8. L.G.O.& B.O. " " 7. T.O.& Q.M.

                                           Capt. & Adjt.,
                                           13th. Northd. Fusrs.,

62 Infantry Brigade O.O. No. 124.   SECRET.

Copy No. 4

20th February 1917.

1. The 13 Northd Fus. and the 1 Lincoln R. will relieve the 12 Northd Fus. and 10 York R. in the Right and Left Subsections respectively on the 22nd February 1917.

2. On relief the 12 Northd Fus. will move to the support line now held by 13 Northd Fus. and the 10 York R. will move into Reserve at HAZINGARBE now occupied by 1 Lincoln R.

3. The relief of the 10 York R. will be completed by 12.30 p.m. The relief of the 12 Northd Fus. by the 13 Northd Fus. will start at 1 p.m. and will be completed by 4.30 p.m.

4. All other details of relief will be arranged by Battn. Comdrs.

5. Officers from the 1 Lincoln R. will reconnoitre the line on 21st instant.

6. Details of fatigues and duty must be handed over to relieving battalions. Work will be interfered with as little as possible. This applies especially to the two parties found by the battalion in Support (B.M.578 - 18th inst) for the T.M.Battery, which will be found on the day of relief by 12 Northd Fus. The daily unloading party of 1 N.C.O and 10 Men, found by battalion in Reserve, reporting at MANSION HOUSE, VERMELLES, at 1.30 p.m., will be found on day of relief by 10 York R.

7. If any alterations in dispositions are made Bde. H.Q. must be informed at once.

8. All trench stores, log books, trench maps etc. will be handed over and lists forwarded to Staff Captain, 62 Inf. Bde. within 24 hours of completion of relief.

9. Gum boots will be handed over and receipts taken, and a statement of the number sent in with Trench Store lists to the Staff Captain.

10. A billeting party will be sent on in advance to HAZINGARBE, by 10 York R. on the morning of the 22nd inst.

11. Completion of relief will be notified to Bde. H.Q. by BAB trench code.

12. ACKNOWLEDGE.

Capt,
Issued by orderly   Actg. Bde. Major,
at 3 p.m.   62 Infantry Brigade.

Copy No. 1 & 2 - War Diary & File.   Copy No. 11 - Quarries Group R.F.A.
"   "   3 - 12 Northd Fus.   "   "   12 - 110 Inf. Bde.
"   "   4 - 13 Northd Fus.   "   "   13 - 111 Inf. Bde.
"   "   5 - 1 Lincoln R.   "   "   14 - 97 Fd. Coy. R.E.
"   "   6 - 10 York R.   "   "   15 - 21 Division.
"   "   7 - 62 M.G.Coy.   "   "   16 - 170 T. Coy. R.E.
"   "   8 - No. 2 M.G.Squad.   "   "   17 - 253   "   "
"   "   9 - 62 T.M.Bty.   "   "   18 - No. 2 Coy. Train.
"   "   10 - Signals.   "   "   19 - 21 Div. Train.

SECRET

13th Northumberland Fusrs. Operation Orders No 6.   Copy No. 1
                                                     21.2.17

1. The 13th Northumberland Fusiliers and the 1st Lincolnshire Regiment will relieve the 12th Northumberland Fusiliers and the 10th Yorkshire Regiment in the right and left sub-sectors respectively on the 22nd February 1917.

2. On relief the 12th Northumberland Fusiliers will move to the support line now held by the 13th Northumberland Fusiliers, the 10th Yorkshire Regiment into reserve at MAZINGARBE, now occupied by the 1st Lincolnshire Regiment.

3. The relief of the 10th Yorkshire Regiment will be completed by 12.30 p.m
The relief of the 12th Northumberland Fusiliers by the 13th Northumberland Fusiliers will start at 1 p.m and be completed by 4.30 p.m

4. The Battalion will relieve the 12th Northumberland Fusiliers in the following order, and at the undermentioned times:-

"C" Company will relieve "C" Company of 12th Northd Fusrs on the right and will pass Battn H.Q at junction of O.G.1 and Devon Lane at 1.30 p.m.

"A" Company will relieve "A" Company of the 12th Northd Fusrs on the left and will pass Battn H.Q at junction of O.G.1 and Devon Lane at 2 p.m

"D" Company will relieve "B" Company of the 12th Northd Fusrs in the centre and will pass Battn H.Q at junction of O.G.1 and Devon Lane at 2.30 p.m

"B" Company will relieve "D" Company of the 12th Northd Fusrs in support and will pass Battn H.Q. at junction of O.G.1 and Devon Lane, at 3 p.m.

Disposition of Company fronts will be as laid down by the Commanding Officer when Company Commanders visited front line with him.

Signals will be relieved by 1 p.m.

The platoon of "D" Company which relieve after dark will remain with the support Company until darkness sets in.

Lewis Gunners will move up with their Companies and the post to which they are attached.

5. Advance parties of one Officer and one N.C.O. per Company will take over all trench stores etc at 12.30 p.m. Triplicate receipts must be signed and countersigned and sent in to the Adjutant by 5 p.m on the 22nd inst.

ALL Gum Boots thigh will be taken over and receipts exchanged for them.

The present trenches and their vicinity now occupied by the Battalion must be left clean and care must be taken to hand over all Gum Boots thigh and trench stores and obtain a receipt for them.

6. Communication Trenches to be used only are CHAPEL ALLEY to O.G.1 and DEVON LANE.

7. All Mess Boxes, Canteen and Orderly Room Boxes, Medicial panniers Kits Dixies etc must be taken down before 12 noon, or after the relief is complete. The Trenches will be policed by both Battalions to see this is carried out and that the communication Trenches mentioned are used only.

8. Immediately each Company's relief is complete, Company Commanders will wire the word "TOP" preceded by his name to Battalion H.Q's.

9. Battalion H.Q's will move at 2.30 p.m. All reports after this hour to Battalion Headquarters at junction of O.G.1 and DEVON LANE.

10. Acknowledge.

H.W. Slton
Captn & Adjt
13th Northd Fusrs

Issued by orderly at 7 p.m
No 1 Copy retained "
 " 2   "   "A" Coy
 " 3   "   "B" "
 " 4   "   "C" "
 " 5   "   "D" "
 " 6   "   L.G.O and B.O.
 " 7   "   Q.M. and T.O.

62 Infantry Brigade O.O. 125.

SECRET.

Copy No. 4

26th February 1917.

1. The 12 Northd Fus. will relieve the 13 Northd Fus. in the Right Subsection on the 27th February 1917.

2. On relief the 13 Northd Fus. will move to the Support Line now held by 12 Northd Fus.

3. The relief will be completed by 12 noon.

4. All other details of relief will be arranged by Battn. Comdrs.

5. Details of fatigue and duties must be handed over to relieving battalions. Work will be interfered with as little as possible. The two parties found by the Support battalion for the T.M. Bty will be found on the day of relief by 13 Northd Fus.

6. All trench stores, log books, trench maps etc. will be handed over and lists forwarded to Staff Captain, 62 Inf. Bde. within 24 hours of completion of relief.

7. Gun boots will be handed over and receipts taken and a statement of the number sent in with Trench Store lists to the Staff Captain.

8. Completions of relief will be notified to Bde. H.Q. in 'B.A.B.' Trench Code.

9. Acknowledge.

Capt,
A/Bde. Major,
62 Infantry Bde.

Issued by orderly at 1 p.m.

```
Copy No. 1 & 2 - War Diary & File.
  "    "   3 - 12 Northd Fus.
  "    "   4 - 13 Northd Fus.
  "    "   5 - 1 Lincoln R.
  "    "   6 - 10 York R.
  "    "   7 - 62 M.G.Coy.
  "    "   8 - No. 2 M.G. Squadron.
  "    "   9 - 62 T.M. Battery.
  "    "  10 - Signals.
  "    "  11 - Quarries Group, R.F.A.
  "    "  12 - 110 Inf. Bde.
  "    "  13 - 111 Inf. Bde.
  "    "  14 - 97 Field Coy. R.E.
  "    "  15 - 21 Division.
  "    "  16 - 170 Tunnelling Coy. R.E.
  "    "  17 - 253    "        "    "
  "    "  18 - No. 2 Coy. Train.
  "    "  19 - 21 Div. Train.
```

62 Infantry Brigade O. O. No. 126.

Copy No. 4

26th February 1917.

1. The 12 Northd Fus. will extend their front as far north as Boyau 92 (exclusive) on the 27th February, relieving troops of the 1 Lincoln R.

2. On completion of this relief the northern boundary of the 12 Northd Fus., Right Subsection, will be Boyau 92 - BRESLAU AVENUE - STAFFORD LANE - CURLY CRESCENT - Jnc. of CURLY CRESCENT and FOSSE WAY - FOSSE WAY to CHAPEL ALLEY - CHAPEL ALLEY (all exclusive).

3. All details of relief will be arranged by Battn. Comdrs. concerned and the relief will be completed by 6 p.m. and will be reported to Bde. H.Q. by wiring the word "SLIP".

4. Trench stores etc. will be handed over and receipts taken, and a list forwarded to Staff Captain, 62 Infantry Brigade, on the 28th inst. Any maps, log books, photographs etc. at the Right Coy. H.Q. of 1 Lincoln R. not affecting the new area of the Right Subsection will be taken to BattN. H.Q. of the Left Subsection.

5. On the afternoon of the 27th February, any troops of 13 Northd Fus. who are north of the boundary set out in para 2, will move into positions south of that boundary. This movement to be completed by 6 p.m.
The above order does not refer to Battn. H.Q. of 13 Northd Fus., which will remain in the present position of Support Battn. H.Q. until the 1st March.

6. The 110 Inf. Bde. will extend their front as far south as Boyau 92 (inclusive) on the 28th February, relieving left front line battalion 62 Inf. Bde. (1 Lincoln R.).

7. On completion of this relief the Southern Boundary of 110 Inf. Bde. Section will be Boyau 92 - BRESLAU AVENUE - STAFFORD LANE - CURLY CRESCENT - Jnc. of CURLY CRESCENT and FOSSE WAY - FOSSE WAY to CHAPEL ALLEY - CHAPEL ALLEY (all inclusive).

8. On completion of this relief the guns of the 2nd H.G. Squadron and the mortars of 62 T.M.Bty., and of the Medium T.M.Bty., which are north of the boundary referred to in para 7, will come under the orders of the B.G.C. 110 Inf. Bde.

9. Further orders in connection with the relief referred to in paras 6 - 8 will be issued later.

10. 62 Inf. Bde. will be relieved by 71 Inf. Bde. in the remainder of the QUARRIES Section on the 1st March. Further orders in connection with this relief will be issued later.

11. Relief of R.A.M.C. Units (other than those of 110 Inf. Bde. Group) will be carried out under arrangements to be made by A.D.M.S.

12. 71 M.G.Coy. and 71 T.M.Bty. will relieve the remainder of 2nd M.G. Squadron and 62 M.G.Coy., and 62 T.M.Bty. in the remainder of the QUARRIES Section on the 28th February. Relief to be completed by 6 p.m.

One man for each M.G. and T.M. emplacement relieved will be left for 24 hours after completion of relief.

On completion of relief

    (i) the remainder of 2nd M.G.Squadron will be withdrawn to NOYELLES and will be placed at the disposal of B.G.C. 110 Inf. Bde., and the H.Q. of 2nd M.G.Squadron will move to the 110 M.G.Coy. H.Q. in VERMELLES.

    (ii) The section of the 62 M.G.Coy. attached to the 2nd M.G. Squadron will join the 62 M.G.Coy. at BETHUNE.

    (iii) The 62 T.M.Bty. will move to NOYELLES.

All other details of these reliefs to be arranged between Unit Commanders concerned.

Completion of relief to be notified to Bde. H.Q. in 'B.A.B.' Code.

13. The working parties of 13 Northd Fus. and 10 York R., attached to 170 and 253 Tunnelling Coys. R.E., respectively, will return to their units on 27 February on relief by units of 6th Division. The 13 Northd Fus. party if relieved before 12 noon will report to Support Battn. H.Q. in CURLY CRESCENT, and will there await the arrival of 13 Northd Fus.

14. The working party of 1 Lincoln R. attached to the 253 Tunnelling Coy. R.E., on relief by troops of the 6 Division on the 27th February, will proceed to MAZINGARBE and await the arrival of the 1 Lincoln R. there on the 28th February.

15. All troops moving East of a line drawn through BEUVRY – SAILLY LABOURSE – NOEUX LES MINES will do so by platoons, at intervals of not less than 200 yards.

Capt,
A/Bde. Major,
62 Infantry Brigade.

Issued by orderly
at 7 p.m.

Copy No.	1 & 2	– War Diary & File.	Copy No. 11	– 71 Inf. Bde.
"	3	– 12 Northd Fus.	" 12	–110 Inf. Bde.
"	4	– 13 Northd Fus.	" 13	–111 Inf. Bde.
"	5	– 1 Lincoln R.	" 14	– 21 Division.
"	6	– 10 York R.	" 15	– 97 Fd. Coy. R.E.
"	7	– 62 M.G.Coy.	" 16	–170 T. Coy. R.E.
"	8	– No. 2 M.G.Squad.	" 17	–253 " " "
"	9	– 62 T.M.Bty.	" 18	– No. 2 Coy. Train.
"	10	– Signals.	" 19	– 21 Div. Train.
			" 20	– 94 Bde. R.FA.
			" 21	– 64 Field Amb.
			" 22	– 65 Field Amb.
			" 23	– Town Major, MAZINGARBE.

SECRET

13th NORTHUMBERLAND FUSILIERS
OPERATION ORDERS No 7.   26th Feby 1917

Ref. Map BETHUNE.
Combined Sheet

1. The 12th Northumberland Fusiliers will relieve the 13th Northumberland Fusiliers in the Right Sub-Sector on the 27th February 1917.

2. On relief the 13th Northumberland Fusiliers will move to the Support line now held by the 12th Northumberland Fusiliers.

3. The relief will be completed by 12 noon.

4. The Battalion will be relieved by the 12th Northumberland Fusiliers in the Front line in the undermentioned order and times:- The relieving Companies of the 12th Northumberland Fusiliers will pass Battalion Headquarters at junction of O.G.1 and DEVON LANE as follows.

   Lewis Gunners   5.30 am
   Signals   8.   am
   Right Company   8.   am
   Left   "   8.15 am
   Centre "   8.30 am
   Support "   8.45 am

   The Platoon of Centre Company in NIEUPORT CRATER will be relieved at dusk

5. CHAPEL ALLEY and DEVON LANE will be used ONLY by the 12th Northumberland Fusiliers and will be closed to all other traffic during relief.
   All Mess Boxes, Kits, Medical Panniers and Dixies etc must be taken up either before 6 a.m or after 12 noon; all communication trenches will be policed by both Battalions who will regulate all traffic.

6. WORKING PARTIES. "B" Company will furnish two working parties of Three N.C.O's and thirty men, each party to report to the 62nd T.M. Battery and 62nd Stokes Mortar Battery Officer's Dugout in DEVON LANE at 9 a.m.

7. Companies will take over the same Trenches in the Support line as they previously occupied when in support.

8. Advance Parties of 1 Officer and 1 N.C.O. per Company and the A/RSM will take over all Trench Stores etc at 7 am; the usual receipts must be signed and countersigned.
   All Gum Boots, thigh, must be handed over to the relieving Battalion.
   Trench Store lists must be sent to the Adjutant by 7 p.m tomorrow, 27th inst.

9. No one whatever may pass over the top of the Trenches or shew himself; the Police have strict orders to take the name of anyone disobeying this Order.

10. Completions of relief will be notified to Battalion H.Q's in CURLEY CRESCENT in B.A.B. Trench Code.

11. Battalion H.Q's will move to CURLEY CRESCENT at 11 a.m.

12. Acknowledge.

Issued by Orderly at 8 p.m
   No 1 Copy retained -
   " 2   "   "A" Coy
   " 3   "   "B" "
   " 4   "   "C" "
   " 5   "   "D" "
   " 6   "   L.G.O and B.O.   No 7 Copy Q.M. and T.O.

Captn & Adjt
13th Northd Fusrs

Copy No 1

SECRET

13th BATTALION NORTHUMBERLAND FUSILIERS

OPERATIONS ORDERS No 8   27.2.17

1. The 12th Northumberland Fusiliers will extend their front as far North as BOYEAU 92 (exclusive) on the afternoon of 27th February 1917, relieving troops of 1st Lincs Regiment.

2. On completion of the relief the Northern boundary of the 12th Northumberland Fusiliers right sub-section will be BOYEAU 92 - BRESLAU AVENUE - STAFFORD LANE - CURLEY CRESCENT - JUNCTION OF CURLEY CRESCENT and FOSSE WAY - FOSSE WAY to CHAPEL ALLEY - CHAPEL ALLEY (all exclusive).

3. All troops of this Battalion who are North of the boundary set out in paragraph 2. will immediately move into position South of that Boundary. This movement must be completed by 5 p.m. Battalion Headquarters will remain in its present position.

4. The 110th Brigade will extend their front as far South as BOYEAU 92 (inclusive) on the 28th February 1917 relieving left front line Battalion 62nd Infantry Brigade.

5. On completion of this relief the Southern Boundary of the 110th Infantry Brigade Section will be as shewn in para 2 (all inclusive).

6. The 62nd Infantry Brigade will be relieved by the 71st Infantry Brigade in the QUARRIES SECTION on the 1st March 1917.

7. The Working Parties now attached to the 170th Tunnelling Company will return to their Companies this afternoon.
Company Commanders will immediately report by wire their arrival.

8. Immediately Company Commanders have removed all their men as ordered in para 3 they will wire the word "BOG" preceded by the Officer's name.

Issued by orderly 2 p.m

Captn & Adjt
13th North'd Fusrs

No 1 Copy retained
" 2 " "A" Coy
" 3 " "B" "
" 4 " "C" "
" 5 " "D" "
" 6 L.G.O. and B. O.
" 7 S.O.
" 8 Q.M. and T.O.

S E C R E T.

62 Infantry Brigade O. O. No. 127.

Ref HAZEBROUCK 5a 1/100.000
    LENS 11 1/100.000.

Copy No. 4

27th February 1917.

1.   The relief of the 62 Inf. Bde. in the QUARRIES Section, by the 110 Inf. Bde. and 71 Inf. Bde. will take place as follows :-

28th February.

    (a)   The 1 Lincoln R. will be relieved by troops of the 8 Leic. R, in the Left Subsection. Relief to be completed by 12 noon.
            On relief the 1 Lincoln R. will move to MAZINGARBE.
            All details of relief to be arranged between Battn. Commanders concerned.

    (b)   One Company of the 6 Leic. R. will move into CURLY CRESCENT.

1st March.

    (a)   The 12 Northd Fus. will be relieved by the 9th Norfolks in the Right Subsection. Guides (one for each platoon) will be sent by the 12 Northd Fus. to meet the relieving battalion at VERMELLES Cross Rds. at 9 a.m.
            On relief the 12 Northd Fus. will march to SAILLY LABOURSE.

    (b)   The 13 Northd Fus. in Support will be relieved by one company of the 9th Suffolks. Four guides (one for each platoon in CHAPEL ALLEY and DEVON LANE) will be sent by the 13 Northd Fus. to meet the relieving Company at VERMELLES Cross Roads at 3 p.m.
            On relief the 13 Northd Fus. will march to NOEUX LES MINES.
            Details of reliefs to be arranged between O.C.'s and C.O's concerned.

2.   Orders for the relief of keeps etc. have been issued separately.

3.   All trench maps, aeroplane photographs, trench stores, grenades, S.A.A. etc. will be handed over on reliefs. Trench stores &c. in the Support Battalion area

    (a)   North of Stafford Lane - will be handed over to the 6 Leic. R. An officer of this battalion will report at Battn. H.Q. of the 13 Northd Fus. in CURLY CRESCENT on the morning of the 28th February for this purpose.

    (b)   South of Stafford Lane - will be handed over to the 9th Suffolks on the 1st March.

4. Receipts will be obtained for all trench stores etc. handed over, and lists in duplicate will be forwarded to Staff Capt. 62 Inf. Bde. within 24 hours of completion of relief's.

5. Completion of all relief's will be reported to Bde. H.Q. by 'B.A.B.' Code.

6. Orders with regard to billeting parties, lorries etc. will be issued separately.

7. During the moves H.Q. Platoon will be attached to and move with 10 York R.

8. The working party of the 12 Northd Fus. attached to the 97 Field Coy. R.E. will remain at NOYELLES for the night of the 28th February/1st March and on the 1st March will march to SAILLY LABOURSE and rejoin their unit.

9. All other moves of the 62 Inf. Bde. units will take place in accordance with attached table.

10. Transport will not be brigaded but will move under units' directions.

11. All units will report their arrival at destinations by orderly to Bde. H.Q.

Capt,
A/Bde. Major,
62 Infantry Brigade.

Issued by orderly
at 2 p.m.

Copy No. 1 & 2	=	War Diary & File.
" " 3	-	12 Northd Fus.
" " 4	-	13 Northd Fus.
" " 5	-	1 Lincoln R.
" " 6	-	10 York R.
" " 7	-	62 M.G.Coy.
" " 8	-	62 T.M.Bty.
" " 9	-	H.Q. Platoon.
" " 10	-	No. 2 M.G. Squadron.
" " 11	-	Signals.
" " 12	-	71 Inf. Bde.
" " 13	-	110 Inf. Bde.
" " 14	-	111 Inf. Bde.
" " 15	-	21 Division.
" " 16	-	97 Field Coy. R.E.
" " 17	-	170 Tunnelling Coy. R.E.
" " 18	-	255 " " "
" " 19	-	QUARRIES Group R.F.A.
" " 20	-	No. 2 Coy. Train.
" " 21	-	21 Div. Train.
" " 22	-	64 Field Amb.
" " 23	-	65 " "
" " 24	-	Town Major, HAZINGARBE,
" " 25	-	" " NOEUX LES MINES,
" " 26	-	" " NOYELLES,
" " 27	-	" " SAILLY LABOURSE.
" " 28	-	" " BETHUNE.

12 Northn Fus.
13 Northd Fus.
1 Lincolns R.
10 Yorks Regt.
62 Coy., Machine Gun Corps
62nd Trench Mortar Battery
No. 2 Machine Gun Squadron

SECRET

S.C. 608 - 27th February, 1917

---

1. The usual billeting Parties must be sent well in advance of units, reporting to the following before taking over billets:-

   NOEUX LES MINES)
   NOYELLES   )
   BETHUNE   )   Town Majors
   SAILLY LABOURSE)
   ANNEZIN   )

   ROBECQ)   Maire
   BUSNES)   Maire

   NOTE: The Maire of BUSNES does the billeting for PIERRIERE and MIQUELLERIE, and also L'ECLEME, although the latter town is in the ROBECQ billeting area.

   HAM-EN-ARTOIS   Maire

2. 62nd Infantry Brigade Headquarters in BETHUNE will be at 56 GRAND PLACE, and 7 RUE DE COLLEGE (Office) and at MIQUELLERIE in BUSNES area.

3. It is not known yet whether the 12th Northd. Fus. billet at ROBECQ or ANNEZIN on the 2nd March.
   They will be notified as soon as this information is obtained.

4. One battalion of the 18th Infantry Brigade (11th Essex Regiment) are at present billeted along the two roads which lead from BUSNES to ROBECQ. *from BUSNES to th CANAL* The 10th Yorkshire Regiment will take over these billets.
   One battalion of the 18th Infantry Brigade (14th Durham Light Infantry) are billeted partly in BUSNES and partly in MIQUELLERIE, and one Company near CORNET BOURDOIS. The 1st Lincolnshire Regiment will take over these billets.

5. Lorries have been asked for, and a list will be issued later.

Captain
Staff Captain
62nd Inf. Bde.

12 Northd Fus.
13 Northd Fus.
 1 Lincolns R.
10 Yorks Regt.
62 M. Gun Coy.
62 T. M. Btty.

S E C R E T

S.C. 647 - 28 Feby. 1917

Following lorries have been asked for to-morrow, March 1st :-

12 Northd Fus.	2 lorries (packs)	Trenches to SAILLY
13 Northd Fus.	4 " (blankets and packs)	Trenches to NOEUX LES MINES
1 Lincolns R.	4 " (blankets and packs)	MAZINGARBE to BETHUNE
10 Yorks Regt.	4 " (blankets and packs)	NOEUX LES MINES to ROBECQ.
62 M. Gun Coy.	1 lorry	BETHUNE to ROBECQ
62 T. M. Btty.	1 "	NOVELLES to ROBECQ.

Time & place where lorries will report will be notified later.

Lieutenant
for Staff Captain
62nd Inf. Bde.

12 Northd Fus.
13 Northd Fus.
1 Linc. R.
10 Yorks R.
62 M.G.Coy.
62 T.M.Btty.

S E C R E T

S.G.654 - 28 Feb.1917

Lorries for to-morrow, Mch.1st, will report as follows:-

12 N.F.	2	12 noon	X rds.C.8.c.4.6. VERMELLES
13 N.F.	4	4.30 p.m.	ditto.
1 Linc.R.	4	12 noon	Sheet 36B/L.23.d.8.6. (rd. from these X rds. to L.23.b.2.8. being closed to traffic).
10 Yorks R.	4	11 a.m.	Church, NOEUX LES MINES
62 T.M.Bty.	1	do.	ditto.
62 M.G.Co.	1	do.	Ecole Michelet, BETHUNE

Guides must be sent to lorry rendez-vous if units require to bringing them to a different place for loading.

If units cannot get all their blankets packs on the lorries, they may do a double journey; but the lorry driver must have a written order from an Officer and packs must be left in charge of a guard, to look after them and load them on the return of the lorry.

Capt?
Staff Capt.
62 Inf.Bde.

Ref Maps
HAZEBROUCK 5a 1/100000
LENS 11 1/100000

Copy No.........
SECRET

13th BATTALION NORTHUMBERLAND FUSILIERS
OPERATION ORDERS No 9   28.2.17

1. The relief of the 62nd Inf. Bde in the QUARRIES SECTOR by the 71st Inf Bde will take place as follows:-

2. (a) The 12th Northd Fusrs will be relieved by the 9th Norfolks in the right sub-section. Guides will be sent by the 12th Northd Fusrs to meet relieving Battn at VERMELLES Cross Roads at 9 a.m.
   (b) The 13th Northd Fusrs in support will be relieved by one Coy of the 9th Suffolks. Four guides will be sent by the 13th Northd Fusrs to meet relieving Coys at VERMELLES Cross Roads at 3 p.m.

3. The Battn will be relieved by "D" Coy of the 9th Suffolks who will take over from two Platoons of A and B Coys respectively; immediately the relief is complete A and B Coy Commanders will wire by BAB Code to the Adjutant. On the receipt of this wire the Battalion will vacate the Trenches and proceed by Platoons at 200 yards distance to NOEUX LES MINES.
   Coys will vacate the Trenches as follows:-

   H.Q. Coy   Ref Map Sheets 36A and 36B.
   "D" "   ROUTE through PHILOSOPHE Cross Roads
   "B" "   L. 18.c.95.40 to MAZINGARBE through
   "A" "   Cross Rds L.23.b.6.6 and L 23.c.8.2.
   "C" "   Past Church L.23.c.4.7. through
                      L.22, L.21, L.20, L.14 and L.13 to
                      NOEUX LES MINES.

4. All packs of those in the Trenches will be dumped at a place to be notified later and taken on lorries to NOEUX LES MINES.
   Lorries will also take all blankets from Q.M. Stores.
   Each Platoon will detail a N.C.O. and leave him in charge of the Platoon packs until loaded upon the lorries.

5. The Billeting party to consist of Lieut S.M. HERBERT and 2nd Lieut L.W. BARRETT, C.Q.M. Sgts and 1 N.C.O. or reliable Pte for each Platoon and two for H.Q. Coy will rendevous at PHILOSOPHE Cross Roads at 7 a.m and March to NOEUX LES MINES tomorrow morning

6. All Mess boxes, Orderly Room Boxes, Kits and Dixies etc will be dumped at Cross Roads VERMELLES by the Dressing Station, and Transport Officer will arrange to have a wagon there to take them to NOEUX LES MINES tomorrow evening; the wagon must wait till they are all brought up on the Tramway. A small fatigue party under a N.C.O. must be detailed in charge of each Coys baggage. These parties will march behind the wagon to NOEUX LES MINES.

7. The Transport will proceed in advance tomorrow morning to NOUEX LES MINES.

8. The Regimental Drummers and odd men now at SAILLY LA BOURSE will march under 2nd Lieut PETRIE to NOUEX LES MINES.
   The Drums will not play.

9. All Billets and their vicinity at Sailly, also all Trenches and dugouts must be left scrupulously clean.

10. Receipts must be obtained for all Trench Stores handed over; and sent in to the Adjutant by 7 a.m on the 2nd March.

11. The Battalion will move off from NOUEX LES MINES about 9 a.m on the 2nd March.

12. Immediately on arrival in Billets in NOEUX LES MINES Coy Commanders will report all present or otherwise

13. The Transport Officer will arrange for Mounted Officers horses to be at the Cross Roads PHILOSOPHE at 5.30 p.m.

14. The Duty Company ("D" Coy) will detail a Sergt and 8 O.R. as a fatigue party to take up the Orderly Room boxes to the Dump.

```
Issued by orderly at 7.45.p.m
   No 1 Copy retained.
   "  2   "   "A" Coy
   "  3   "   "B"  "
   "  4   "   "C"  "
   "  5   "   "D"  "
   "  6   "   L.G.O. and B.O.
   "  7   "   Q.M. and T.O.
```

Houghton
Captn & Adjutant
13th Northumberland Fusrs.

WAR DIARY
INTELLIGENCE SUMMARY

Army Form C. 2118.

(Erase heading not required.)

D/4 Bn North Fusiliers Vol 23

Place	Date	Hour	Summary of Events and Information	Remarks and references to Appendices
BOYELLES	July 1st		The Battn remained in bivouac near BOYELLES until the evening when A & C Coys took over the C line of posts from 6 to 11 from the 33rd Division and B and D Coys moved up into CONCRETE and STAFF trenches respectively where units of the 50th Division were relieved.	51.B.S.W. 1/20,000
	2.		The Battalion headquarters moved up at 9 A.M. to N.35.C.2.4 and the Battn. became Bde support to the 62nd Bde. The 10th Battn. Yorkshire Regt. being in the front line on the right and the 1st Battn. LINCOLNSHIRE REGT in the front line on the left; the 62nd Bde now being the left Bde of the 21st Div; the 110th Bde being in the right subsector. Battn. transport remained at in T.13.6 near BOYELLES.	
	4.		A & C Coys were relieved by two Coys of the 13th Battn. mostly Fusiliers (the Battn. in Bde Reserve), and moved from C Post 6-11 to HIND trench (about T.6.A) and STAFF trench (about T.5.B) respectively. The Battn remained in Bde support until July 7th.	
HINDENBURG LINE.	4-7.			3 3
	7.		The Battalion relieved the 10th Battn. Yorkshire Regt. in the right subsector of the Bde front, the relief was completed by midday. The Coys then occupied the following positions: A Coy trenches U.1/1 from the SENSEE River to V.1.C.55.35 to V.1.C.10.55: B Coy in BUCK and CLAW trenches from V.1.C.10.55 to V.1.C.55.35: D Coy from V.1.C.55.35 to V.1.C.10.55: C Coy in support in HIND trench from V.7.A.55.75 the Junction of CLAW trench and PUE LANE at V.1.A.4.5. Battn. Headquarters at T.6.B.25.00. to 7th LANE T.6.D.07.65.	6
	8-15.		12th Battn. Northumberland Fusiliers remained in the right subsector of the 62nd Bde front; there was a good deal of shelling, but conditions in this sector were now those normally prevailing in trench warfare. The total casualties for 8 days were 1 killed and few wounded.	2/Lt Sedgwick reported for duty on July 12 from the 3rd D.E.'s (Queens Bays).

WAR DIARY
or
INTELLIGENCE SUMMARY
(Erase heading not required.)

Army Form C. 2118.

Instructions regarding War Diaries and Intelligence Summaries are contained in F. S. Regs., Part II. and the Staff Manual respectively. Title Pages will be prepared in manuscript.

Place	Date	Hour	Summary of Events and Information	Remarks and references to Appendices
HINDENBURG LINE	July 16		The 12th Northumberland Fusiliers were relieved in the front line by the 1st Battn EAST YORKSHIRE Regt 64th Bde; upon relief the Battn moved back to 7. camp at MOYENVILLE, when the 62nd Bde remained in Divisional Reserve. The following awards were made to the 12th Battn Northumberland Fusiliers in respect of special work done on the night of June 16th, Lieut E. M. PHILIP, M.C. awarded the D.S.O. Capt E. H. Griffith M.C. R.A.M.C. (attached 12th MNId Fusrs) Bar to Military Cross. MAJOR the Rev. J. B. MARSHALL C.F. (attached 12th MNId Fusrs) the Military Cross, No 18/1382 Sgt J. G. Stephenson awarded the D.C.M. Lt-Col P./Stevenson D.S.O. proceeded to England on special leave, Major J. J. EDIMANN D.S.O. assumed command of the Battalion.	51. B.S.W 20.000
	July 19		A draft of 11 O.R joined the Battn from the 31st I.B.D. The Battalion rested and carried out training from July 16th – July 24th at 9. camp MOYENVILLE.	D.R's W.B.MARSH G.N.EDMONDS
	24		The Battn relieved the 15th Battn Durham Light Infantry of the 64th Bde in Bde reserve at BOYELLES; the Battn took over huts 6–10 and B & D Coys – Battn HQrs – & platoon returned to T.13.B. A & C Coys relieved A and C Coys into huts 6-10 , A Coy and C Coy less one platoon returned to B and D Coys relieved at T.13.B; one platoon of C Coy was placed at the disposal of the officer commanding the bivouac at T.13.B.	reported upon the 7 Corps Reinforcement Depot July 22.
	28		The Battn in the Bde left subsector to wire SNIPE trench & moved up to SHAFT trench. 2nd M.M. Brodie M.C. wounded on June 3rd died of wounds in a Base Hospital. Lt BRODIE joined the Battn in June 1916 and was awarded the Military Cross for gallant conduct near HULLUCH on Feb 22.	

Army Form C. 2118.

WAR DIARY
or
INTELLIGENCE SUMMARY
(Erase heading not required.)

Instructions regarding War Diaries and Intelligence Summaries are contained in F. S. Regs., Part II. and the Staff Manual respectively. Title Pages will be prepared in manuscript.

Place	Date	Hour	Summary of Events and Information	Remarks and references to Appendices
BOYELLES	July 1917 29-31.		The Battn remained in Bde Reserve, working & carrying parties being found. The actual strength in Officers & men with the battalion on July 31st was 22 Officers & 463 O.R. J McLennan Major Comdg 12th (S) Bn. Northumberland Fusiliers	51. B.S.W. 1 20,000

www.ingramcontent.com/pod-product-compliance
Lightning Source LLC
Chambersburg PA
CBHW080853230426
43662CB00013B/2096